INFORMAL WOMEN WORKERS IN THE GLOBAL SOUTH

Formalising employment is a desirable policy goal, but how it is done matters greatly, especially for women workers. Indeed, formalisation policies that do not recognise gendered realities and prevailing socio-economic conditions may be less effective and even counterproductive.

This book examines the varying trajectories of formalisation and their impact on women workers in five developing countries in Asia and Africa: India, Thailand, South Africa, Ghana and Morocco. They range from low- to middle-income countries, which are integrated into global financial and goods markets to differing degrees and have varying labour market and macroeconomic conditions.

The case studies, using macro and survey data as well as in-depth analysis of particular sectors, provide interesting and sometimes surprising insights. Despite some limited success in providing social protection benefits to some informal workers, most formalisation policies have not really improved the working conditions of women workers. In many cases, that is because the policies are gender-blind and insensitive to the specific needs of women workers.

The impact of formalisation policies on women in developing countries is relatively under-researched. This book provides new evidence that will be applicable across a wide range of developing country contexts and will be of interest to policymakers, feminist economists and students of economics, labour, gender and development studies, public policy, politics and sociology.

Jayati Ghosh is Professor of Economics, University of Massachusetts at Amherst, USA. She was previously Professor of Economics at Jawaharlal Nehru University, New Delhi, India. She has taught and researched for over three decades in areas of development economics, international economics, gender and macroeconomics. She has won several national and international awards for her research and advised governments at different levels, international organisations and social activist groups on economic policy issues.

Routledge IAFFE Advances in Feminist Economics

IAFFE aims to increase the visibility and range of economic research on gender; facilitate communication among scholars, policymakers and activists concerned with women's wellbeing and empowerment; promote discussions among policymakers about interventions which serve women's needs; educate economists, policymakers and the general public about feminist perspectives on economic issues; foster feminist evaluations of economics as a discipline; expose the gender blindness characteristic of much social science and the ways in which this impoverishes all research—even research that does not explicitly concern women's issues; help expand opportunities for women, especially women from under-represented groups, within economics; and encourage the inclusion of feminist perspectives in the teaching of economics. The IAFFE book series pursues the aims of the organization by providing a forum in which scholars have space to develop their ideas at length and in detail. The series exemplifies the value of feminist research and the high standard of IAFFE sponsored scholarship.

15 **Economics and Austerity in Europe**
    Gendered Impacts and Sustainable Alternatives
    Edited by Hannah Bargawi, Giovanni Cozzi and Sue Himmelweit

16 **Women, Work and Gender Justice in the Global Economy**
    Ruth Pearson

17 **Gender and Risk-Taking**
    Economics, Evidence and Why the Answer Matters
    Julie A. Nelson

18 **Global Women's Work**
    Perspectives on Gender and Work in the Global Economy
    Edited by Beth English, Mary E. Frederickson and Olga Sanmiguel-Valderrama

19 **Informal Women Workers in the Global South**
    Policies and Practices for the Formalisation of Women's Employment in Developing Economies
    Edited by Jayati Ghosh

20 **The Political Economy of Same-Sex Marriage**
    A Feminist Critique
    Bronwyn Winter

For more information about this series, please visit www.routledge.com/ Routledge-IAFFE-Advances-in-Feminist-Economics/book-series/IAFFE

INFORMAL WOMEN WORKERS IN THE GLOBAL SOUTH

Policies and Practices for the Formalisation of Women's Employment in Developing Economies

Edited by Jayati Ghosh

Routledge
Taylor & Francis Group

LONDON AND NEW YORK

First published 2021
by Routledge
2 Park Square, Milton Park, Abingdon, Oxon OX14 4RN

and by Routledge
52 Vanderbilt Avenue, New York, NY 10017

Routledge is an imprint of the Taylor & Francis Group, an informa business

British Library Cataloguing-in-Publication Data
A catalogue record for this book is available from the British Library

Library of Congress Cataloging-in-Publication Data
Names: Ghosh, Jayati, editor.
Title: Informal women workers in the global south : policies and practices for the formalisation of women's employment in developing economies / edited by Jayati Ghosh.
Description: 1 Edition. | New York : Routledge, 2020. | Series: Routledge IAFFE advances in feminist economics | Includes bibliographical references and index.
Identifiers: LCCN 2020033947 (print) | LCCN 2020033948 (ebook) | ISBN 9780367545994 (hardback) | ISBN 9780367545987 (paperback) | ISBN 9781003089841 (ebook)
Subjects: LCSH: Women--Employment--Developing countries. | Informal sector (Economics)--Developing countries. | Sex discrimination in employment--Developing countries. | Labor policy--Developing countries.
Classification: LCC HD6223 .I54 2020 (print) | LCC HD6223 (ebook) | DDC 331.409172/4--dc23
LC record available at https://lccn.loc.gov/2020033947
LC ebook record available at https://lccn.loc.gov/2020033948

ISBN: 978-0-367-54599-4 (hbk)
ISBN: 978-0-367-54598-7 (pbk)
ISBN: 978-1-003-08984-1 (ebk)

Typeset in Bembo
by MPS Limited, Dehradun

CONTENTS

List of figures   *vii*
List of tables   *viii*
List of contributors   *ix*

1 Introduction: The gender implications of formalising
   informal activities   1
   Jayati Ghosh

2 Insecurity of women workers and the chimera
   of formality in India   34
   C.P. Chandrasekhar, Jayati Ghosh, Nancy Yadav and
   Shreya Sharma

3 Growing informality and women's work in South Africa   68
   Hameda Deedat

4 Does formalisation improve women's work conditions?
   A review of the regulatory regime for contract farming
   and domestic trade in Ghana   88
   Dzodzi Tsikata and Promise Eweh

5 Striving for formalisation: Gender and youth aspects
   of informal employment in Morocco   137
   Mouna Cherkaoui and Taoufik Benkaraach

6 The socio-economic complexities of formalisation
of women's employment in Thailand 174
Jessica Vechbanyongratana, Yong Yoon,
Warn Nuarpear Lekfuangfu and Peera Tangtammaruk

Index *211*

FIGURES

1.1	Share of informal employment in total employment, by gender	2
1.2	Men and women workers face similar extent of informality	2
1.3	Informality is high even in non-agricultural activities	3
1.4	Rates of informality vary across the developing world	3
1.5	Informal employment by type of production unit	7
2.1	Worker to population ratios in rural and urban India	38
2.2	Wage distribution of workers interviewed	54
2.3	Social security of surveyed workers	57
3.1	Sectoral shares in GDP and Employment (2018)	70
3.2	Social protection indicators in South Africa, 2018	71
4.1	Access to a financial institution account	115
4.2	Access to a mobile money account	116
4.3	Savings at a financial institution	116
4.4	Saved with a savings club or persons outside family	117
4.5	Borrowing from a financial institution	117
4.6	Borrowed from family or friends	118
6.1	Sectoral value added (% GDP) in Thailand, 1969–18	176
6.2	Employment and wages by industry and gender, 2018	177
6.3	Monthly labour income for formal and informal workers, 2011–16	178
6.4	Incidence of informality by worker type, 2016	187

TABLES

2.1	Women's wages as per cent of men's wages	39
2.2	Structure of employment in 2011-12	42
2.3	Conditions of employment in 2017-18	43
2.4	Employment status of surveyed workers (in number, figures in brackets are percentages of total)	52
2.5	Number and percentage of workers in relevant category in registered enterprises earning below minimum wages	56
4.1	Informal employment in Ghana (2000, 2010)	96
4.2	Some global certification bodies with key influence on contract farming regulation in Ghana	110
5.1	Real GDP growth, unemployment and youth unemployment in Morocco 2008-18	139
5.2	Women beneficiaries of the active employment programmes in 2016	159
5.3	Logistic regression model of informal employment	168
5.4	Final logistic regression model of informal employment	169
6.1	Distribution of hours, monthly labour income, and hourly wages for formally and informally employed full-time domestic workers and cleaners, 2016	189
6.2	Real monthly wages for Thai manufacturing subsectors by gender, 2011–16	200

CONTRIBUTORS

Taoufik Benkaraache is a professor at the Faculty of Legal, Economic and Social Sciences of Mohammedia-Casablanca and Director of the Intelligence Research Laboratory at Hassan II University in Casablanca, Morocco. His research interests include economic and business intelligence, territorial economic development and innovation.

C. P. Chandrasekhar was Professor of Economics at Jawaharlal Nehru University. He has worked on finance, industry, development and political economy at national and international levels.

Mouna Cherkaoui is Professor of Economics at the University Mohamed V, Faculty of Law, Economics and Social Sciences in Rabat Agdal. Her research interests include subjects in international economics, poverty and inequality. She has advised governments and international organisations on these and related issues.

Hameda Deedat is Acting Executive Director of NALEDI, and has been a gender and social activist for more than 30 years. Her advocacy and research have focused on economic and social justice issues, some of which are gender, water, climate change and the just transition, 4IR vs Future of work and BRICS.

Promise Eweh is a PhD Candidate at the Institute of African Studies, University of Ghana. He looks forward to a future of research focusing on issues in African development.

Jayati Ghosh is Professor of Economics, University of Massachusetts at Amherst, USA. She was previously Professor of Economics at Jawaharlal Nehru University, New Delhi, India. Her research includes work on international economics, macroeconomics, political economy of development and gender issues.

Warn Nuarpear Lekfuangfu is Assistant Professor of Economics at Universidad Carlos III de Madrid, Madrid, Spain.

Shreya Sharma holds an MA in Development and Labour Studies from Jawaharlal Nehru University, New Delhi, India. She has previously worked at the Ministry of Labour and Employment, Government of India and with organizations like Self-Employed Women's Association.

Peera Tangtammaruk is Assistant Professor of Economics, Srinakharinwirot University, Bangkok, Thailand.

Dzodzi Tsikata is Research Professor and Development Sociology Director at the Institute of African Studies, University of Ghana, Legon.

Jessica Vechbanyongratana is Assistant Professor of Economics at Chulalongkorn University, Bangkok, Thailand.

Nancy Yadav is a research scholar at the Centre for Economic Studies and Planning, Jawaharlal Nehru University, New Delhi, India. She has worked on women's autonomy and factors affecting it; and is currently working on subcontracting in India's manufacturing sector.

Yong Yoon is Assistant Professor of Economics at Chulalongkorn University, Bangkok, Thailand.

1

INTRODUCTION

The gender implications of formalising informal activities

Jayati Ghosh

I The global incidence of informality

According to the International Labour Organization (ILO), around 60 per cent of all employment in the world is informal, and most of this is in informal sector enterprises that rarely if ever get the benefit of any government subsidies or protection even in periods of crisis.[1] This is much more of a problem in the developing world, where informal workers account for as much as 70 per cent of all employment—meaning that at least two out of every three workers are informal.

There is a widespread perception that women are more likely to be in informal employment than men, but the aggregate data suggest otherwise. Figure 1.2 actually suggests the opposite; men are marginally more likely to be informal workers than women, possibly because several public services that provide formal employment tend to hire more women (albeit in lower paid positions on average).

The other common perception is that informality is higher in developing countries because of the greater significance of agricultural employment. But this is dispelled by Figure 1.3, which show that even in non-agricultural activities, informal workers predominate in the Global South, to the extent of making up more than 60 per cent of all such workers.

Within the developing world, there are significant variations across regions, as Figure 1.4 indicates. The highest incidence of informal employment for both men and women is to be found in Africa, but it is also true that some countries in other regions have particularly high rates of informality. For example, in India, nine out of ten workers are informal, higher than the average for Africa, even though the ratio is much lower for the Asia-Pacific region as a whole.

It is this combination of the widespread prevalence of informality of employment contracts, combined with the ever-increasing evidence, that informal

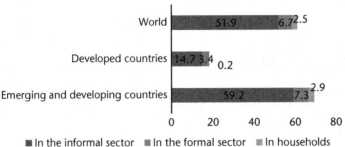

Share of informal in total employment (%)

FIGURE 1.1 Share of informal employment in total employment, by gender
Source: Women and Men in the Informal Economy: A Statistical Picture, Geneva: ILO, 2018.

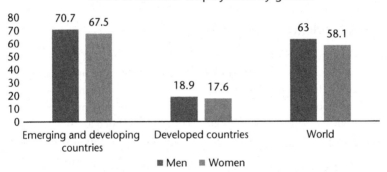

Share of informal employment by gender

FIGURE 1.2 Men and women workers face similar extent of informality

workers are disproportionately adversely affected in period of crisis and economic slowdown or contraction, which has made formalisation a desirable goal for both governments and civil society. However, the specific goal of formalisation can vary, and there is quite a difference between formalising *employment* and for-malising *enterprises*. Trade unions and civil society organisations have been much more concerned with formalisation of employment, to protect and enlarge workers' rights. In its barest form, informality is essentially the absence of worker protection, and so it is not surprising that those interested in the empowerment of workers (whether men or women) should strive for greater formalisation of work.[2] Formalisation enables workers' associations to form and assists workers in fighting for their rights by providing a legal and regulatory framework within which their struggles can occur. By contrast, informal workers typically cannot or dare not try to organise and have little or nothing in the form of legal cover in their struggles. However, governments are usually much more focussed on the formalisation of enterprises, rather than on the contracts of workers. They see the proliferation of

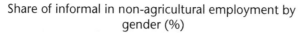

Share of informal in non-agricultural employment by gender (%)

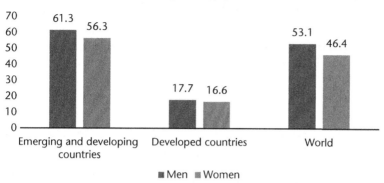

FIGURE 1.3 Informality is high even in non-agricultural activities

Share of informal employment by developing region (%)

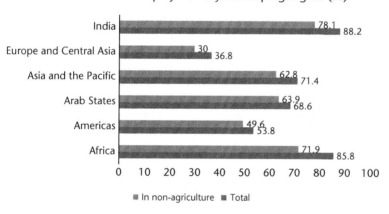

FIGURE 1.4 Rates of informality vary across the developing world

informal enterprises as undesirable because it enables greater evasion of taxes, and because such enterprises are harder to regulate in other ways, so bringing them into the ambit of regulatory structures is seen desirable and moving towards a "modern" economy.

Even in terms of their stated objectives, goals and good intentions are never sufficient to ensure the success of formalisation policies. The legal and institutional processes whereby formalisation is sought to be achieved, and the macro-economic, social and labour market conditions under which such policies are undertaken also matter greatly. If policies aimed at formalisation do not recognise the broader socio-economic and cultural contexts, they may end up worsening the employment and livelihood conditions of the very workers who are sought to be protected.

This is obviously true in general, but it is particularly true for women workers in informal activities, who tend to be disadvantaged in ways that are not recognised by public policy because of the gender construction of societies.[3] Typically, women informal workers have both different initial conditions and different constraints when compared to men informal workers. As self-employed workers or those running small or micro enterprises, they tend to lack assets and titles to property; this in turn reduces access to other facilities and enabling features such as bank credit and government programmes; they are more likely to face social restrictions on the types of activities they can engage in; they have greater difficulty in dealing with patriarchal officialdom and bureaucracy. As workers, women typically operate in more adverse labour market conditions, with lower wages; they also usually have on average lower educational attainment; they tend to be more vulnerable to harassment of various sorts within employment situations in both formal and informal enterprises; they are called upon to perform much more unpaid labour on a regular basis within the household and extended families; they are more likely to face patriarchal constraints upon their mobility and the types of employment they can seek to engage in. The responsibilities of unpaid work within households continue to weigh much more severely on women, requiring greater amounts of their time and effort, and thereby affecting their patterns of labour market participation. All of these features obviously affect the possibilities and nature of formal employment, but they also determine the contours of engagement in informal employment as well. Essentially, the crucial features of relational inequality and power imbalance are strong determinants of both women's employment patterns and the official policies designed to change them. As a result, formalisation policies that do not take into account these very different conditions and constraints may not be effective or may even be counterproductive for the concerned women workers. That is why a gender perspective is essential when considering processes of formalisation.

This argument is developed in more detail in this volume, which examines the processes of formalisation and their implications with a gender lens, through a comparative assessment of five developing countries in Asia and Africa: India, Thailand, South Africa, Ghana and Morocco. These studies assess the gendered impact of formalisation policies, with a special focus on women workers, in different developing countries with varying economic characteristics. They also use a mix of methods to assess both the conditions of informal workers and the effect of formalisation policies. While the countries considered here have very different economic and labour market conditions, all the studies find that the impact of formalisation policies tends to be much more complex than is generally perceived, and that the effect on informal women workers in particular can even be the opposite of what may be intended. At one level this appears to be surprising, given the unequal conditions for women's employment described above, since formalisation and coverage under laws and regulations could counter many disadvantages of women workers. While this is true to a limited extent, the studies find that the positive impacts on women workers tend to be much lower than anticipated; there are often negative impacts that were not expected. Several factors contribute to such outcomes: overall macroeconomic conditions and the state of demand for labour; the existing structure of labour markets and the extent of informality; the social and cultural forces affecting women's involvement with paid employment of different sorts; the nature of existing legal and other institutions; the extent to which government regulations can be enforced; the ability of informal women workers to organise and engage in collective action in their own interests; the perverse incentives that may arise from particular policies and regulations; and much else.

What emerges as common across all these experiences is the lack of appropriate gender perspectives in the formulation and implementation of such policies. Some of this occurs because of the all-too common gender-blindness of official strategies. But even when they seek to recognise gender differences, and sometimes even when they are specifically directed at women workers, they may inadvertently result in unanticipated or undesired outcomes. This means that the gendered implications of formalisation policies must be considered in a holistic way, in the wider political economy and socio-cultural context. The studies in this volume seek to do this. While they cover only five countries in Asia and Africa, because they are quite different, they allow for more general conclusions to emerge that may have some relevance to other developing countries as well.

II Defining the informal economy, informal work and informal workers

It is necessary, at first, to define formality, informality and formalisation and to consider some of the conceptual underpinnings of these definitions as they are used in official statistics, in government policies and in public perception. These concepts have evolved over time as the ideas of informal economy and informal employment have become both sharper and more sophisticated; Chen (2012) provides a succinct historical overview of these different approaches and perceptions.

In its most basic form, the informal economy is the diversified set of economic activities, enterprises, jobs and workers that are not regulated or protected by the state. The concept originally applied to self-employment in small unregistered enterprises and was thereafter expanded to include wage employment in unprotected jobs. However, there is wide variation in definitions of the unorganised or informal sector, which mostly attempt to draw boundaries between organised and unorganised and formal and informal by differentially focusing on differences in features such as technology, employment size, legal status and organisational form. Sometimes this is simply based on size—such as enterprises employing less than say five or ten workers are seen as being "unorganised." Other definitions are usually based on legal status—such that those enterprises that are registered with the relevant authorities are seen as part of the formal sector.

Informal employment is a large and possibly even more heterogeneous category. Many different types of employment belong under the broad umbrella "informal." This includes employment in informal enterprises as well as outside informal enterprises—in households or in formal enterprises. It also includes the self-employed and the wage employed and within these broad categories, the sub-categories according to status in employment, and covers a wide range of different occupations that also encompass very different income groups.

Following ILO (2013) and Chen (2012), informal employment can be described as consisting of the following types:

A. Persons employed in the informal sector (including those who are formally employed in the informal sector):

   - Employers in informal enterprises.
   - Employees in informal enterprises.
   - Own-account (self-employed) workers in their own informal enterprises.
   - Contributing family workers working in informal enterprises.
   - Members of informal producers' cooperatives, that is those that are not formally established as legal entities.

B. Persons in informal employment outside the informal sector, specifically:

   - Employees in formal enterprises not covered by social protection through their work, including contract workers, temporary and part-time workers, unregistered or undeclared workers, home-based workers, sub-contracted or out-workers.
   - Paid domestic workers not covered by social protection through their work.
   - Contributing family workers working in formal enterprises.

Workers are considered to have informal jobs if their employment relationship is, in law or in practice, not subject to national labour legislation, income taxation, social protection or entitlement to certain employment benefits (advance notice of dismissal, severance pay, paid annual or sick leave, etc.). The reasons may be the following: non-declaration of the jobs or the employees; casual jobs or jobs of a limited short duration; jobs with hours of work or wages below a specified threshold (e.g. for social security contributions); employment by unincorporated enterprises or by persons in households; jobs where the employee's place of work is outside the premises of the employer's enterprise (e.g. outworkers without employment contract); or jobs, for which labour regulations are not applied, not enforced, or not complied with for any other reason. Certain types of wage work are more likely than others to be informal. These include employees of informal enterprises, casual or day labourers, temporary or part-time workers, paid domestic workers, contract workers, unregistered or undeclared workers and home-based workers who are part of industrial outsourcing chains.

Figure 1.5 provides a matrix that indicates the relationship between informality of enterprises and of employment. This is useful because it brings out the complexity of the relationship. Thus, informal employment contains the following kinds of jobs: (1) own-account workers employed in their own informal sector enterprises (cell 3); (2) employers employed in their own informal sector enterprises (cell 4); (3) contributing family workers, irrespective of whether they work in formal or informal sector enterprises (cells 1 and 5); (4) members of informal producers" cooperatives (cell 8); (5) employees holding informal jobs in formal sector enterprises, informal sector enterprises, or as paid domestic workers employed by households (cells 2, 6 and 10); (6) own-account workers engaged in the production of goods exclusively for own final use by their household (cell 9). Employees holding formal jobs in informal sector enterprises (cell 7) should be excluded from informal employment.

III Approaches to formalisation

Increasing formalisation of employment was earlier seen as an inevitable and desirable attribute of the development process—but the experience of different countries over the past half century shows that development trajectories may be much more complex and less linear. The earlier, rather simplistic approach to formalisation that assumed that the shift to more formal economic activity would be a necessary concomitant of the development process has been jettisoned for

Production units by type	Jobs by status in employment								
	Own-account workers		Employers		Contrib-uting family workers	Employees		Members of producers' cooperatives	
	Informal	Formal	Informal	Formal	Informal	Informal	Formal	Informal	Formal
Formal sector enterprises					1	2			
Informal sector enterprises (a)	3		4		5	6	7	8	
Households (b)	9					10			

FIGURE 1.5 Informal employment by type of production unit

Note: Cells shaded in dark grey refer to jobs, which, by definition, do not exist in the type of production unit in question. Cells shaded in light grey refer to formal jobs. Unshaded cells represent the various types of informal jobs. Informal employment: Cells 1–6 and 8–10. Employment in the informal sector: Cells 3–8. Informal employment outside the informal sector: Cells 1, 2, 9 and 10.

Source: Report of 15th International Conference of Labour Statisticians

some time now in the wider development literature. It is now clear that there can be many different paths, not all of which are necessarily socially desirable. Four broad trajectories of formalisation can be identified, each of which has quite different implications for the well-being of workers and the conditions of work:

1. The classical or Kuznets-Lewis trajectory, whereby the processes of economic growth and development automatically generate more formal activity and formal work as part of broader structural transformation. This occurred in several now-developed countries in the past but is much rarer today.
2. A process of false "formalisation," whereby (some) informal activities get subsumed by formal enterprises as part of their accumulation strategies. This implies that the formal sector relies on such dualism and continued informality to keep its own costs low through outsourcing, and so there is no real incentive to reduce the extent of informality.
3. A reverse trajectory, whereby formal activities become more informal, whether to avoid taxes or regulation, or because of external competitive pressure.
4. A desirable process of formalisation brought about by policies and processes that ensure the economic and financial viability of small-scale activities and improve the wages and working conditions of hitherto informal workers.

In general, formalisation of informal work is seen to be inherently desirable by almost all stakeholders, but often for completely varying reasons. Increasingly, governments in the developing world see this as an end in itself, and in this, they are generally supported by trade unionists, activists and other civil society organisations—as well as those actually involved in informal work. However, it should be noted that the shift from informal to formal employment can occur in several different ways, and this depends on which of the following approaches is given importance by the government: (1) to regulate informal enterprises; (2) to regulate informal employment; (3) to provide social protection to informal workers; (4) to create more jobs in formal sectors and activities; and (5) to increase the viability of informal enterprises and productivity and incomes of informal workers.

Obviously, the third, fourth and fifth approaches are the most desirable in terms of progressive and sustainable formalisation of work over the process of economic development. But these are much more difficult and medium term or long term in nature, and require macroeconomic and development policies that put first emphasis on good quality job creation rather than GDP growth per se. Such strategies also require the state to put in more fiscal resources and in general play a more activist role. That is why the most common approach to formalisation has been to avoid the harder path and instead seek simply to regulate microenterprises and provide some forms of protection to informal workers. However, this strategy is not only less effective in itself; it also has significant gendered implications, in some cases even making things worse rather than better, particularly for women informal workers.

With respect to informal enterprises, including own-account enterprises (or self-employment) of the very smallest kind, governments tend to prioritise registration, which is seen to enable monitoring, taxation and generally bring enterprises under the purview of government regulation. It is also believed that this helps enterprises to get more access to formal institutions such as banks, input and marketing boards, government subsidies and incentives, etc., and gives them greater stability and viability by recognising their property rights and enabling them to operate with enforceable commercial contracts. While the evidence on this is mixed, this is nevertheless the most common approach to formalisation.

With respect to informal workers, there has been a more complex approach on the part of most governments in the recent past. On the one hand, it is seen as desirable to ensure that all workers are brought into regulatory regimes, including labour regulations and worker protection, and to provide some social protection; on the other hand, the focus of most states has been on greater labour flexibility and labour market deregulation, which is somewhat at odds with the earlier objective. Therefore, there has been a tendency, especially among governments in the developing world, to try and provide some forms of social protection (such as access to healthcare or pensions) that are publicly provided and therefore apply more generally to workers irrespective of their form of employment, or are specifically directed to informal workers but without requiring employers to bear the burden of such provision.

From the point of view of informal enterprises, the benefits of formalisation have to be weighed against the costs. Costs are those of registration and subsequent compliance with regulations, including those that raise costs such as on labour, and of course increased taxation, in the form of both direct and indirect taxes. The benefits for the enterprises themselves range from coming under the umbrella of enabling legal and regulatory frameworks (such as being allowed to operate in a particular space without harassment, enforceable commercial contracts, clear default and bankruptcy rules and limited liability) to being able to access public infrastructure and services, to increased access to institutional finance. For microenterprises and self-employed people, the freedom to operate without harassment and without fear of violence of different kinds may be among the most significant gains—but this depends crucially on the kind of public strategy and the extent of formalisation that does occur.

For informal workers, it can be expected that the benefits are in general likely to outweigh the costs, since the benefits can include legal recognition and protection as workers, the various rights that should come with being formally employed, such as freedom from discrimination, receiving legal minimum wages, benefiting from occupational health and safety measures, regulating conditions of work, receiving employer contributions to health and pensions and even realising the right to organize and bargain collectively. Therefore, it is not workers but employers who would be less willing to formalise in this case. The flexibility with respect to time and location of work that is often mentioned as a reason for some people choosing informal work is only relevant in a tiny minority of cases: in most

situations, informal work involves longer hours with less control over either location or conditions of work, and with significantly less pay, so that the choice
element is only applicable to a favoured few. All other workers who are engaged
in informal work are effectively rationed out of formal employment. Once again,
the extent to which formalisation of employment meets these laudable conditions
depends on the strategies used, the degree to which public policy actually pushes
these goals, and the forms and effectiveness of mobilisation of workers and civil
society.

There are strong gender differences in both the nature of informal employment
and its implications, which in turn mean that strategies of formalisation also play
out in different ways for men and women informal workers. For example, with
respect to enterprises, one important issue is that the costs of formalisation tend to
be much higher for women running microenterprises, while the benefits are less
apparent and generally lower, because even within the formal system women tend
to own fewer productive assets, receive less credit, are less equipped to handle
complex accounting requirements and deal with formal taxation. Even when they
are able to, women tend to receive much less institutional credit than men, and are
forced to rely on traditional moneylenders or very expensive microcredit. Because
of the social perceptions around gender and patriarchal attitudes pervading officialdom at all levels, such women tend to be much more subject to the whims and
caprices of enforcers on the ground. They are therefore much more likely to suffer
when there is "over-regulation" and especially when such over-regulation is associated with corruption. Furthermore, there are concerns about physical and
sexual security of women microentrepreneurs especially when they are engaged in
work in public spaces (such as street vending) which are rarely resolved by the acts
of registration and coming under the purview of regulatory bodies.

Kanbur (2009) described four types of possible economic responses on the part
of informal enterprises to regulation: (1) to stay within the ambit of the regulation
and comply; (2) to stay within the ambit of the regulation but not comply; (3) to
adjust activity to move out of the ambit of the regulation; and (4) among those that
are outside the ambit of the regulation in the first place, no need to adjust. While
the first category is very clearly in the realm of formalisation, the other three are
not—but importantly, they are all quite different, and therefore combining them
all for purposes of analysis or official policies is not useful. While the second category refers to those enterprises that are more likely to be classified as engaged in
"illegal" activities because of not conforming to regulations, the nature of the
regulations may be such that there could be a grey area between the second and
third categories. With respect to the first three categories, the choice of whether to
comply or not with regulations clearly depends on the costs/benefits of compliance vis-à-vis those of non-compliance. One important issue that is often
missed is that formalisation may lead to an increase in costs for enterprises, which
can make them less able to compete in markets characterised by extremely low
margins. In the case of women running informal and micro enterprises, the costs of
compliance are often higher, because they are more likely to have difficulties

fulfilling various legal and regulatory criteria; while the benefits of compliance may be uncertain and transient. Indeed, this emerges from several of the experiences of street vendors and other women engaged as micro entrepreneurs described in the chapters that follow.

With respect to the formalisation of employment and associated contracts, there can be no question that the extension of worker protection laws and social protection to cover informal workers is in general highly desirable. However, when they are sought to be imposed without regard for the implications for the financial viability of the small employers who employ them, they could have the unintended effect of reducing paid employment. This is particularly so when such regulatory efforts are not linked to wider strategies that link worker protection with attempts to improve the productivity of workers and improve demand conditions for their employers. This has been noticed in the case of women workers, for example, when attempts to ensure basic rights such as maternity benefits lead to employers' backlash resulting in fewer employment opportunities for women workers, which means that such policies need to be developed along with other supportive measures and institutional conditions.

Another possibility is the opposite situation, when there is effectively lack of regulation even when the rules and regulations exist on paper, essentially because of lax or insufficient monitoring and enforcement, because of paucity of public resources or corruption. This then means that laws and regulations—such as minimum wage laws or requirements that employers pay into the social security funds of workers—are simply not implemented. In conditions where even informal paid jobs are effectively rationed because of very low rates of aggregate employment generation, such flouting of rules may occur with the explicit or implicit support of the workers themselves, who may be desperate to receive wages, however low. In addition, women workers are found to be disproportionately unaware of their rights and entitlements, and this tends to make them more vulnerable to such exploitation.

So how do formalisation strategies actually play out for women workers in different contexts? What are the policy pitfalls to avoid and which strategies appear to be more effective in ensuring greater gender justice and empowerment of women workers? These questions are considered with specific reference to five different developing countries in Asia and Africa, in the next section. The essential features of labour markets and the nature and gendered impact of formalisation efforts in these countries are described briefly below.

IV The countries considered in this volume

India

India is remarkable even among developing countries, for the extreme prevalence of informality in economic activities as well as in employment. Despite rapid GDP growth in India since the 1980s, there has not been any noticeable expansion of decent work opportunities for India's relatively young labour force, nor of more formal employment. Growth has not been associated with much employment generation, and in fact the employment elasticities of output growth have actually declined as the economy has become more exposed to global competition that was supposed to have favoured more labour-intensive activities. The share of manufacturing in both output and employment has remained stubbornly constant at relatively low levels. Low productivity work continues to dominate in total employment, so in the aggregate there is little evidence of labour moving to higher productivity activities. Interestingly, this is true across sectors, such that low productivity employment coexists with some high value added activities within all of the major sectors, and there are extremely wide variations in productivity across enterprises even in the same sub-sector. The expected formalisation of work and the concentration of workers into large-scale production units has not occurred—rather, there has been widespread persistence of informal employment and increase in self-employment in non-agricultural activities. Most striking of all, the period of rapid GDP growth has been marked by low and declining work force participation rates of women, unlike most other rapidly growing economies. In the past two decades, this has reflected a shift of women into unpaid work within households (including activities like collection of fuelwood and water, along with usual care activities).

The latest labour force survey for 2017–18 revealed further deterioration in labour market conditions, with absolute declines in employment, driven by women's job losses especially in rural areas. Open unemployment rates also reached historic highs of 6.1 per cent in aggregate, with the unemployment rate for educated women at 20 per cent and that for young urban women at 27 per cent—truly remarkable rates in a society with no provision for any unemployment benefit. An estimated 68 per cent of workers were employed in the informal sector, and more than 90 per cent of all workers were informal (including those working in the formal sector). Women workers were overwhelmingly informal (around 95 per cent of all women workers and 85 per cent of non-agricultural workers). In general, they were clustered in the lowest paid of informal activities as well, with around half of them being self-employed and one-third working as helpers in family enterprises. Even among the relatively privileged category of regular employees in non-agricultural activities, only 29 per cent had written contracts (while the ratio for regular women workers was higher at 33 per cent than for men at 28 per cent, there were fewer women in such work). 55 per cent of men workers and 50 per cent of women workers were not eligible for paid leave. 52 per cent of women workers were not eligible for any form of social security benefit, compared to 49 per cent of men workers. These dire conditions existed before the pandemic struck; conditions are likely to be much worse after the pandemic and the brutal lockdown further destroyed livelihood opportunities.

While the general perception is that the informal economy exists because low wages allow it to compete with the formal sector in various activities, in fact there are many examples in which informal units are not in competition with formal enterprises, but actually service their requirements. (The vast, unorganised "logistics" apparatus offering services such as transportation and catering, which supports the India's IT and IT enabled services sector, is one example.) In the process, low wages in the informal economy help to sustain profits in the formal sector. This fits in with what has been found in many other studies of the linkages between formal and informal sectors across the world (Chen and Carre, 2020; ILO, 2016).

The Indian government's policies directed towards formalisation include those seeking to regulate informal enterprises; regulate informal employment; provide social protection to informal workers; create more jobs in formal sectors and activities; and increase the viability, productivity and incomes of informal enterprises and workers. In general, they have all had only very limited success, and have barely made a dent in the sea of informality that still dominates economic activity in India.

Two recent and drastic attempts to formalise informal enterprises are particularly noteworthy: the drastic demonetisation of "high value" currency notes (of Rs 500 and Rs 1,000) in November 2016; and the chaotic imposition of the Goods and Services Tax (GST) from July 2017. The first abruptly removed 86 per cent of the value of currency in circulation in a dominantly cash economy without speedy or adequate remonetisation, which led to a collapse of liquidity and consequent collapse of many informal activities. The associated push to digitisation of transactions, even in the absence of supportive infrastructure and institutional conditions, failed in its objectives but also significantly added to the costs faced by informal units and workers. The badly planned, hasty and poor implementation of the GST, which was designed to bring more enterprises into the tax net and bringing them into the regulatory sphere even while supposedly simplifying their operations, also sharply added to costs of informal enterprises operating on very low margins and reduced demand for their output. Both these measures have been extremely adverse for informal enterprises, causing their costs to increase and disrupting down existing supply chains. Since most informal activities operate on very thin margins, many have been simply unable to cope with the associated higher costs and have bowed down to competitive pressure from larger units. This has in turn also affected informal wage employment, and reduced demand for such workers, making it harder for them to find even poor quality paid work.

While this is true across all informal enterprises, matters have been even worse for women running microenterprises or operating as self-employed, such as those engaged in street vending and petty services. In addition to sharply increased costs of operation, they are disadvantaged because fewer of them have bank accounts and even those who do still find it next to impossible to get loans for productive purposes, other than tiny amounts of microcredit at high interest rates. They also find it more difficult to cope with the various requirements posed by formal institutions, whether for engaging in digital transactions or for filing of returns, and so on. This means that they have to rely on intermediaries for such actions, further adding to their costs.

Measures to improve employment conditions and social protection for informal workers have been limited and largely ineffective. The stark evidence for this is that the Indian government itself continues to rely heavily on informal workers for some of its major schemes and other public spending, both directly and through outsourcing of some of its responsibilities. The most obvious examples are in the National Health Mission and the Integrated Child Development Scheme (ICDS), both of which rely on women workers who are grossly underpaid, with remuneration well below minimum wages. This is made possible through the cynical classification of such workers are "volunteers" who are paid "honoraria" rather than wages, even though these women workers are effectively the basis on which both programmes run. The Accredited Social Health Activists who underpin the National Health Mission that supports public primary health care and the *anganwadi* women workers and helpers who are the mainstay of the Integrated Child Development Services providing nutrition and care to pregnant and lactating mothers and infant children, have been waging a prolonged struggle to be recognised as public employees with associated rights. But this movement has not yet met with success, despite some successes in raising the honoraria (which are still well below minimum wages). In addition, there are increasing numbers of other "voluntary" workers (mostly women) associated with various government schemes, and some are even completely unpaid. The unwillingness of the government to recognise its own workers and formalise their status is in sharp contrast with the stated aim of formalising other workers in the private sector. Even in this attempt at formalisation, the focus has been on regulatory measures, without concern for their impact on viability of microenterprises and associated livelihood.

A survey conducted in the National Capital Region of Delhi for this study found that most workers (and especially women workers) were simply unaware of basic legal and other provisions designed to improve their conditions, such as the Unorganized Workers' Social Security Act, 2008 or even the Maternity Benefits Act. Legal minimum wages were rarely implemented, including in formal enterprises that hire informal workers on a casual basis. A striking finding was that of the mobility of workers between formal and informal employers, and the general fluidity of the labour market, such that strict distinctions between the two categories seemed irrelevant, especially when the law is observed mainly in the breach even for many formal enterprises. Attempts to provide access to credit for microentrepreneurs, which would enable them to set up enterprises that could become formal, have been limited by poor coverage and the tiny amount of the average loan that does not allow for any meaningful investment.

Thus far, therefore, Indian attempts at formalisation have not just been largely unsuccessful but even counterproductive, especially for women workers. While this does reflect the wider context of an extremely weak labour market with poor demand conditions, it is also the result of poor design, worse implementation and little attention to the social contexts within which such attempts have been made, specifically gendered social relations.

South Africa

Unlike many other developing countries, the South African economy can be described as highly formal—but with a rapidly increasing informal economy, so that it is being transformed from a once predominantly vibrant formal sector to a much more mixed economy of formal and informal activities. Informalisation of employment is occurring both in the traditionally formal sectors of the economy, that is, manufacturing, retail, nursing, transport, security, cleaning, refuse removal, agriculture amongst others; and within conventionally informal sectors, such as street vending, waste pickers, domestic workers, transport (Uber and Taxify services). Increasing informality within formal sectors expresses itself through outsourcing, precarious working conditions, contracting, part time work, labour broking and moonlighting. Some sectors have historically been characterised by informality due to the nature of work, such as domestic work, farm work and sex work. But there are others that have become more informal over time, such as street vendors/traders, parking guards or attendants, waste pickers both on landfill sites and in urban areas, security guards, cleaners, as well as migrant and local artisans informally employed in the formal sector.

In the aggregate, South Africa has a higher rate of open unemployment and a lower rate of informal employment than other countries in Sub-Saharan Africa and other developing regions. In 2018, the labour force participation rate for women (aged 15–64 years) was 64 per cent, while for men it was 74 per cent. However, unemployment in South Africa has remained extremely high at nearly 28 per cent in 2017, and as high as 37 per cent using the "expanded definition" that includes discouraged workers. Labour market conditions have deteriorated recently: open unemployment increased by 2 million people in the decade between 2008 and 2017, while employment increased by only 1.6 million in the same period. In the last quarter of 2018, the unemployment rate for women was estimated to be as high as 41 per cent for women and 33 per cent for men. Youth unemployment is particularly high: 55 per cent of those in the 15–24 years age cohort are openly unemployed, and 88 per cent of youth (nearly one out of every ten young persons) with school degrees are unemployed.

In 2018, total informal employment represented approximately 18 per cent of non-agricultural employment. A somewhat surprising feature of the South African labour market is that women workers are more likely to be in formal employment than men. In late 2018, 22 per cent of male non-agricultural workers were in informal employment, compared to only 16 per cent of women non-agricultural workers.[4] Around 30 per cent of men workers and 27 per cent of women workers are members of trade unions, a low proportion but still higher than in many other countries, including the others in this comparative study. Male union members are disproportionately likely to be permanently employed with regular contracts, especially in construction and mining sectors. Female unionisation is highest in private households (domestic workers) and in the public sector. As expected, access to leave, pension and medical aid benefits are higher amongst unionised workers, especially those in the formal sector.

The often contradictory implications of government intervention in informal activities are especially evident in some economic sectors. Street vendors and other market workers (who are dominantly women) provide a telling example. They are affected by a multiplicity of actors: governments (municipalities or other levels) who regulate their use of public spaces; collective associations regulating the operations of local markets; and the private suppliers from whom they buy goods. Public infrastructure policies often result in marketplace evictions. Street vendors and the organisations that represent them have to negotiate with local, regional and national authorities, in contexts in which such authorities tend to be oblivious of street vendors, and generally dismissive of the direct and indirect impact of their policies or bye laws on street vendors' core economic activity. The most visible impact is the extent to which access to public spaces for vending, storing or producing (e.g. cooking) goods for sale are impacted or hindered by existing or new legislation. Through processes of formalisation, local governments control access to these spaces for vendors, who are then forced to conform or face the wrath of the law through fines or having their stalls demolished. Such formal access for vendors is usually accompanied by the need for applying for trading licenses and paying market fees, but rarely takes into account issues like access to transportation, toilet facilities and ensuring safety in public spaces, which can be especially important for women. These are evidently formalisation measures that operate against the interests of the (self-employed) women informal workers, also because they are undertaken without sensitivity to the workers' needs. In this context, only active mobilisation and collective bargaining by street vendors (with the assistance of organisations like WIEGO and Streetnet) can play a role in generating a context for statutory negotiations.

Similar tendencies of generating unanticipated negative consequences for informal workers were evident in the case of waste pickers. An attempt by the city of Johannesburg to create formal employment in the waste sector, by organising the recognised but informal "reclaimers" (waste pickers) working on landfill sites into co-operatives and allowing them to compete with private waste companies, was not successful because these newly formed co-operatives were not able to compete in the tendering process with the private companies, many of which relied on informal workers. The process required reclaimers to operate within a business model framework, assisted by externally driven training programmes that were not in sync with their skills and orientation. Once again, organisations like WIEGO played facilitator and mediator roles between the workers and the city. This intervention was crucial to the city recognising the invaluable contributions made by reclaimers and the informal economy. However, other examples from other South African cities emphasise that issues of access to and control over physical space in which to carry out their activities (including storing material and undertaking sorting and recycling work) remain a critical difficulty for informal workers in waste and recycling activities, which formalisation attempts rarely take into account.

A particularly interesting example of informal work of women in South Africa is that of informal (illegal) miners. Many women working as artisanal miners to replace or supplement their traditionally undervalued, female work, saw artisanal mining as a means to escape the gender discrimination experienced in various facets of life, in both the productive and social reproductive spaces. Despite facing worse terms than men workers, women described their work positively, emphasizing the ability to choose flexible hours of work, allowing for breaks and being able to determine the pace of work.

There are over a million domestic workers in South Africa, of which the overwhelming majority (96 per cent) are women. Unfortunately, less than 1 per cent of them are unionised. Unionised domestic workers are more likely to receive minimum wages. However, overall, the working conditions of domestic workers are significantly inferior to those of the median worker: less than a quarter have written contracts or any kind of paid leave, less than 5 per cent have access to any pensions or retirement funds, and less than 1 per cent receive any kind of medical assistance or health insurance. In this context, and given the difficulty of implementing minimum wages in extremely informal household settings, the recent increase in minimum wages for domestic workers is welcome but needs to be supported with mobilisation and organisation.

The South African case makes it starkly clear that organising and mobilising are central to processes of desirable formalisation, and their absence tends to be associated with undesirable formalisation. Of course, labour organisations need to be supported by appropriate laws and regulatory processes, but these must be sensitive to the specific needs and requirements of the women workers. It is worth noting that despite such challenges, domestic workers, farm workers and security guards have successfully managed to organise themselves into unions, be covered by the national minimum wage legislation and in some cases even engage in collective bargaining.

Ghana

Like India, Ghana's economy is overwhelmingly dominated by informal work and informal enterprises, with a diminishing proportion of the workforce engaged in formal work. The structure of the economy and its labour relations have been reinforced by economic liberalisation policies since the 1980s that have sought to limit the role of government in the economy, promote the private sector, loosen the regulation of economic activities and labour relations and promote free markets in goods and services.

The Ghanaian population and labour force have expanded rapidly over the past few decades. Participation in economic activities is also quite high, with rates for males and females being nearly equal, especially in recent decades. However, around 90 per cent of all workers are estimated to be in informal activities, whether self-employed (around 56 per cent) or in family enterprises (20 per cent) or as paid workers (18 per cent). The rural informal economy has a substantial proportion of Ghana's self-employed workers, mainly in agriculture, fishing and fish processing, and rural agro-based processing activities and collection of forest products. Work in the informal economy is generally gender segmented both in rural and urban areas. While agriculture involves both men and women, albeit in different activities, fishing is predominantly male and fish processing is mostly done by women. Agro-processing is largely women's work, while forest products workers are mostly male. The urban informal economy is made up of services, dominated by women; construction, with predominantly male workers; and industry, which consists mainly of manufacturing and extractive industries. There is widespread gender segmentation of labour forms in the informal economy, that is, wage work (casual, permanent), self-employment, communal labour, family and child labour and apprenticeships.

Several indicators point to a change in the structure of the labour market. In 1960, male participation in economic activities exceeded that of females by 18 percentage points whereas the corresponding figure for 1970 was nearly 10 percentage points. These large differences have disappeared over the years, with female participation in economic activities even surpassing that of males (although the differences are insignificant) in 1984 and 2010. In 2013, male LFPR was 80 per cent compared to 75 per cent for women, while employment rates in 2010 were nearly the same at 95 per cent for men and 94 per cent for women. The highest rate of unemployment (10 per cent) was recorded in 2000. Unlike the case of South Africa, slack in the labour market in Ghana is reflected in underemployment and a preponderance of informal work, rather than open unemployment or discouraged workers who drop out of the labour force. Indeed, informality is arguably the most visible aspect of employment and the Ghanaian economy as a whole.

While the informal economy has been the dominant source of employment for the expanding working population, government regulation has stressed *enterprise* formalisation. But it has not been accompanied by specific strategies and activities that are capable of formalising informal *employment*. This is evident from the analysis contract farming and domestic trading, two sectors that provide the bulk of informal employment in Ghana. Interestingly, workers in these sectors also face worse conditions of employment in terms of the standard criteria for formality, than the average across workers in all sectors.

Contract farming involves interactions between agribusiness (formal enterprises) and small- and medium-scale farmers (the informal economy). There are different variants of contract farming. In most cases, farmers participating in these schemes operate on their own land, but there are instances in which the agribusiness, besides its supply of production requirements, also provides producers with land. In this case, the most important factor that farmers contribute to the production process is their labour. There are other variants in which farmers assume nearly all the risks that are associated with production. In this case, the contract is centred on the marketing of produce (typically horticultural products) after harvesting has been undertaken. Contract farming has been strongly endorsed by successive governments in Ghana and has become an important model for the penetration of agribusiness into farming communities with a large share of women workers. Government policy does little to formalise the informal nature of contract farming. However, firms that work with contract farmers are required to adhere to the regulations of the sector in which they operate. While firms with export-oriented crops and products operate under regulatory regimes of international regulatory bodies of which they are members, the regulation for domestically oriented-marketing firms and their contract farmers are determined and regulated by the firms themselves.

The analysis of some specific agribusiness operations shows that they do generate employment in local communities—not only for the farmers involved in contract farming, but also for other local residents who are able to find employment at factories or processing centres. Furthermore, employment was generally available to women; in fact, in many of the cases, employment at processing centres was dominated by women. However, the majority of workers were employed as temporary labour to undertake specific activities during the production or harvesting season such as picking and cleaning fruits. There were opportunities for permanent employment (decent work), but these were extremely limited and were more likely to benefit a handful of men in technical and managerial positions. The regulation of contract farming itself was primarily based on international certification initiatives signed on to by agribusiness firms. These were generally concerned with environmental and biodiversity conservation, although some (like the Fair-Trade certification) prohibited the use of children and pregnant women as labour.

In general, the emphasis on production and marketing contracts improved the quality of products, introduced farmers to global production standards and brought some minimal consciousness about labour conditions on farms, which are usually not considered in smallholder agriculture production. However, these only pertain to export-oriented crops and their contract farmers. On the downside, exposure to global value chains increased the burdens and risks contract farmers carried, without protection from the vicissitudes of export commodities trade. Gender issues were not articulated clearly in the contract farming schemes. The only exception was one case in which pregnant women and children were not expected/allowed to work on contract farms. Regulations were also silent on wage differences between women and men on contract farms. Typically, wages were determined by community standards, and not by contracting firms, which led to the persistence of gender wage gaps. Other silences and gaps in the contracts included any mention if leave periods, overtime payments and use of family labour on farms.

The contract farming regimes in the four cases were fraught with implementation challenges, including the inability of the agri-businesses to supervise all the farmers they engaged with. Due to their limited human resources and the fact they have to work with smallholders scattered across several communities, firms were unable to monitor farmers' adherence to the specified procedures required to meet production standards. Companies were more effective with regard to marketing, as farmers' produce could be rejected for not meeting the required standards. Additionally, the inability of companies to meet their obligations (supply of inputs and making credit available) in a timely manner imposed additional constraints on production. For farmers who have to produce crops organically, the labour and chemical use restrictions are additional challenges. Other major reported challenges include the inability of companies to buy all produce (especially during the peak agriculture harvesting season), low prices and delays in payment. The cases showed that contract farming arrangements were not a viable approach to formalising informal employment, and that major gender concerns were not addressed. The study suggests that contract farming in Ghana is probably an example of a process of "false formalisation," in which (some) informal activities of contract farmers get subsumed in formal agri-business enterprises as part of their accumulation strategies. In effect, the formal sector (in the form of agri-business firms) relies on the informality in the operations of contract farmers to keep their own costs down.

Domestic trading in Ghana comprises two broad types of activities: trading activities operated by persons from both authorised (district markets and rented stalls) and unauthorised structures; and street vending. There is much diversity within these two broad types. For instance, street vending can range from highly mobile sellers of cold water to less mobile cooked food sellers who pack up their table tops and cooking utensils at the end of each day. There are also market traders who, in a bid to increase interaction with buyers, might also engage in street vending. However, there are other groups of traders who do not fall neatly into any of the two broad categories. This includes women who combine household reproductive duties with trading, selling their wares in corner shops attached to residential accommodation or on table tops in front of houses.

Domestic trading in Ghana is generally regarded as the space of, and for, women, although more men have moved into this activity in recent years. The preponderance of women has been attributed to the nature of the work that enables them to combine this with their gender specific reproductive duties, the low skill and capital requirements of trading and a supposedly strict separation in economic functions in which men are responsible for agricultural production or fishing whereas women are responsible for the marketing of produce. However, it is found that in general, women workers dominate the over-crowded survivalist segments of the trading sector, while their entry and participation in small but more capital-intensive segments is restricted. Segmentation of the informal economy is clearly evident in domestic trading. In many of the large metropolitan and municipal areas, traders who lack sufficient capital and the right social networks end up operating from unauthorised structures or as street vendors, and these are disproportionately women.

The regulation of domestic trading in Ghana involves three main actors: namely, the state, local governments and traders' associations. In domestic trading, the extension of credit to operators has been prioritised over formalisation of work although evidence about access to, and actual gains from participation in these services is inconclusive. More importantly, local governments are more concerned with generating revenue from traders through taxes, although traders are generally dissatisfied with market and other infrastructure.

The state's role in affecting the conditions of retail trade has been important at the level of policy as well as because of institutional reforms in the banking and financial sectors. Part of the reasoning behind these reforms was to increase access to credit, especially for microenterprises. Indeed, the number of operators in the formal financial sector has expanded, but the impact of the reforms can be described as moderate. High interest on loans, and the failure of some financial institutions in recent years have implied that traders and other actors in the informal economy are either excluded or cannot rely on these systems. As a result, informal arrangements for banking and insurance continue to be important.

Local governments are more influential in regulating domestic trading than the state. However, their interactions with traders revolve around revenue generation, urban planning and city management. Enhancing and expanding market infrastructure is a major challenge in many districts, although trading comprises one of the most important sources of revenue. Also, concerns about urban planning and city management lead local governments to embark on demolitions and forced relocations. Confrontations between street vendors and district assembly guards are quite regular and may in some areas comprise a part of the daily life of street vendors. These activities disrupt the livelihoods of street vendors who are more likely to be women, and to be poor. In response, traders' associations comprise one of the few organisations that seek to promote the interests and welfare of traders. They are an important source of informal social protection, providing their members with support which prevent them from exiting trading when they experience shocks.

Thus, like contract farming, the formalisation of trading under the current regulatory practices is limited. In the absence of any serious attempts at formalisation, workers engaged in the informal economy continue to lag behind their counterparts in formal employment in the areas of entitlements to maternity leave, social security, and the rights to organise, among others.

Morocco

Morocco has experienced a period of relatively rapid growth, which resulted in reduction of poverty as well as structural transformations of the economy with new sectors emerging such as agri-business, automotive industries, aeronautics and pharmaceutical industries. However, the economy still remains highly dependent on agriculture and has not created sufficient employment opportunities for the growing labour force. This has meant that informal employment continues to be significant, and more young people and women have been pushed into informal activities.

There are striking differences between men and women in work participation. In 2016, the employment rate was 65 per cent for men and only 21 per cent for women. The difference between men and women was higher in urban areas, with employment rates for men and women being 59 and 13 per cent, respectively. While occupational mobility is very high for both men and women, women workers are more likely to shift from inactivity to informal or unpaid work and also more likely to move to worse job status. More than a quarter of young people are not working and not being educated, and this rate is four times higher for young women (44 per cent) than for young men (12 per cent).

Minimum wage laws apply to workers in the formal sector. Overall, wage employment increased significantly from 38 per cent in 2000 to 47 per cent in 2016, but this was mostly in informal activities. However, employment in the informal sector is not feminised: the share of women's informal employment in 2014 was only 10.5 per cent, compared to 17 per cent for overall non-agricultural employment. Women have a higher propensity to work in the industrial sector where they hold one in five jobs, while in the services sector, they account for 14 per cent of total employment.

Within informal activities, self-employment predominates, as nearly 80 per cent of permanent workers in the informal sector are self-employed; 68 per cent are own account workers and 11 per cent are employers. However, the share of paid employment has increased since 2014, especially in rural areas. Other indicators show a high presence of informality. Less than a quarter of employed men and women have medical coverage related to their work, and in rural areas the ratio was more than 90 per cent. Only 20 per cent of employees are covered by the pension system, with large disparities depending on residence, sector and professional status. Less than one-third of workers have a formal written contract, with young people and non-graduates disproportionately engaged in non-contractual employment. Unpaid employment is particularly important among employed women, around 40 per cent of whom worked without pay in 2018, compared to less than 10 per cent of men. Unpaid work is even higher among rural women, with 70 per cent of them working without remuneration. Women are also more likely to receive low wages. Those working in urban areas are more likely to suffer from low wages and excessive work time.

At the aggregate level, the share of young female workers who are informally employed is higher than that of young male workers. The informally employed represent a higher percentage of young workers residing in rural areas compared to young workers residing in urban areas. In rural areas, young female workers are almost all informally employed (97 per cent). Formal employment in the youth population increases with age. It also rises with education; however, only the higher education level protects from informality, while lower levels of education show high shares of informal employment. The type of education received seems to also matter in terms of access to formal jobs: attending private school increases the chance of being formally employed and studying the French language increases the chance of men being formally employed. Parental job status is a good predictor of formal versus informal employment among youth. The fact that the father or mother holds a formal job increases the probability that the person's employment will be formal rather than informal, and this holds true for both men and women. However, the mother's job status has more influence on both sons and daughters. The average wage of the informally employed youth is significantly lower than that of the formally employed youth.

There have been numerous attempts in Morocco to implement formalisation policies. The strategies include active labour market policies and employment policies aimed at making labour formalisation less costly; laws for certain workers like domestic workers; and laws to encourage self-entrepreneurs.

Since 2005, a large number of active employment programmes have been introduced, including programmes aimed at encouraging formal wage employment. One programme exempts firms from the employer's and employee's social security contributions and professional training tax for a period. Another encourages firms and associations to hire job seekers on permanent contracts through exemptions from social security contributions and income tax. The TAEHIL programme aims to increase employability through contractual training for job seekers.

A total of 65 per cent of the 2016 beneficiaries of the TAEHIL programme and almost 50 per cent of the 2016 IDMAJ beneficiaries were women. Some programmes (IKRAM 1 and IKRAM 2, MINAJLIKI and WADIYATI) are specifically geared toward women. Studies of the IDMAJ programme have found benefits for the beneficiaries, through greater incidence of permanent contracts and reduction in average duration to find sustainable employment, as well as benefits in terms of salary, the type of work contract and access to social security cover. However, these programmes still cover a relatively small number of workers and youth. While well-designed active employment programmes can help secure employment to a number of job seekers, it has been found that the more educated have a greater likelihood of benefitting from these programmes and that women can be relegated to the least interesting programmes.

The law for domestic workers came into force in late 2018 and was largely based on the ILO Convention on Domestic Workers, with some differences. It requires an employment contract that must be signed and legalised by both parties, specify if it is a fixed term contract or one with unlimited duration, the nature of the work, weekly hours of work (limited to 48 hours per week for those over 18 years and to 40 hours per week for those aged 16-18 years) with weekly and annual holidays, and state the salary which must be equal to at least 60 per cent of the minimum wage. Social security benefits are to be paid by employers, but the impact of this provision has been hindered by delay in the relevant decree. Sanctions in the form of fines are provided if the employer does not respect the signed contract.

However, since the law came into force, only 300 employment contracts linking a domestic to her/his employer have been filed, and most of them are by foreign employers residing in Morocco. Domestic workers are reluctant to sign employment contracts, partly because of a wait-and-see attitude by employers, partly because of the fear of losing other social security benefits and partly because of the concern that signing the contract will prevent them from quitting their jobs at any time. There is also the impact of the role of intermediaries in the hesitation of employees to sign an employment contract. An additional reason for this may be that the law only seems to address one type of domestically employed person, whereas there are at least four types. There are women (sometimes relatives of their employers) who permanently live with their employers and work without remuneration, only receiving food, clothing and on occasion a limited amount of money. There are young women who work for a monthly wage well below the minimum wage, who often do not negotiate or receive the wage, which is given directly to their parents, with negotiations conducted by brokers who set wages and working conditions. There are women who hire themselves out on a daily basis, as well as those who receive weekly or monthly wages for specific tasks like cleaning. It is difficult to ascertain the rights of women relatives working as domestic employees or to ensure 60 per cent of the minimum wage to domestic employees living outside the major cities. As a result, the law is struggling to gain public support and have a significant impact on domestic workers.

The Moroccan Law dealing with the status of the self entrepreneur was adopted in 2015. The law gives a number of advantages to self-entrepreneurs: they are exempt from the obligation to register in the commercial register and keep extensive accounts; they can work from their residences or in premises operated jointly by several companies; they obtain social coverage from the date of registration; and they receive a number of fiscal advantages like protection from value added tax and low rates of income tax. The status is attractive especially for young people, and more than half of self-entrepreneurs are between 15 and 34 years old. Two-thirds are men and one-third are women. While the law alone is not sufficient to significantly reduce informality, it has given the opportunity to some to formalise their activity. Nevertheless, despite the numerous advantages and procedure simplifications introduced by the law and some success, the objective in terms of the self-entrepreneurs interested by this status has not been achieved.

Survey data point to differences in "values," which are stronger when different work status is considered, rather than when gender is taken into account. Agreements or disagreements with statements dealing with whether men and women should be given the same job opportunities and salaries, whether men should have more right to a job in case of job scarcity, whether men should be the main provider and whether married women should work outside the house are rather similar between men and women but are quite different among women formally and informally employed and slightly different between formally and informally employed men.

This analysis of the Moroccan case suggests that even the most well-intentioned schemes and laws may fail in their goals if the specific social contexts and the gender construction of the society is not taken adequately into account.

Thailand

Thailand presents a striking contrast to the other countries in this study. The most significant difference is macroeconomic in nature: Thailand has been experiencing an economic boom that has also been accompanied by significant increases in employment, to the point where it could be said that the economy is close to full employment, which in turn has been reflected in rising real wages. Some essential structural features of the labour markets are similar to the other countries studied here. While the proportion of people who were employed informally witnessed a gradual decline in recent years, informal sector employment still accounts for the majority of the employment in Thailand, at 56 per cent in 2016. There are large wage gaps according to type of employment, with the average wage for formal workers 40 per cent higher than that for informal workers in 2016, and by gender, with women workers earning 12 per cent less than men workers in formal employment and 21 per cent less in informal activities. However, the Thai experience highlights the complexity of issues around formalisation, for both units and workers

Thailand's attempts to formalise have focussed both on enterprises and on the provision of social security schemes to a wide range of workers, including those in informal work and self-employment. For example, the coverage of the voluntary Social Security Fund was extended to informal workers, and as of 2017, there were 2.25 informal million workers in the Scheme, which provides some non-occupational injury or sickness benefits, maternity, invalidity, death, unemployment, old-age and child support, depending on the package chosen. The Universal Health Care system (popularly known as the 30 Baht for All Scheme) is even more universal in nature, as it is available to every citizen, although it does not cover ethnic minorities, stateless persons and foreign migrant workers. The Scheme covered 99.95 per cent of the Thai population in 2017. There are also some targeted non-contributory social protection schemes, such as for the disabled, the elderly and for those with HIV-AIDS, as well as those below some income/asset criteria.

However, these strategies do face certain barriers. For one, the very provision of universal health care, which is clearly eminently desirable in itself, provides a default option for every citizen and therefore disincentivises enrolment in contributory schemes, even though the benefits derived from social security go beyond medical insurance. The inflexibilities and time required for reimbursement or accessing benefits are also not appealing for informal workers who value time (since this implies loss of incomes) and convenience. In addition, informal workers may encounter a fiscal trap due to the formalization process, which may require the payment of income tax or at least the filing of tax returns. Self-employed individuals working with formal enterprises may have some tax withheld from their incomes, which, especially when combined with social security contributions, reduces current incomes while benefits from social security are to be realised only in the future.

Therefore, in some cases, the inflexibility of the formalisation schemes becomes a significant disincentive for workers, especially women workers. For example, the recent effort of the government to formalize online shops (both wholesalers and retailers) and Prompt-Pay registration has had untended effects on female informal workers, since the informal activities in this sector are dominantly run by independent women workers, who would now be required to report their income to the state and be subject to various regulations.

Domestic housekeepers and domestic cleaners and helpers who largely work inside private homes in Thailand are overwhelmingly informally employed: 71 per cent of domestic housekeepers and 91 per cent of domestic cleaners and helpers are informal employees without any type of social security coverage, compared to 80 per cent of cleaners and helpers in hotels and other businesses who are formally employed. Consistent with conventional wisdom, informal workers generally work longer hours and earn less on a per hour basis than their formal counterparts. While all domestic workers reported problems in the workplace, such as issues with pay, arduous work and no benefits, informal workers had additional complaints about not having any days off. Nevertheless, there were several women workers who preferred informal work in private homes, not because of wages or access to social security, but because of the work environment, ease of tasks, flexibility (despite long hours), lower costs associated with travel and accommodation and even access to low or no interest informal credit. This points to the importance of considering preferences relating to flexibility and other more personal benefits over other workplace amenities that are more easily provided in an informal setting than in private firm settings.

Sex workers present a different set of concerns, since prostitution is criminalised in Thailand. The law forbids selling sex, pimping and running a "prostitution establishment" and punishes the sex worker for selling sex (with a maximum fine of 1,000 baht) but not the customer for purchasing sex—except in cases when minors are involved. This obviously poses problems for formalisation: being informal does not necessarily mean illegal, but illegality usually makes formalisation tricky. There are obvious negative consequences for the sex workers because of such illegality: legitimate "service providers" (especially women) working in entertainment venues struggle to determine their legal status; the law enables the violation of many other rights of sex workers, such as the rights to equal protection under the law, to work, to have access to social services and the right to the highest attainable standard of health; it acts as a barrier for sex workers, who want to seek help from local authorities when targeted with violence and harassment but have to keep these abuses, along with their work, hidden for fear of being arrested; and of course it does nothing to diminish the physical and mental abuse of sex workers and their human rights, by brothel owners, clients, etc.

It has been argued that legalising prostitution in Thailand would allow sex workers to register with the government authorities allowing them to undergo regular medical checks for sexually transmitted diseases, be subject to taxation and labour laws, and contribute to social security schemes, while regulation also would make it easier to control the minimum age of those entering the trade. However, it is also the case that a majority of sex workers conceal their work status not only for fear of being arrested by police, but because of the possibility of being stigmatised and discriminated against in society, since the perception of sex workers is generally negative. As such, many sex workers feel that formalising and regulating (or indeed legalizing) sex work will not change the situation much because many would insist on keeping their anonymity, both for financial reasons (i.e. untaxed earnings) and societal reasons (i.e. taboo and stigmatisation). Some even argue that formalisation could actually drive prostitution further underground rather than reducing it, thereby making it even more dangerous. It is evident that the Thai law as it applies to the sex industry is old and outdated, and legislation needs to be revised to actively protect those who enter into the sex industry without being criminalised, stigmatised and marginalised. However, legalisation, formalisation and regulation are elusive on a practical level, not least because of social stigma, discretion and crime, but also because there seems to a general lack of political will to drastically change the industry.

V The way forward: insights and policy recommendations

This study was undertaken and completed well before the COVID-19 pandemic swept across the world, but the insights it provides are still likely to have significant relevance for the post-pandemic world. The case studies presented here provide a sobering assessment of the benefits of even the most well-intentioned formalisation policies, particularly with respect to their impact on women workers. To put it starkly, many official measures designed to increase formalisation of work have essentially failed to improve the conditions of workers, particularly women, and even those that can be deemed to be successful have been very limited in scope and coverage. This is not to say that there have been no successes at all, but rather that these successes have not been sufficient to change the basic conditions of the labour force in situations of widespread informality. In addition, many government schemes to provide some "formal sector-type" benefits to workers such as pensions are merely limited substitutes for formalisation, but these are often mistakenly identified as evidence of actual or effective formalisation. Furthermore, in labour markets with a high degree of informality, there is often a lot of fluidity in workers' conditions, and they can move across formal/informal employment without really changing their basic circumstances.

Of course, government interventions that are designed to provide social security to unorganised workers vary in impact according to labour market conditions, extent of regulatory power and monitoring of the government, political will, etc. Lack of awareness of many laws and schemes, as well as the sheer difficulty of accessing entitlements, still operate against the interests of informal workers, and this is especially the case for women, since gender blindness or lack of concern for the specific and varying circumstances of women workers makes formalisation less effective or even ineffective.

The analysis provided thus far points to some broad conclusions that also have important policy implications, as specified below.

The significance of the macroeconomic context

One absolutely crucial point to note is that the impact of formalisation policies is hugely dependent on the overall macroeconomic and labour market contexts. The contrast between Thailand and the other countries considered here makes that amply apparent. Thailand is the only country that was experiencing not just a macroeconomic boom, but also an employment boom, expressed in rapidly growing employment and rising real wages. This has had significant effects on other features of the labour market that are often seen as more structural, such as the gender wage gap, which has reduced (and even disappeared for some sectors). In a situation of such a tight labour market, it is often the case that it is easier to bring in and enforce formalisation measures. But it could also be that even informal employers are forced to offer better conditions, more social protection, and so on, so that the differences in wages and working conditions between formal and informal employment become less stark.

All the other countries considered here show much more slack in the labour market, with the high presence of open or disguised unemployment, and evidence of decreased demand for workers in the recent past. This is true even of the countries like India and Morocco that were otherwise experiencing rapid output growth. This aggregate lack of productive employment opportunities obviously makes it harder to implement formalisation policies, since workers desperate for livelihoods will be forced to accept even relatively poor conditions in informal work and official monitoring of such employment can be difficult if not impossible. The collapse of economic activity and employment because of the pandemic and lockdowns have made matters significantly worse, especially for women; therefore the dangers of women workers being rationed out of available wage employment and being forced to undertake even more unpaid labour within homes, are even greater than before. Employment generation strategies therefore have to recognise these likely outcomes and factor in specific policies accordingly.

Recognising what genuine progressive formalisation means

Governments seek to bring both enterprises and workers into the ambit of formalisation, often for different reasons. The differences between these two types of formalisation are considered below, but it is also important to note that neither need necessarily create better conditions for those engaged in informal activities. In the case of small and micro-enterprises and self-employment, costly registration and tax requirements without the rights, benefits or protections that should accompany formalisation are not particularly beneficial. Similarly, taxation or enforced registration of informal enterprises without benefits, such as in the Indian GST or in other flat tax systems where own-account workers may have to pay the same taxes as big businesses, or obligations to register with different departments in cumbersome procedures, all operate to worsen the conditions of those involved in informal activities. In all such laws and regulations, women engaged in such activities are worse off, partly because they typically have lower levels of literacy and numeracy, fewer social networks to access the relevant bureaucracy, and are more likely to be threatened or abused during the process of enforcement. Similarly, in several of the cases considered here (such as South Africa and Ghana), rules with respect to location, zoning, phyto-sanitary conditions, etc., had substantial negative effects for small traders and street vendors, with women workers disproportionately hit by these laws and regulations. Therefore, such policies should not be seen as examples of progressive and desirable formalisation without more detailed consideration of the actual implications.

With respect to workers, governments often use other indicators to suggest that more workers are getting the benefit of formal employment. But in fact, the case studies show that any one measure of formalisation (such as paid leave or social security or written contract) is very inadequate as a genuine measure of decent work, and workers characterised as being in formal contracts according to any one of these indicators can typically face extreme insecurity of tenure and exploitation in various ways. So these should not be seen as genuine progressive formalisation either. In some cases, over-zealous governments impose conditions that are designed to encourage worker formalisation but actually operate against the interests of workers, such as unrealistic educational requirements for informal workers, unrealistic legal requirements for informal workers, preconditions that are difficult to meet, costly bureaucratic requirements that are effectively unaffordable for most informal workers. Such measures actually operate against the interests of workers, and once again women workers who are less likely to meet the criteria fare worse in such situations. Indeed, as Chen and Carre (2020, 8) note, much official policy is based on "the presumption that informal workers are not 'real' workers with a place in labour law and with shared concerns around which they can coalesce, mobilise and organise for collective action and bargaining with actors and institutions that impact on their activities. This perspective has led, in many countries, to significant 'blinders' in employment standards and labour law, especially the law on representation rights."

The formalisation of enterprises versus formality for workers

It is often believed that when enterprises are formalised, workers would automatically benefit because they would necessarily become formally employed, be subject to minimum wage laws and receive protection from various legislations, including those relating to job security and various forms of social security.

However, the case studies show that this is not the case. The Indian experience is especially stark in this regard, showing that even formal enterprises continue to hire workers on completely informal terms, often without even any written contracts, and that there is a high degree of fluidity across formal and informal employment.

Indeed, attempts to formalise enterprises and economic activities (rather than employment) can often be counterproductive, reducing their competitive position and thereby even threatening their survival and so affecting employment adversely. This was found to be true for contract farming in Ghana, as well as demonetisation and GST implementation in India. Genuinely progressive formalisation policies that improve the conditions of workers, especially women workers, need to recognise that the focus must be on precisely on such workers, and on laws, rules and policies to improve their wages and working conditions that can be implemented without harming their employment prospects.

Framing laws and regulations appropriately

There are several issues to bear in mind when framing formalisation laws and policies, including both economic and social context. Some cases of apparently pro-women measures can operate to their detriment, such as in the case of the law on private employers providing maternity benefits for their women workers in India. This is obviously an essential requirement for all women, and formal public employment in India already provides maternity benefits in the form of paid leave. However, private employers especially in the informal sector have not been as keen to provide this benefit. The imposition of a law requiring paid maternity leave to be provided to all women workers, while certainly desirable in principle, may not work in the expected way. In the Indian context, with an extremely slack labour market wherein employment prospects are poor, this has simply meant that private employers choose not to hire women. In informal contexts where job security is also not ensured, it could even mean the loss of employment for women—exactly the opposite of what is intended. Therefore, it is necessary for policies to be nuanced to take into account such considerations. It could be argued that it is necessary for some state participation in the costs of such maternity leave, to ensure that women workers are not at the receiving end through loss of employment.

The need to avoid oppressive or punitive regulation

It was found across the case studies that some regulations, particularly of small and micro enterprises that have little in the form of financial assets or technical expertise, can be counterproductive and oppressive, in extreme cases even leading to closure of units and loss of livelihood. This was true of street vendors (dominantly women) across the countries studied, who were subject to rules and regulations that effectively served to oppress them and inhibit their operations. It was also true in the case of agriculture in Ghana, whereby small holders found it difficult to compete with companies engaging in contract farming. The GST imposition raised compliance costs dramatically and squeezed out many small producers from the supply chain, and here again women were found to be disproportionately affected both as microentrepreneurs and as workers. So all such regulations—even the most well-intentioned—need to be considered carefully in terms of how they will affect the people concerned, and specific note must be taken of the differential positions of women workers both as microentrepreneurs and self-employed, and as workers.

Social context, rigidities of formalisation in the context of gender relations

Even with the most careful and sensitive policy approach, there is no getting away from the fact that formalisation necessarily introduces rigidities into labour relations. Most of the time, this is a good thing, as it reduces possibilities of exploitation and oppression, and this is especially valuable for women workers whose bargaining positions are weak. However, precisely because of the inevitable rigidities, there may be some situations in which women workers prefer informal work. The example of Thailand highlighted how some domestic workers prefer informal arrangements, not only because it keeps them out of the tax net, but also—and perhaps even more importantly—it allows greater flexibility in working conditions and leave that can be negotiated interpersonally with individual employers. (Once again, it is true that employers are much more likely to be suitably flexible in the context of a tight labour market.) Similarly, it was observed in the case of sex workers, that workers' resistance to legalisation and formalisation (even when it would otherwise benefit them) emerged from a societal context of possible stigma and discrimination associated with such work.

In general, social and cultural contexts are critical to understand and incorporate when examining formalisation strategies, which means in turn that one-size-fits-all policies are unlikely to be either effective or desirable.

The urgent imperative of universal social protection

The essential requirement of universal social protection is more evident than it has ever been, and the massive dangers created by its absence have been brought out sharply by the COVID-19 pandemic and its more worrying outcomes. Across the developing world, including in our study countries, informal workers have been economically devastated and received very little by way of compensation for the incomes lost during this period. They also continue to remain exposed to greater health risks, not only through their work and because of the spread of the virus, but also because other health concerns are not adequately addressed during this period. Income deprivation is also associated with falling into poverty and inadequate nutrition, creating conditions for greater vulnerability to disease. This is not simply a concern about inequality and welfare, since the nature of infectious diseases is that they remain a social threat as along as anyone anywhere is infected.

Informal workers—and most particularly women, both unpaid and paid working women—are among those most deprived of basic social security, health security and access to affordable health services. Reproductive health services and child immunisation, both absolutely essential requirements for social survival, have been especially neglected across the developing world during the pandemic, with extremely adverse implications. The need for universal social protection that goes beyond employment contracts is therefore one that is not only about ensuring the rights of women, but also the very survival of societies.

The importance of mobilisation and association

The huge role played by mobilisation and awareness emerged in several of the case studies. In Ghana and South Africa, the associations of street traders have been critical in ensuring both the rights of such workers and preventing some particularly egregious cases of injustice. In India, it was found that only those workers who were associated with a trade union or an NGO engaged in mobilisation had awareness about several of their rights granted by law, including with respect to minimum wages, paid leave and social security. Therefore, the role of trade unions, NGOs and social movements may be absolutely essential to ensure progressive formalisation.

Notes

1 The ILO considers a worker to be informal if s/he is a worker whose social security is not paid for by the employer, is not entitled to paid annual leave and paid sick leave; or works in a household; or owns and runs an informal enterprise, typically in the form of self-employment, but also including micro-enterprises. More elaborate definitions are provided below.
2 Bear in mind that employment is only a subset of the broader category of work. Work also includes unpaid activities done within households and communities or for purely personal consumption, while employment is only that part of work that is remunerated.
3 This is also true of other socially disadvantaged groups about whom public policies tend to be blind, such as those disadvantaged by race, ethnic group, caste, language, migration pattern and so on. Indeed, these cross-cutting inequalities and their effects are evident in several of the case studies in this volume.
4 South Africa Quarterly Labour Force Survey for October–December 2018.

References

Chen, M. A., 2012. The Informal Economy: Definitions, Theories and Policies. WIEGO Working Paper No. 1.

Chen, M., Carre, F. 2020. The Informal Economy Revisited: Examining the Past, Envisioning the Future. Routledge Taylor and Francis.

Kanbur, R., 2009. Conceptualizing informality: regulation and enforcement. *Indian J. Lab. Econ.* 52 (1), 33–42.

Vanek, J., Chen, M. A., Carré, F., Heintz, J., Hussmanns, R., 2014. Statistics on the Informal Economy: Definitions, Regional Estimates & Challenge. WIEGO Working Paper (Statistics) No. 2. Available from: https://www.mypsup.org/library_files/ downloads/WIEGO%20-%20Statistics%20on%20the%20Informal%20Economy%20- %20Definitions%20Regional%20Estimates%20and%20Challenges.pdf, last accessed on 3 January 2020.

2

INSECURITY OF WOMEN WORKERS AND THE CHIMERA OF FORMALITY IN INDIA

C.P. Chandrasekhar, Jayati Ghosh, Nancy Yadav and Shreya Sharma

I Introduction

In this chapter, we consider how gender inequality is expressed in the Indian labour market and analyse various official attempts at formalisation of work. The Indian experience presents a striking example of the failure of formalisation policies in the context of a sluggish labour market with significant underemployment and open unemployment and poor regulatory practices.

There are many paradoxes of the recent pattern of growth in India. India is remarkable even among developing countries, for the extreme prevalence of informality in economic activities and in employment. Despite rapid GDP growth in India since the 1980s, there has not been any noticeable expansion of decent work opportunities for India's relatively young labour force, nor of more formal employment. The (already low) employment elasticity of output growth declined, even as the economy was more exposed to global competition that was supposed to have favoured more labour-intensive activities. In recent years, it has even turned negative, as aggregate employment declined between 2011–12 and 2017–18. Growth did not generate employment diversification, as most workers (especially women workers) remain stuck in low value added but arduous work in agriculture and low-grade services. The share of manufacturing in both output and employment has remained low, and low productivity work continues to dominate in total employment. Even within sectors, there are extremely wide variations in productivity across enterprises. Over several decades of rapid income growth, the expected formalisation of work and the concentration of workers into large-scale production units has not occurred—rather, there has been widespread persistence of informal employment and increase in self-employment in non-agricultural activities. Most striking of all is that the period of rapid GDP growth has been marked by low and declining workforce participation rates of women, in a pattern that is unlike almost any other rapidly growing economy in any phase of history over the past two centuries.

This does not mean that workers in the informal economy in India have simply been excluded from formal activity—rather, they are deeply integrated into it both directly and indirectly. The perception that the informal economy exists because low wages allow it to compete with the formal sector in a host of non-agricultural activities is misplaced. In many instances, the informal economy is not in competition with the formal sector, but actually services its requirements, through subcontracting and provision of various inputs and service activities. In this way, low wages in the informal economy help sustain profits in the formal sector.[1]

There is strong evidence of substantial increases in subcontracting by the formal manufacturing industry to more informal production arrangements since 2001 (Bairagya, 2010; Kesar, 2017; Sahu, 2010; Sundaram et al., 2012). This provides greater flexibility to formal operations and lowers their costs because of the ability to suppress net incomes in informal enterprises. The value chains evident in a number of important exporting industries in sectors as varied as readymade garments, gems and jewellery, automotive components, leather and leather products and sports goods, which are often co-ordinated by large and possibly multinational corporate entities, provide evidence of the significant and increased contribution of informal activities to what are seen as formal sector production (Damodaran, 2010). These are only some examples of a wide and pervasive process of extremely close intertwining of formal and informal sectors, and the effective subsidisation of the formal sector by low-paid informal activities.

Furthermore, labour markets in India are massively determined by the ability of employers to utilise social characteristics to ensure lower wages to certain categories of workers. Caste and other forms of social discrimination have a long tradition in India, and they have interacted with capitalist accumulation to generate peculiar forms of labour market segmentation that are unique to Indian society. Studies (such as Thorat 2010Human Rights Watch, 2007; Shah et al., 2006; Thorat, 2010; Thorat et al., 2009) have found that social categories are strongly correlated with the incidence of poverty and that both occupation and wages differ dramatically across social categories.

Gender-based differences in labour markets and the social attitudes to women's paid and unpaid work are also reflections of this broader tendency (Ghosh, 2009; Mukherjee, 2012). Most socio-economic indicators point to the low status of women in the Indian society. The widespread perception that women's work forms an "addition" to household income and, therefore, commands a much lower reservation wage is common to both private and public employers. Women workers typically receive significantly lower wages for similar work (on average 60 per cent of men's wages) pointing to one of the highest aggregate gender wage gaps in the world. In public employment, the use of underpaid "voluntary" women workers receiving well below minimum wages has become institutionalised in several major government programmes to deliver essential public services of health, nutrition, support for early child development and even education. Furthermore, the role played by the unpaid labour of women in contributing not only to social reproduction, but also to what would be recognised as productive economic activities in most other societies has been absolutely crucial in enabling this particular accumulation process.

This is the broad political economy context in which successive governments have introduced various measures to "formalise" the economy by bringing more producers and workers into the ambit of formal regulations—or at the very least to try and increase the number of workers classified as "formal workers". Unfortunately, most of these measures have not taken into account or addressed macroeconomic factors that affect the rate and pattern of employment generation. Nor have they sought to change the specificities of Indian labour markets, which rely on existing forms of inequality (such as those based on caste and gender) that lead to varying outcomes for different types of workers. As a result, as will be seen below, the impact of most of these measures has been marginal at best, and at worst even counterproductive, in terms of improving the conditions of women informal workers.

The chapter is organised as follows. In the next section, we examine the broader context of employment trends and women's work in India. The third section considers the relative extent of formal/informal activity and organised/unorganised sectors. The fourth section is a brief description of some of the recent schemes and programmes of the government with respect to formalisation. The fifth section contains the results of a primary survey of workers conducted in the Delhi National Capital Region (NCR) region over August-October 2018, to assess how these efforts at "formalisation" affect women workers. The final section contains some brief conclusions and highlights their relevance for policy.

II Employment patterns

As noted earlier, a remarkable feature of the recent growth trajectory of the Indian economy was the absence of employment generation. The economic strategy of the past two decades essentially relied on large corporate investment to deliver more investment, and therefore more growth, productivity and formal sector jobs. At least, that was the goal. And in pursuit of this goal, it was believed that the large private corporate sector needs to be incentivised in every possible way: through access to relatively cheap credit (much of which has not been repaid), provision of subsidised inputs, amenities, land, natural resources—and of course, cheap labour. It also meant that banks were encouraged to lend more, which they did in the state of euphoria that takes over in a boom. State-owned commercial banks were actually pushed into risky lending for long-term investments, something that commercial banks are not really supposed to do.

This strategy actually worked for a while, especially during the boom of the 2000s, when GDP grew rapidly and investment rates picked up pushing growth up further. The economic boom of the decade 2003–2012 was one in which even the global financial crisis caused only a temporary blip, and it created a complacent belief that this trajectory could run for ever. But there were many adverse fallouts of this particular path: terrible environmental damage, growing bad loans with banks, rising inequality and a proliferation of "scams" that were the by-product of all these incentives being offered to big capitalists. Also, the boom did not generate the expected increase in good-quality employment: even as real GDP increased at the rate of 7–9 per cent per year, formal jobs barely increased at all, and even informal work grew at the slow rate of around 2 per cent per annum while the potential labour force expanded much faster. Real wages did increase until 2011–12, but the share of wages in total national income fell (Ghosh, 2015). What is worse, when the boom ended around 2012, there was a progressive decline in investment rates and GDP growth also decelerated. The decline in investment rates was partly due to reduced access to credit because of the weight of the bad loans in the banking system and projects that were held up or delayed because of environmental and legal concerns. But the biggest reason for the slowdown was insufficient expansion of domestic demand because wage incomes were suppressed. It is ironic that the strategy to deliver more profits to corporates by suppressing wages ended up reducing potential profits by shrinking the potential market. The focus on large companies also left out the micro, small and medium enterprises that provide the bulk of employment in the country.

The slowdown was particularly driven by the drastic demonetization of November 2016, which abruptly removed 86 per cent of the value of currency in circulation without providing enough replacement cash until a year later. The ostensible goals of this bizarre move—getting rid of corruption, removing counterfeit notes and forcing people to shift to digital transactions—were not realized, but it did manage to deal a body blow to informal activities, which run dominantly on cash (Ghosh et al., 2017). Nine months later, the hasty and botched implementation of a poorly designed Goods and Services Tax (GST) further added to the woes of small enterprises, which found it hard to remain viable. These adverse tendencies in the macroeconomy have continued and even intensified to the end of 2019, as most macro and sectoral indicators indicated significant economic slowdown.

For all these reasons, the number of those in paid employment actually shrank (according to official surveys) between 2011–12 and 2017–18, by an estimated 9 million—an unprecedented process in an economy in which GDP was supposedly growing at between 6 and 8 per cent per year. As Figure 2.1 indicates, the worker–population ratios of both men and women declined over this period, in both rural and urban areas. The decline for women was particularly stark, and worth noting because recorded work participation of women was already so low.

One of the difficulties with discussions on employment in India is the tendency to conflate employment and work. But employment is only that part of work that is remunerated, and in India, a vast amount of work is actually unpaid and often not even socially recognised. This is especially true of women's work. There has been much discussion of the significant decline in women's workforce participation rates, which have generally been declining since the mid-1990s. Various

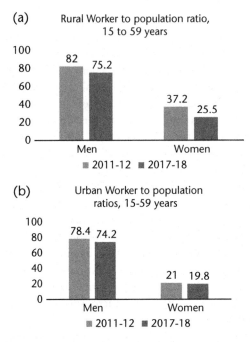

(a) Rural Worker to population ratio, 15 to 59 years

(b) Urban Worker to population ratios, 15-59 years

FIGURE 2.1 Worker to population ratios in rural and urban India
Source: NSSO (2013, 2019).

explanations have been offered for this, from more young women being engaged in education (which is still not enough to explain the decline) to rising real wages that have allowed women in poor households to avoid or reduce involvement in very physically arduous and demanding work with relatively low wages. Implicit in this discussion is a notion of a household-level backward bending supply curve, which allows women (including in poorer families) not to "work" for outside income when their economic conditions allow it.

However, these numbers relate to recognised employment, even if it is informal or self-employment. Until 2011–12, survey reports included more detail on some categories that were described as "not in the labour force": Code 92 (attended to domestic duties only) and Code 93 (attended to domestic duties and also engaged in free collection of goods such as vegetables, roots, firewood, cattle feed, etc., water collection, sewing, tailoring, weaving, etc. for household use) both of which essentially involve women working in unpaid ways. If these are included in the definition of work, then more women worked in India than men! In 2011–12, the total women's work participation rate was as high as 86.2 per cent, compared to 79.8 per cent for men. In fact, the decline in women's employment rates really reflects a shift from paid to unpaid work. A significant share of such unpaid women workers (40 per cent in rural areas and 22 per cent in urban areas in 2011–12) were dominantly involved in fetching water for household consumption, an activity that took more time than before. More than half of the poorest women had to do this, as well as to collect biofuels for cooking as they did not have access to or could not afford other fuel (Chakraborty, 2018) indicating that the absence of basic amenities was an important factor driving the increase in unpaid work. In addition to these extended domestic tasks, there are the various activities associated with the "care economy": care of the young, the old, the sick and the differently abled; cooking, cleaning and generally looking after healthy adults—all of which are dominantly seen as the responsibility of women in the household. Nearly two-thirds of these unpaid women workers reported that they had to perform these necessary tasks because there was no one else in the household to do them.

This lack of recognition of a significant part of the work dominantly provided by women has several important economic and social implications. The unpaid–paid continuum of women's work serves to devalue both women and the work they do. Thus, when women do enter labour markets, their wages tend to be lower than those of men—not only because they are willing to work for lower wages but because so much of their work is available for free. India has one of the largest gender gaps in wages to be found anywhere in the world, with women's wages on average only around two-thirds that of men's wages. In addition, the occupations in which women dominate tend to be lower paid—and the wage penalty extends even to men doing similar work, such as in the low-paid care sector. This is certainly true of private employers. But in India, as noted earlier, even the government has used these gender-segmented labour markets to provide public services on the cheap, by employing "volunteer" women workers in various schemes that are really about providing basic social services of health and nutrition. This contributes to a general invisibility of women's work, which extends into paid work as well. Once again, this has been found to be true of both private and public employers, as significant activities undertaken by women are simply not perceived as necessary elements of production and remain unrecognized and unpaid. Table 2.1 indicates how aggregate gender wage gaps have changed over time.

These trends in gender wage gaps reflect gendered patterns of occupational concentration, through differential access to occupations, with women workers

TABLE 2.1 Women's wages as per cent of men's wages

| | Regular workers | | Casual workers | |
	Rural	Urban	Rural	Urban
1993–94	59.6	79.8	65.4	57.1
1999–2000	73.9	82.3	64.4	59.4
2009–10	62.6	81.9	68.0	58.3
2011–12	62.5	77.9	69.2	60.8

Source:Chakraborty (2018) Daily money wages computed from NSS Surveys on Employment and Unemployment 50th, 55th, 66th, 68th round unit level data.

overwhelmingly concentrated in low-paid and informal jobs. The gaps in the public sector resulted from the government's extreme reliance on the underpaid labour of contractual women workers relative to permanent employees in implementing various critical policies in health, nutrition and education. Even in the private sector, gender differentials were explained primarily by differences in occupational structures, alternatively termed as horizontal segregation. In rural areas, more women were involved in the male-dominated manufacturing industry where gender gap in wages were high; in urban areas, more urban women were involved in domestic work in private households.

The bulk of rural women recognized workers (almost 75 per cent) are engaged in agriculture. Among non-agricultural workers, most women are engaged in medium and low/unskilled occupations: in food and tobacco processing, textiles, garments, leather, shoemakers and related workers and machine operators. Among unskilled women workers, construction work experienced a boom because of the public rural employment guarantee programme or the MGNREGA, which was implemented from 2005. There were also increases in women workers as head-loaders in brick kilns and wholesale markets. Among less skilled and unskilled women workers in urban areas, most were wage workers employed as in sales, services, manufacturing, mining and construction sectors. Women working as salespersons dominated this category. Within personal services, the dominant occupations were of hairdressers, personal care, housekeeping and restaurant service workers and travel- and tourism-related work. Such employment does not break the stereotypes associated with women's work as most of these services are extensions of care work which women have been performing historically, and in fact reinforces the gender stereotypes in occupations in altered, more commercialised contexts. Among unskilled service workers, domestic workers, cleaners and launderers are the most important occupations for women. But even here, men have better working conditions: commercial cleaning in offices and hotels employs more men compared to women and commands higher wages than the household-based domestic services (Mitra, 2017).

The most important points to note about the broader macroeconomic context within which formalisation attempts are being made in India are therefore the following: there is enormous and growing slack in the labour market; there have been absolute declines in employment in the recent past as well as high and rising open unemployment rates; for those in employment, there is a dominance of insecure and poorly paid employment under relatively adverse working conditions; and the economy continues to rely hugely on unpaid labour, especially performed by women. The economic slowdown up to the end of 2019 increased open unemployment and slack in the labour market; thereafter, the spread of the COVID-19 pandemic and the containment attempts that involved very stringent lockdown and restrictions on mobility have further worsened the labour market conditions for women, with dramatic declines in employment and increases in open unemployment (Vyas, 2020).

III Formal and informal sector activity in India

Informality is an overarching feature of the Indian workforce, with around 95 per cent of workers estimated to be informal. As noted in the introduction, such workers are to be found in both formal (organised) and informal (unorganised) enterprises, and therefore it is useful to distinguish between the characteristics of informality across enterprises and workers. This is more difficult than it sounds, partly because of the overlapping datasets available on sectors variously described as the small-scale sector, the unorganized sector and the informal sector. The small-scale sector, which is defined as consisting of units with fixed investments lower than a changing, specified ceiling, and which are registered with the relevant government agency, is identified to target government support for smaller units. In manufacturing, the unorganized sector is defined as consisting of units that employ less than 10 workers if using electricity or less than 20 workers if not using electricity, which are not subject to the Factories Act. In other sectors, it is defined in organisational terms and consists of proprietary and partnership enterprises, as well as those run by non-corporate entities such as self-help groups, trusts and non-profit institutions.

Periodic surveys by the National Sample Survey Organisation (NSSO) capture the non-organised sector under heads such as the "unorganised sector," the "informal sector" or "unincorporated enterprises." They also capture the distribution of workers according to formality, determined by whether they have formal contracts and conditions of work. For enterprises, the most recent data for non-agricultural enterprises relate to 2015–16 (NSSO 73rd Round survey of Unincorporated Non-Agricultural Enterprises). This survey excluded construction, which accounts for a substantial and rising share of non-agricultural employment, 30 per cent in 2011–12, most of which is men working in the unorganised sector. The survey suggested that there were 111 million workers (including part-time workers) working in unincorporated non-agricultural enterprises excluding construction, or about a quarter of the workforce of 459 million workers employed in that year. Urban workers accounted for 55 per cent of the total. Such non-construction unorganised employment was more or less equally distributed across manufacturing (32 per cent), trade (35 per cent) and "other services" (33 per cent). So there were 36 million workers engaged in unorganised manufacturing in 2015–16, compared to only 14.2 million "employees" (with 11.1 million workers) in the registered manufacturing sector.

Women workers are heavily concentrated in only some activities, even in the unorganised sector. Within unorganised manufacturing, 71 per cent of women workers were concentrated in just 3 out of 25 sectors: tobacco products (3 per cent), textiles (17 per cent) and wearing apparel (29 per cent). In unorganised trade, 95 per cent of women workers were engaged in retail trade, which constitute one of five activities. And in "other services," more than 70 per cent of women workers were engaged in 3 of 15 sectors: food service activities (20 per cent), education (41 per cent) and human health and social work (11 per cent). In all of these areas, self-employed workers running "own account enterprises" without hired labour overwhelmingly dominated, with very low levels of earnings.

An important reason for the persistence of unorganised economic activity is the absence of employment opportunities in the formal economy in a country that provides no social security to the vast majority. People have no choice but to work if they and their families have to avoid starvation. If agriculture does not provide the required opportunity, they find something to do in the non-agricultural economy, even while earning low incomes.

Despite these relatively "primitive" characteristics, it would be mistaken to assume that the unorganised sector exists in a separate realm in which there is no interaction or only competition with the organised sector. The common implicit perception is that the informal economy exists because low wages allow it to compete with the formal sector in a host of non-agricultural activities varying through manufacturing, construction and trade. In fact, the large relative size of the informal economy suggests that this "ability to compete" cannot be the sole explanation. There are many areas where the informal sector is not only in competition with the formal sector, but actually services its requirements, as noted above. The vast, unorganised "logistics" apparatus (offering services such as transportation and catering) that supports the India's IT and IT-enabled services sector is one example. In the process, low wages in the informal economy help sustain profits in the formal sector.

Turning now to formality of workers rather than enterprises, as noted above, the overwhelming bulk of the Indian workforce is informal, with women disproportionately concentrated in such employment. Furthermore, informality is pervasive in both organised and unorganised sectors, suggesting that simply ensuring that enterprises become "formal," registered or organised does not ensure that their workers will be under formal contracts and receive other benefits of formality. Table 2.1, Table 2.2 shows that even in the organised sector, there was a significant proportion of informality in terms of work contracts. While informal employment dominated in private unorganised activity, within organised private enterprises, more than half of the workers had informal contracts. In the organised public sector, nearly a quarter of such workers were informal.

Most women workers—more than four-fifths—operate without even the most basic and minimal requirements of formal employment, such as a written contract,

TABLE 2.2 Structure of employment in 2011–12

| | Public | | Private | |
	Informal	Formal	Informal	Formal
Unorganised	25.6	74.4	94.5	5.5
Organised	23	77	54.3	45.7
Total	24.3	75.7	88.7	11.3

Source: NSSO Survey of Employment and Unemployment, 2011–12.

paid leave or any kind of social security provided by the employer. Table 2.2, Table 2.3 suggests that the biggest gender gap was in the absence of paid leave, with women workers suffering much more from this—ironic considering that most such women also face the double burden of household work and various family responsibilities. The gender gap was lowest in the existence of written contracts, as men workers seemed to be just as disadvantaged in this respect. There was a marginally higher share of men workers who had access to social security, but even this was mostly in the form of registered participation in a provident fund of some sort, which does not necessarily require that the employment itself occurs in a formal setting. Furthermore, the various forms of social security (such as access to health coverage or provident funds) are often of very little amount and do not serve to provide much protection in periods of genuine need or other extreme situations like the COVID-19 pandemic, as will become evident below.

IV Official strategies for formalisation

Policies directed towards formalisation in India can be categorised according to their objectives, which typically cover one or more of these goals: (1) to regulate informal enterprises; (2) to regulate informal employment; (3) to provide social protection to informal workers; (4) to create more jobs in formal sectors and activities; and (5) to increase the viability of informal enterprises and productivity and incomes of informal workers. In what follows, we consider some recent policies of the Government of India that seek to meet one or more of these goals.

Unorganized Workers' Social Security Act (UWSSA), 2008

This relates to social protection coverage and is an umbrella legislation covering various schemes. The UWSSA, 2008 was enacted by the Indian Parliament following various debates on the conditions of work for various occupations such as domestic workers and street vendors. The Act mandated that there would be registration of all unorganised workers, including home-based workers, self-employed workers or even wage workers within the unorganised economy, by the District Administration, as the first step to including unorganised workers within

TABLE 2.3 Conditions of employment in 2017–18

	Rural men workers	Rural women workers	Urban men workers	Urban women workers
Without written contract	71.7	58.5	72.7	71.4
Not eligible for paid leave	58.1	47.9	53.1	51.8
Not eligible for any kind of social security	51.9	55.1	47	50.1

Source: NSSO Periodic Labour Force Survey, 2017–18.

any possible social security net. By introducing legal provisions for registration and issuance of smart ID cards to unorganized workers, the Act was supposed to enable the provision of social security through already existing Acts and policies, such as Indira Gandhi National Old Age Pension Scheme, National Family Benefit Scheme, Janani Suraksha Yojana, Handloom Weavers' Comprehensive Welfare Scheme (Mahatma Gandhi Bunkar Bima Yojana), National Scheme for Welfare of Fishermen and Training and Extension, Aam Admi Bima Yojana, Rashtriya Swasthya Bima Yojana and Atal Pension Yojana. State Governments could look beyond the basic social security provided by the Central Government (officially life and disability cover, health and maternity benefits and old age pension, though these have rarely been provided to most people).

Therefore, the Act lists those social security schemes that target Below Poverty Line (BPL) workers, which were active at the time of its passage. These are mostly universal schemes, benefits of which are extended to citizens meeting the eligibility criteria and are not focused on workers or working women in any way. The only women specific scheme included under the law is concerned with maternity benefits for all women. The benefits of the schemes are to be provided to all women of certain categories or within certain institutional frameworks, rather than to workers of any kind.[2] There is nothing else that considers the conditions that women face as workers, such as equal pay, decent work conditions, occupational safety or prevention of sexual harassment. Apart from some particular schemes such as the Handloom Weavers' Comprehensive Welfare Scheme, which relate to certain occupations, the schemes within the Act's Schedule are in no way specific to the workforce. Since the schemes listed under the Act do not refer to any new schemes for the unorganised workers and most of the schemes looks at BPL workers, informal workers who are above the poverty line but outside of any social security net are left uncovered.

There has been very poor implementation of the Act. There are no legal penalties for violation of any section of the Act and no time bound regulations for active participation of the states or Centre for any aspect of the law. A fundamental aspect of the Act, the registration of workers and the issuance of smart ID cards, was only initiated in 2018, a decade after the law was passed. The nationwide database for unorganized workers is to be seeded with Aadhaar, the controversial biometric-based Unique Identity number. Hence, provision of benefits of all the social security schemes to the unorganized workers would firstly require the workers to possess an Aadhaar card to begin with, even though this has been found to be very exclusionary especially for manual workers whose biometrics may not match and others who have been denied benefits because of clerical errors like misspelled names and/or addresses.

Maternity Benefits Act (1961), Amendment 2017

This Act aims to provide maternity benefits to women workers in establishments (factories, mines plantations or shops) employing more than 10 workers over a period of 12 months (20 workers in establishments without electricity) for a period of 1 month before and a period of 6 weeks after childbirth and to provide for wages during maternity leave and other health benefits. The Act prohibits the employer from employing a woman during the six weeks post the day of the delivery, miscarriage or medical termination of pregnancy. The employee is also subjected to the responsibility of abstaining from work during the specified periods. The Act provides for the employee to draw wages during her maternity leave, calculated on the basis of the past three months of work. There is also a provision for medical bonus to the employee along with creche facility at the workplace.

The law relates to women workers who are registered with an employer, leaving most of the workforce (especially informal workers) outside its ambit. The establishments eligible for inclusion under the Act are determined by the size of the workforce employed. The Act excludes daily wage workers, casual workers, self-employed workforce and even unregistered waged workers from being possible beneficiaries of maternity benefits—even though informal workers with unregulated wages and working hours are most susceptible to lack of such benefits. By mandating that women need to have been employed for a period of 80 days during the 12 months of employment, casual or daily wage workers are excluded, since this part of the workforce is neither registered, nor is their association with one single employer always that long. Since the Act excludes the informal workforce in the country, the implementation of the act is restricted to the small fraction of the formal sector.

The Maternity Benefits Act put the responsibility of the provision of benefits on the employer. This has been known to become a disincentive for hiring women, and concerns have been expressed about this and about the associated tendency among employers to avoid regularisation of women workers so as to avoid the costs associated with maternity leave. Since there is no part of the law which talks about a parity in paternal leave, the Act creates a degree of disadvantage for the employer employing women who may access maternity benefits. With the provision of paid leave and creche facilities only for women workers, the Act assumes that child rearing is solely a woman's responsibility and thereby reinforces patriarchal stereotypes.

The NULM was launched in 2013 with a focus on urban poor households, to enable them to access self-employment and skilled employment. The policy is targeted at the urban poor (Below Poverty Line or BPL), with possible expansion to include families of "disadvantaged groups like SCs, STs, women, minorities, disabled, etc. subject to a maximum of 25 per cent of the above urban poor population." The NULM mandates at least 30 per cent of women beneficiaries in each component, including skill training, placement, self-employment, credit cards for enterprise development, capacity building for trainees, as well as institutional development for Self Help Groups (SHGs) for women.

There is special attention to SHG development for women in urban areas, to further the goal of increased financial inclusion and financial empowerment of possible "women entrepreneurs." The self-employment programme extends support for the establishment of micro and small enterprises, with a ceiling of ₹2 lakh for individual enterprises and ₹10 lakh for group enterprises, through the provision of loans to entrepreneurs through banks and SHGs. By providing interest rate subsidies and making the microenterprise itself the collateral, NULM seeks to facilitate credit access to self-employed workers. Over and above the interest rate subsidy, a 3 per cent subvention is provided to all women SHGs who repay their loans in time.

The programme has been implemented in at best a very half-hearted manner, with very low funds allocation and limited coverage. Even when funds are provided, there has been little attention to dealing with practical problems such as insufficient financial literacy of possible beneficiaries, especially women and those from marginalised sections of society. Lack of awareness has also impacted implementation, and there has been little effort to ensure that all those eligible for the programme are aware of the requirements and possible benefits. The relevant data are not even available in the public domain. For example, while the NULM focuses on street vendors with provisions for periodic surveys as well as registration of street vendors, there appears to be no information on this mandated database. On the administrative side, the State Mission Management Unit and the City Mission Management Unit lack representation of women despite requiring representation from the Health and Family Ministries.

Pradhan Mantri MUDRA Yojana

MUDRA stands for Micro Units Development and Refinance Agency. The MUDRA Yojana was launched in April 2015, to provide institutional finance up to ₹10 lakh to the non-corporate, non-farm small and micro enterprises. These loans are given by commercial banks, Regional Rural Banks, small finance banks, cooperative banks, micro finance institutions and non-bank financial institutions, and the refinance facilities are provided by MUDRA. The declared aim of the MUDRA scheme is "funding the underfunded." As providing collateral security is one of the major hurdles for small enterprises in securing institutional finance, under this scheme banks have been mandated not to insist on collateral for loans up to ₹10 lakh to units in the micro, small enterprises sectors. It was expected that MUDRA loans would boost employment as the micro and small enterprises are considered as the main engine of employment generation in India. In order to boost women's entrepreneurship, women are offered loans at reduced interest rates (by 25 basis points [bps]).

Under the MUDRA scheme, loans are provided under three categories: Shishu loans up to ₹50,000; Kishor loans ranging from ₹50,001 to ₹5 lakh; and Tarun loans ranging from ₹5 lakh to ₹10 lakh. Until 21 September 2018, 14 crore (14,09,58,241) people were given loans under the scheme till 21 September 2018.[3] There have been reports that the absence of a collateral requirement has encouraged some corrupt managers to lend out fraud loans.

More than 70 per cent of the loans have been sanctioned to women. However, women are concentrated in the lowest amount loan category (Shishu, up to

₹50,000). More than 70 per cent of the smallest (up to ₹50,000) loans were sanctioned to women. Women's share in the Kishor loan category was less than 20 per cent and it was only a little more than 10 per cent in the Tarun loan category. Even for these loans, there is no certainty that the sanctioned amount was used by women themselves, as it is often the case that family member uses the amount sanctioned in the name of women in order to take advantage of lower interest rates on loans given to women.

Stand up India

This is another government scheme to boost entrepreneurship, launched in April 2016 to promote entrepreneurship among Scheduled Castes/Scheduled Tribes (SC/STs) and women in non-farm activities by providing them bank loans between ₹10 lakh and ₹1 crore without collateral for setting up a new enterprise (greenfield projects). All banks are mandated under this scheme to ensure that every branch must give two loans—one to a Dalit or Adivasi and one to a woman—to help them set up a new business enterprise. In case of non-individual enterprises, at least 51 per cent of the shareholding and controlling stake should be held by either an SC/ST or woman entrepreneur.

This scheme has not been implemented seriously by most banks. Between 5 April 2016 (when this scheme was launched) and 24 September 2017, only 6 per cent of the 130,000 bank branches in the country had provided Stand Up India loans to SC or ST individuals.[4] Only a little more than 60,000 loan accounts were opened in the two years since the launch of this scheme.[5] Only around half of the sanctioned loans were actually disbursed, implying poor implementation.

The Street Vendors (Protection of Livelihood and Regulations of Street Vending) Act, 2014

Street vending is an important part of the informal economy across urban India. The aim of the Street Vendors Act, 2014 is to enable the street vendors to pursue their livelihoods in a safe, harassment-free environment. It aims to do this through a registration system and by creating a system of local management and self-governance to protect the vendor's rights. This act upholds the constitutional principle, namely the right to equality in Article 14 and the freedom to pursue any profession, trade and business in Article 19(1)(g).

Section 22 of the Act mandates the formation of a Town Vending Committee (TVC), which must conduct surveys within the area under their jurisdiction for the identification of all the street vendors. Such surveys are to be carried out every five years and the lists of all the identified vendors have to be accommodated in the vending zones. A total of 40 per cent of the representation in the TVC should be from the street vendors, with minimum one-third representation of women so as to avoid marginalisation of women in the committee decisions. The Act prohibits eviction or relocation of street vendors until the survey is complete. The street vendors are to be provided with certificates that grant them the right to carry on street vending in their prescribed vending zones. This Act therefore emphasises the legitimacy of street vending as a profession and seeks to provide freedom for them to operate within regulated zones.

While this Act looks good on paper, it does not really reduce the hardships of street vendors, because of almost complete lack of implementation, which has been evident even in the major metro cities. Most street vendors are not even aware about the existence of this Act and continue to experience local official harassment and suffer from petty corruption. In addition, the concerns about safety and security of women vendors are inadequately addressed in the Act.

The EPF is the main scheme under the Employees' Provident Funds and Miscellaneous Provisions Act, 1952, and is supposed to cover all establishments with 20 or more persons employed. In addition, some other organisations are covered (subject to conditions and exemptions) even if they employ less than 20 persons each. The Act defines an "employee" as "any person who is employed for wages in any kind of work, manual or otherwise, in or in connection with the work of an establishment and who gets his wages *directly or indirectly from the employer*, and includes any person employed by or through a contractor in or in connection with the work of the establishment and engaged as an apprentice, not being an apprentice engaged under the Apprentices Act, 1961 (52 of 1961) or under the standing orders of the establishment." Recently, the numbers of workers registered with the Employees Provident Fund Organisation (EPFO) has come to be seen as a significant indicator of formalisation of workers, and this view has been actively promoted by the central government as well as by the head of the EPFO.

Under this scheme, an employee has to pay a certain contribution, matched by his/her employer, that leads to a lump sum payment (including interest on the principal) on retirement. The current contribution is 12 per cent of basic wage (in some cases plus dearness allowance plus retaining allowance), paid by both employee and employer. An employee's contribution goes directly into the EPF, while the employer's contribution goes into the EPF, the Employees' Pension Scheme and the Employees Deposit Linked Insurance Scheme, as well as administrative costs. The scheme is meant to be mandatory for workers earning less than ₹15,000 per month (increased from ₹6,500 in December 2017), and optional for those earning above this limit if the employer agrees and this is officially approved.

A worker can withdraw the total balance of sum of contributions plus interest (when she/he is 55 years old. The withdrawal is tax free. A total of 90 per cent of the balance can be withdrawn after 54 years. There are withdrawal benefits upon leaving service after putting in less than ten years but more than six months of service. An employee who is out of work for at least 60 consecutive days can also withdraw the full balance. If a male worker dies, his widow can get a pension of half the average wage of the previous five years, with a minimum monthly pension of ₹1,000, ₹250 for children and ₹750 per for orphans.

Since 2014, the EPFO has allocated a Universal Account Number to each worker to ensure portability across employers, and this is now being linked with the Aadhaar number. This is also meant to help in easy transfer and withdrawal of claims. At best, this scheme provides a bare minimum of social security that does not cover most aspects of formalisation of contracts as considered here. Therefore, treating it as a proxy for formal employment may be problematic for several reasons. Registration with the EPFO persists even when the employee/employer concerned have stopped making payments and ends only with the final withdrawal. Therefore, while new entrants are recorded, dropouts are not. The database is meant to provide "real time" data, but it has been subject to frequent and extensive revisions that leave the quality of the information in doubt. Most of all, there appear to be serious concerns with the EPF scheme with respect to coverage, knowledge about their rights and entitlements on the part of employees, and therefore potential for denial of these entitlements by employers. Our survey in NCR Delhi found extensive lack of knowledge among EPF-registered workers about any benefits due to them, as many of them simply viewed the EPF contribution as a tax on their salaries and did not even know the procedures for accessing these funds.

Demonetisation and digitisation of payments

The drastic demonetisation move of 8 November 2016 was ostensibly directed towards the elimination of 'black money' and corruption, the spread of counterfeit notes and their use in the financing of terrorist activities, but it did not actually meet any of these goals. However, as is now widely accepted, it did result in major disruption of the economy, loss of jobs and incomes and considerable material distress (Ghosh et al., 2017; Reddy, 2017), especially in the informal economy and in agriculture. Since more than 95 per cent of transactions were estimated to occur in cash before this move, the result was the collapse of purchasing power for a considerable period of time, which froze a number of markets, diminished demand, disrupted economic activity and led to loss of livelihood and employment.

Since then, the case for demonetisation has also been made on the grounds that the shift from cash to bank and digital payments would enable more tax collection in future (still an unproven claim) and, most importantly, that the move would reduce dependence on cash transactions in favour of digital transactions that would in turn assist in the formalisation of economic activities and employment. Therefore, along with measures to restrict cash-based exchange, the government sought to promote and incentivise non-cash transactions. These measures ranged from the purely coercive (not putting enough currency notes back into the system, imposing limits on cash withdrawals from bank counters and ATMs, banning cash transactions of more than ₹200,000), to the threatening (declaring that all withdrawals of cash beyond a certain limit would be monitored by the tax authorities), to the placatory (reducing or eliminating charges for digital transactions when dealing with public agencies, offering to speed up the installation of point-of-sale machines), to the incentivising (offering tax benefits and discounts for certain transactions, periodic 'lucky draws' with financial rewards for those who made cashless transactions).

Even before the demonetisation exercise, efforts had been underway to accelerate digitisation. Despite these and the demonetisation shock, efforts to accelerate the shift to digitised transactions have failed to move away from the trend that was already in place before demonetisation. The constraints range from inadequacies in physical and banking infrastructure to poor connectivity, to still insufficient banking access (especially among women) and the emerging higher costs of mobile transactions. It is certainly true the greater reliance on cashless transactions can bring more of the economy under the ambit of the fiscal authorities, and thereby enable greater taxation, which may appear desirable in general. However, insofar as this imposes taxes on transactions per se, it is undeniably regressive and the costs fall disproportionately on the poor relative to their incomes. Significantly, the extraction implicit in the fees levied by the banks and fintech companies providing the services underlying cashlessness, including the mobile or e-wallet companies that appear to have been among the biggest beneficiaries of the demonetization shock, is also regressive. It amounts to a transfer of income from all consumers and producers, including the poor who really cannot afford it, to banks and a few fintech companies engaged in e-commerce and mobile wallet services. Insofar as wage payments are digitised, this can be an advantage for workers to avoid underpayment and ensure minimum wages. However, it now appears that even such systems can be gamed or circumvented to pay less than minimum wages and sometimes even less than the declared emoluments.

There are also reasons for women workers to prefer cash payments in particular contexts, given gendered power relations within families. In fact, the demonetisation exercise was remarkably gender blind and did not appreciate the specific circumstances of many women that led them to suffer disproportionately from that measure. Within households, women are much less likely to have bank accounts in their own names, and therefore if they want to maintain privacy and control over their own resources they are often forced to keep their own cash holdings. The drastic move to invalidate currency that amounted to 86 per cent of the value of currency in circulation meant that many women were forced to reveal—and in the process, lose control over—their small hoardings of cash that they had meticulously kept aside away from male members of the household, for specific personal purposes or for welfare of children. There were several cases of violence and domestic abuse of women when such cases were discovered by men in the household. The loss of privacy that is associated with the shift away from cash transactions is therefore more than just a matter of individual preference: in unequal contexts in which relational power is significant, it can have real and severe adverse implications especially for women.

Goods and Services Tax

The GST regime was put in place by the government in July 2017, after only three months' preparation, even though the required infrastructure and compliance systems were not yet ready. The new tax regime was supposed to help central and state governments mobilise more resources while integrating the national market. Forced formalisation would be part of the process, as units and agents that had remained outside the indirect tax system would gradually be incorporated, requiring them to report revenues and pay taxes.

The GST is essentially a hybrid version of the Value Added Tax (VAT), modified to suit the complexities of a federal system. VAT is administered by computing tax payable at the relevant rate on sales receipts of firms at each stage of a production process, with provision for the offset of similar taxes paid by it as reflected in invoices of purchases made by the firm from its input suppliers. This was expected to render the implementation of the tax easy and improve compliance, since suppliers would have to declare the prices and taxes on their sales of goods and services to enable upstream producers to claim their offsets. This was supposed to formalise almost all economic activity in the country, since companies would choose to deal only with those that are GST compliant.

However, the system was poorly conceived and designed, and very badly implemented. As a result, its impact on unorganised and informal activities has been extremely adverse. Instead of a simple uniform system, it is extremely complicated with seven rates varying from 0 to 28 per cent (0, 0.25, 3, 5, 12, 18 and 28 per cent) and changing classifications. Compliance is difficult and costly. Cumbersome reporting procedures that require filing frequent online returns force small enterprises to turn to paid, professional assistance. This online system has proved to be unreliable and not user friendly. While enterprises below a certain turnover can avoid cumbersome GST formalities and pay tax at a fixed rate of turnover, the reporting requirements and complexities of the system significantly increased costs, especially for small enterprises. Many units with small margins have had to close down or live in constant fear of scrutiny and punishment because they evade tax procedures. Somewhat surprisingly, GST has also failed on the revenue mobilisation front. While it is regressive in nature and adds to inequality, the new regime has not delivered the promised revenues, and GST collections have been consistently below targets. Yet prices of goods and services have not come down. Overall, the impact of GST on small enterprises has been adverse, even when they fall below the threshold required for compliance, since this has affected supply chains and markets faced by these enterprises.

V Results from a primary survey of workers in Delhi NCR

A small survey to capture some of the working conditions of informal workers, especially women, and assess how they were affected by formalisation policies, was undertaken in the Delhi NCR.[6] A structured questionnaire was used, which gathered information about the socio-economic status of workers, detailed information about their work (relating to nature of work, wages, hours of work, paid leave, place of work, union participation, availability of crèche facilities at work, occupational safety, availability of social security, occupational history of workers). In order to assess the government's attempts at formalisation, questions were asked on impact of particular government schemes, policies and interventions. The questionnaire also gathered information on awareness about certain labour laws. Keeping in mind the specificity of occupations, there were separate questions for different occupations. While the primary survey was not intended to be representative in nature, the results were checked against the evidence emerging from secondary data sources. Since the focus was on women workers, fewer men were surveyed, but other men were also questioned informally regarding their work. The data collection from the survey was supplemented with numerous informal discussions with workers, stakeholders, researchers and activists, and detailed notes were made of these conversations.

Profile of survey respondents

The survey covered 120 workers (90 women and 30 men) in Delhi NCR in August and September 2018. Table 2.4 shows the employment status of workers interviewed. In total, 29 regular/salaried workers were interviewed, 21 women and 8 men. They included 3 domestic workers (all women); 26 workers (18 women and 8 men) in a factory/enterprise; and 20 casual or daily wage workers (14 women and 6 men) working in garment factories and as construction workers. The self-employed workers interviewed included 7 retail traders (3 women and 4 men), 30 street vendors (23 women and 7 men), a male broom factory owner and 4 women providing services (1 woman owned a beauty parlour, 2 women owned restaurants, and 1 woman was providing tuition services).

A total of 19 home-based workers (16 women and 3 men) were interviewed, who typically were working through a contractor. Of the 16 women, 4 were involved in home-based deseeding of figs, 9 were involved in home-based toy making and packaging, 2 were working as home-based tailors and 1 woman was

TABLE 2.4 Employment status of surveyed workers (in number, figures in brackets are percentages of total)

Employment status	Female	Male	Total
Regular/salaried	21 (23.3)	8 (26.6)	29 (24.1)
Casual labour	14 (15.6)	6 (20)	20 (16.7)
Self-employed: street vendors, retail traders and service providers	30 (33.3)	12 (40)	42 (35)
Self-employed: home-based	16 (17.8)	3 (10)	19 (15.8)
Recently Unemployed	9 (10)	1 (3.33)	10 (8.33)
Total	90	30	120

involved in making and packaging of electrical coils; 3 men were involved in home-based broom making. All these workers were working on piece rates. The survey included ten recently unemployed persons, nine women and one man. Of the recently unemployed, two were home-based garland makers, who had been rendered unemployed because the garland making activity had gone out of business, six (five women and one man) recently unemployed workers were garment factory workers, one was a call centre worker and one was a street vendor woman, who had left street vending because of low earnings and was looking for some other work.

Approximately 70 per cent of the workers surveyed were under the age of 40 years. In total, 54 per cent of the women workers interviewed were not literate, whereas around 13 per cent of the men workers interviewed were not literate. Only around 25 per cent of the workers had more than secondary education. A total of 92 per cent of the workers interviewed were Hindu and 5 per cent were Muslims. There was one worker each from Buddhist, Christian and Sikh religions in the survey. In total, 25 per cent of the workers were OBCs, 22.5 per cent were SC and around 5 per cent were STs. Around 23 per cent of the workers did not know their caste category.

More than 70 per cent of the workers were married, approximately 2 per cent and 4 per cent of them were divorced/separated and widowed, respectively. Only 15 per cent of the workers originally belonged to Delhi/Delhi NCR; 85 per cent of the workers were migrants, 50 per cent from UP and Bihar and 15 per cent from Gujarat. Around 65 per cent of the workers interviewed were first-generation migrants, and 20 per cent of the workers were second-generation migrants. More than 90 per cent of the first-generation male migrant workers came to Delhi in search of work, compared to only 50 per cent of the women migrant workers. Around one-third of women migrants cited marriage as the reason for migration.

Wages and conditions of work

Figure 2.2 shows stark variations in earnings across gender and across occupations. Across all occupations, male workers had higher earnings as compared to their female counterparts. Female casual workers and home-based workers had the lowest earnings, with half of them earning less than ₹5,000 a month. The median earnings of the female self-employed home-based workers were only ₹1,800 per month, compared to ₹15,600 for male home-based workers. The women home-based workers in the survey were engaged in low-paying activities such as toy-making and packaging and deseeding of figs, while men were involved in broom-making. Even in the same locality, women were working for much lower wages as compared to men, and when they packaged brooms, they earned significantly lower wages. The women mentioned that broom-making work was paid higher than their packaging work, as it was the principal source of income for work undertaken by the men of the household. The women, if in any way associated

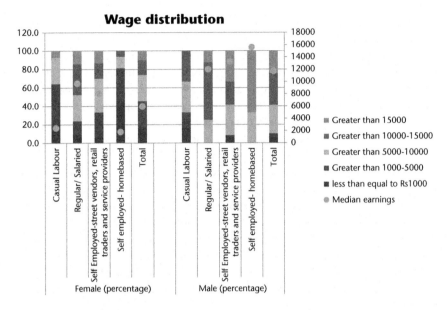

FIGURE 2.2   Wage distribution of workers interviewed

with the occupation of broom-making, were engaged in the packaging of the brooms and working at factories with regular wages but not actually making any brooms or earning in the same bracket as the men. Some women also claimed that their own home-based work of packaging toys was more for keeping themselves occupied at home, as their husbands did not approve of them working at factories but they still wanted to earn some money. Gender segregation in the nature of work was observed even among casual workers. In the garment factories, casual men workers were employed as helpers, supervisors, etc., whereas women were employed for thread cutting, sewing and other hand work. The work done by men workers fetched higher earnings. The casual construction workers interviewed reported that men and women workers were usually hired for different types of work, but men got higher wages even if they were hired for the same work as women.

A total of 88 per cent of the workers interviewed were below the tax threshold. Street vendors, home-based workers and even factory workers were not making enough to be included in the brackets for income tax. For the self-employed, 25 out of 30 women (83 per cent) were below the tax threshold, while in case of men, it was 6 out of 12 (50 per cent). The concentration of women in low-paying jobs such as home-based packaging work and daily wage work at factories results in fewer women making enough to be included in the income tax brackets.

A significant proportion of the respondents (40 per cent of the women and 73 per cent of the men) were working at registered enterprises, while 23 per cent of the women were not sure whether the enterprises they were working at were registered or not. There were 2 regular/salaried women workers, 16 home-based women workers and 2 recently unemployed women workers. But it was found that employment in the formal sector does not necessarily ensure formal employment, as workers in the formal sector were increasingly being hired on informal contracts. A total of 64 per cent of the women casual workers and 50 per cent of the men casual workers interviewed were working in the registered enterprises. The casual garment factory workers in Kapashera (a suburb of Delhi) reported that regular worker in factories were increasingly being replaced by casual workers hired on an informal basis, so that the employers could avoid their responsibility of providing social security and job security to workers. Among self-employed workers, nearly 58 per cent of the men interviewed had registered their enterprise/establishment whereas a very low percentage (only 16 per cent) of the self-employed women had registered their enterprise. Only one of the street vendors was registered. The women working as home-based workers at piece rates did not know whether they were working for a formal or an informal enterprise. Only three home-based men workers were interviewed and all three were working with a registered enterprise, with higher wages than women home-based workers in the same locality. Overall, women were more likely to be working in informal work, and for lower wages.

Delhi NCR is considered to be the most prosperous part of the country attracting migrants from all over because of the prospects of higher wages. Nevertheless, it was found that many surveyed workers did not receive the legal minimum wages. Out of the 120 people surveyed, 27 were employed in Haryana (monthly minimum wages of ₹8,541 in survey period), 83 in New Delhi (monthly minimum wage of ₹13,896) and 10 in Uttar Pradesh (monthly minimum wage of ₹5,750). In total, 84 workers (70 per cent of the surveyed workers) were not getting minimum wages; 28 of them worked in registered enterprises (18 women and 10 men, 23 per cent of the total workers). As many as 77 per cent of female casual workers working in regular enterprises were earning below minimum wages, while only 1 male casual worker working at a registered enterprise had lower wages than the legal minimum. Not just casual workers, but also a very high percentage (62 per cent) of the regular/salaried workers working in the registered enterprises were earning lower than minimum wages.

As apparent from Table 2.5, 50 per cent of the women workers and 45 per cent of the men workers working in the registered enterprises were earning less than minimum wages. Clearly, there is severe lack of implementation of the minimum wage laws, which is confirmed by aggregate national sample surveys. Even in enterprises and factories operating in industrial hubs, there was lack of awareness of legal minimum wages. Obviously, if the workers are not aware of a regulatory mechanism of this kind, they are unlikely to demand their legal wages.

Indian labour laws require workers doing overtime work to be paid double the wages for regular working hours. Implementation of this policy was not uniform or universal as various workers reported diverse experiences when it came to overtime wages. Some workers were not being given overtime work, other workers did overtime work but the same wages as for regular working hours, still

TABLE 2.5 Number and percentage of workers in relevant category in registered enterprises earning below minimum wages

	Occupation	Number	Percentage
Female	Casual labour	7	77.8
	Regular/salaried	10	62.5
	Self employed	1	20
	Total	18	50
Male	Casual labour	1	33.3
	Regular/salaried	5	62.5
	Self employed	3	42.9
	Self-employed: home-based	1	33.3
	Total	10	45.5

others worked overtime with no additional pay. For self-employed occupations such as street vendors and home-based workers, 50 per cent of the men and 54 per cent of the women interviewed reported the lack of regulated working hours. Such workers often worked beyond 8 hours on many days and also had days with much fewer hours of work. In total, 18 per cent of the women and 20 per cent of the men said they did not work overtime; 20 per cent of the males reported that they got over time wages on working overtime, while the corresponding figure for females interviewed was lower, at 15 per cent. More interestingly, 7 per cent of the males reported that they worked overtime and did not get overtime wage of any kind while the figure for women was at 11 per cent. Therefore, among the workers interviewed, not only was the percentage of males receiving overtime wage on engaging in overtime work higher than the category of women, but there was also a larger percentage of women not receiving overtime wage on engaging in overtime work as compared to men. There were also cases of workers reporting overtime work not being made available from the employer's side, for which the males in the category were 3 per cent and the females were 1 per cent. For the regular workers surveyed, the percentage of males and females not working overtime was at 50 per cent and 40 per cent, respectively. While 38 per cent of the males did overtime work and got corresponding overtime wages, the percentage of such females was at 50 per cent. A total of 13 per cent of men and 10 per cent of women worked overtime without getting overtime wages.

Social security provision

Figure 2.3 shows social security levels of different workers. Casual workers and self-employed-home-based workers were the most vulnerable in terms of lack of social security. More than 50 per cent of the casual workers were working in the formal sector, but despite this their work was most precarious, without job security and social security. In our survey, only five women workers availed some social security, and these were from government sources rather than employer-provided.[7] Most of

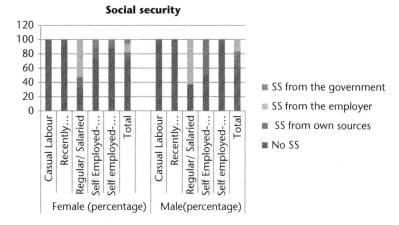

Social security

SS from the government
SS from the employer
SS from own sources
No SS

Female (percentage) | Male(percentage)

FIGURE 2.3 Social security of surveyed workers

the workers were not even aware of the plethora of government schemes and the mechanisms through which they can avail them. Male workers, with 20 per cent, recorded more than double the percentage of females accessing private social security, 9 per cent. Most of the respondents accessing private social security had life insurance through LIC or other private insurance providers.

Among the regular/salaried workers, only 52 per cent of the women and 62 per cent of the men were getting social security in the form of EPFO, and Employees State Insurance Corporation (ESIC) from their employment. Of the 21 women and 8 men regular/salaried workers, 12 (57 per cent) women and 4 (50 per cent) men had four days of paid leave in a month. In total, 32 per cent of the women and 36 per cent of the men had paid leave. Only 35 per cent of the women and 50 per cent of the men in regular/salaried work had a written contract. None of the casual labour, contract labour and recently unemployed (in their previous employment) had a written contract. Even regular/salaried workers working in the formal sector did not have all of these conditions of formal work. What is more, the absence of any relation between the formalisation of the enterprise and the formalisation of work existed at all levels of skills and earnings.

Floating between "formal" and "informal" work

There was a certain degree of fluidity recorded in the daily wagers and contract workers of the Kapashera area. The movement of daily wagers in and out of regular employment at the factories in the area was a characteristic shared by many workers engaged in factory work. Due to no regulation on notice period or severance packages for employees, almost all workers had at some point or the other been fired without much notice and had subsequently lost access to their social security given by the previous employer. These workers would then enter the group of daily wagers, looking for work on a daily basis, without access to the wages, social security or benefits they enjoyed as contracts workers. The transition from one category to another could span a few months or even days as there is no regulation of the recruitment process in any way. A worker employed formally for three months could be working as a daily wager for the next five months and turn back to formality as the opportunity came up, only to enter the informal work-force with subsequent possible retrenchment.

The three cases below provide examples of how the boundaries between formal and informal employment appear to be fluid and unmarked, particularly from the perspective of the worker.

Case 1: KK, a young woman aged 22 years, is a first-generation migrant from Bihar who moved to Delhi three years ago after marriage, when she and her husband moved to Delhi for work. She worked as a casual worker in January and February and then was employed in regular work as a security guard from April to June, when she went to visit her village for personal reasons for a month. This caused her to be dismissed from work, even though she had asked for leave for some time and the employer had verbally guaranteed that she could have her job back when she re-turned. That promise turned out to be false, but since the promise to retain her was only verbal, she had no recourse when she was effectively dismissed. Since she re-turned in mid-July, she had been seeking work as casual worker in daily wage work for factories in the Kapashera area, until the day of the interview in mid-August. Her employment as a security guard gave her the option of enrolling for EPF and ESI. However, she decided to take higher wages in hand because she presumed that she might get fired at any point, with her money stuck in the social security account, and because of her need for more money in hand for running her household. She was paid ₹11,500 for the 2-2.5 months she worked as the security person (Haryana minimum wage is ₹8541). When interviewed, she was seeking employment as a casual worker, cutting thread in factories at daily wages of ₹250.

Case 2: PM, woman aged 29 years, is a first-generation migrant from Mathura, who moved to New Delhi 11 years ago for education and then stayed on for em-ployment. She was unmarried with a post-graduate degree, and was working under client management for a leading designer label in the country since 2013. She was highly paid, with a monthly wage of ₹100,000, but on a completely informal contract. She had no access to any form of social security, as the employer did not provide for pension funds or any form of insurance, including for health care. She worked six days a week, including overtime work on her regular days of work but got overtime wages only sporadically. Rather than paid leave, the employer offered extra pay for ten days in each quarter of the year, with the option of taking ten days leave in each quarter instead of the regular monthly salary. There were no provisions for medical or casual leave. The respondent had worked for another fashion brand in the past with social security coverage and paid leave, but shifted to this more well-known brand despite worse contractual conditions.

Case 3: VK, woman aged 30 years, is a first-generation migrant from Madhya Pradesh, who moved to Delhi in 2008 for work. She was unemployed at the time of the interview and seeking work as a daily wage worker due to lack of opportunities as a regular worker. She had a job as a security guard, with EPF and ESI benefits along with maternity leave. Due to issues with the timing of work, she left that job and became a salesperson at a leading Indian supermarket chain. Her association with the supermarket varied with the marketing periods of different brands that were active at the supermarket. Therefore, she was working within an apparently formal workplace, with designated hours of work, in an organised manner, but her association with the brands changed within weeks or even days. The income she earned came in through the brands, along with any social security benefits, if the brand provided these, but the working period, leave and other workplace rules were governed by the supermarket. Therefore, her wages varied according to the brand she was working for at the time. In one instance, she even acquired EPF and ESI benefits for six months as a salesperson for an international brand at the floor of the supermarket chain. However, subsequently she lost these, when the brand she covered changed.

These examples provide a glimpse of the way workers tend to move in and out of different degrees of informality. Even when the employment is supposedly in a regular form, as with the woman security guard, it can be easily terminated, and the supposed benefits of formality such as some social security may not accrue. The level of employment and income does not necessarily have an effect on the formality or informality of the worker, as seen in Case 2. Despite being an employee of a very high-end employer, the respondent shifted from a type of employment with a much higher degree of formality to another workplace which lacked social security, designated leave and overtime wages. Case 3 is particularly interesting, as it shows that being a part of an apparently organised and well-functioning workplace, such as a supermarket in a mall, does not guarantee the kind of formality that is understood to be associated with these largely organised workplaces. The worker moved in and out of the social security net while doing effectively the same job, for the same number of hours, at the same place, for years. Her wages and conditions of employment varied as her principal employer varied over this period, even as she continued to work in exactly the same location, the supermarket.

This peculiarity of the fluid movement of workers persists irrespective of the scale and type of employment. The precariousness of work in these cases operates despite, and at times because of, the apparent sense of formality that these workplaces might propagate. This is a very important feature, because it means that formalisation measures that stress that enterprises themselves should become formal need not have any impact in terms of the greater formality of employment contracts or the protections available to workers in these enterprises.

Demonetisation, digital payments and banking

In large parts of the economy, demonetisation operated to destroy or dramatically reduce incomes available in informal activity, at least for six months or so (Ghosh et al., 2017). However, the impact seems to have been much less marked among respondents in this survey, possibly because of the specific circumstances operating in the NCR of Delhi, which is a megacity with the highest per capita income in the country. A total of 75 out of 120 respondents reported that there was no significant effect of demonetisation on their work, or the availability of work. The wages for factory workers were paid in the new notes and street vendors and home-based workers also reported their earnings to be in the newly minted currency. Those whose work and incomes were negatively affected by demonetisation were mostly among those who were self-employed or managing small own-account enterprises, especially street vendors who faced issues in sales due to the currency crunch. For these self-employed workers, the effect of the policy was experienced not just immediately but for many months after it was introduced.

The expansion of digital payments has been cited as a central goal of the demonetisation exercise, but the workers interviewed did not show any increase in tendency to engage in digital payments before or after demonetisation. A total of 86 per cent of the surveyed workers did not participate in any kind of digital payments or online banking. Among the women interviewed, only 13 per cent had ever used any form of digital payments while a higher percentage of surveyed men (30 per cent) used digital payments through their phones or participated in online banking for their accounts. The respondents did not attribute the usage of digital payments to demonetisation, and (barring two) those who did not participate in digital payments earlier were not spurred by demonetisation to start doing so. Lack of literacy, of smartphones, and the ability to make payments and indulge in transactions without using digital means were the common reasons reported for this.

Banking was more prevalent, but not really for credit access. Only 78 per cent of the women and 83 per cent of the men interviewed had bank accounts; 45 per cent of the women workers and 40 per cent of the men workers interviewed had ATM cards, but 19 per cent of the women and 3 per cent of the men did not use their ATM cards on their own. Only 15 per cent of the workers had ever taken formal credit. Most of the workers were not eligible for formal credit because of their low incomes, and so had to rely on informal credit with higher interest rates. Around 30 per cent of workers had taken credit from informal sources, typically to cover medical emergencies, marriage expenses and consumption shortages.

Union participation and awareness of laws and government schemes

Of the 120 workers interviewed, only 18 workers (15 per cent) were a part of union, 16 women and 2 men; 12 were street vendors, 5 were regular/salaried workers and 1 was casual worker. The home-based workers interviewed did not have any union, despite working in the same locality. The precarious nature of work and the widespread unemployment prevented casual workers from forming unions. The 12 street vendors were a part of a trade union named Self-Employed Women's Association (SEWA). The street vendor workers associated with SEWA were more aware about relevant laws, were financially literate and had access to credit at low interest rates (through SEWA cooperatives). These workers were financially literate in the sense that they could go to banks themselves and get their work done. These workers had taken loans for expanding their work and for consumption and medical purposes at low interest rates from SEWA cooperative banks. SEWA has also lobbied to get a fixed place in a special women's market (Mahila Bazaar) for the women street vendors. The regular workers associated with a union reported that the union had prevented unjustified firing of workers, and delays in their salaries. So workers associated with a union were found to be more empowered, but such workers were in minority even in regular/salaried work.

In the survey, we enquired whether workers were aware of two critical laws, the Minimum Wage Act and the Sexual Harassment Act, and found that more than 50 per cent of the women workers surveyed and more than 60 per cent of the men workers surveyed were not aware about them. In any case, they had little idea of how to ensure implementation if these laws were openly flouted by employers.

A critical legislation for street vendors is the Street Vendors (Protection of livelihood and regulation of Street vending) Act, 2014. This act mandates the formation of Town Vending Committees which are supposed to conduct a survey of all street vendors every five years and accommodate them in a designated vending zone. However, in our survey, we found that this legislation lacks practical implementation. None of the street vendors interviewed in Delhi were covered by any survey by the TVC. Only one male street vendor in Delhi NCR had been covered by a survey and was given a fixed place and a vending cart by the local authorities. Despite the existence of the law, most of the street vendors interviewed did not have a fixed place in markets. In Raghubir Nagar market, the street vendors had to go early in the morning at around 2–3 AM to reserve places. Basic amenities such as shelter, drinking water and sanitation were not available at the vending sites. The street vendors reported that local authorities extort money from them in some markets. SEWA has played a major role in organising these workers and provided a fixed place of work to some of these workers in a Mahila Bazaar (women's market), pointing to the importance of non-state actors in formalisation.

Jan Dhan Yojana (Pradhan Mantri Jan Dhan Yojana) was aimed at financial inclusion by opening zero balance accounts across all commercial banks and providing ATM, overdraft, short-term credit and insurance facilities. While the initiative has been lauded for making banking facilities accessible, with at least one family member in 90 per cent of the households getting access to a bank account, there are several lacunae. Women are still disproportionately excluded from formal banking. The scheme also seems to fall short of achieving other objectives of providing short-term credit and insurance facilities. In our survey, 80 per cent (77 per cent women and 83 per cent men) of the workers interviewed had bank accounts. However, none of the workers with Jan Dhan accounts had access to the insurance and credit facilities provided by this scheme—in fact, they were not even aware of the existence of these facilities. Most of the workers had little or no savings.

The Unorganised Workers Social Security Act, 2008 described in a previous section has the potential to be a critical legislation for informal workers. However, we found in our survey that most of the workers were not even aware about the existence of these schemes. Only three workers were found to have availed of any benefits under this scheme. Two street vendor women were availing government old age pensions, and one woman home-based worker had received maternity benefits through the district administration.

We asked whether the workers were enrolled in schemes like MUDRA, Stand up India, Rojgar Protsahan Yojana, Deendayal Antayodaya Yojana or other government schemes. None of the workers interviewed had enrolled in these or in any other government scheme. So workers even in the NCR, arguably the most developed part of urban India, were not benefitting from the plethora of government schemes available for them and typically were not even aware of these schemes.

VI A brief postscript on the impact of the pandemic

The overwhelming preponderance of informality and lack of social and legal protections for workers—especially women workers—were already evident in India well before the COVID-19 pandemic struck. The low effectiveness of various laws and interventions designed to provide some greater access to protection and provide greater formalisation to workers has emerged quite clearly from this study. If further confirmation were needed, this was massively provided by the impact of the pandemic. Even more significant than that, perhaps, has been the terrible impact of the draconian lockdown measures, which were announced with only four hours' notice and the subsequent rather brutal implementation, which disproportionately affected informal activities. Those in self-employment as well as those without any formal recognition or proof of employment were typically deprived of any income or livelihood for nearly three months. Overnight, the self-employed lost the opportunity to earn their own living; casual workers lost the tenuous employment that provided them some wages by the day, week or fortnight; piece-rate and home-based workers either did not get any more orders or could not fulfil or deliver their work for payment. Even thereafter, the partial lifting of restrictions in a collapsing economy did not lead to much revival of incomes, which remained well below the pre-lockdown levels.

Women among such workers were inevitably the most vulnerable. During this period, in absolute numbers more men lost jobs than women, but that was because of the huge existing gender gap in employment, which as we have seen had grown substantially over the previous decade. But even so, they were more likely to lose jobs during the lockdown and downturn in economic activity. Longitudinal surveys conducted over this period suggest that the women who were employed pre-lockdown were around 20 per cent less likely to be employed than similarly placed men (Deshpande, 2020). There is also evidence that there was a significant increase in the hours that women spent on domestic work, because many goods and services could no longer be outsourced because of falling household incomes. The lack of compensation for loss of income, and the extreme fragility of employment for informal workers, made it all the more evident that such widespread informality was a major underlying feature of the denial of basic rights to such workers. The need for a progressive, equitable and gender-sensitive strategy for formalization therefore became even more obvious and urgent.

VII Conclusions

Some important conclusions emerge from this consideration of the Indian experience. First, the Indian government's major focus has been on formalising enterprises rather than employees, to the detriment of the conditions of informal workers. Our study found that formal organised sector enterprises increasingly hire workers on informal contracts (and sometimes on no written contract at all) and the nature of the enterprise provides no guarantee of formal employment with workers' minimum rights protected. Rather, attempts to formalise enterprises can often be detrimental to workers, negatively affecting their livelihood and denying them some employment. Demonetisation and GST implementation both clearly damaged livelihoods, employment and wages of informal workers and had especially adverse effects on women.

Thus far, most official formalisation strategies have failed, not just because of inadequate design, but largely because of poor implementation. Legislation designed to ensure minimum wages, regulation of working hours and overtime wages, attempts to ensure social security and other forms of social protection and so on, are all essential and if properly enforced, would particularly benefit women informal workers who tend to face the lowest wages and worst conditions. But are these mostly honoured in the breach, and workers themselves are often not aware of the provisions of such laws and rules and have no recourse when they are openly flouted. These gaps are even greater in the case of women workers, who are among the most disadvantaged even among informal workers and self-employed.

Government schemes to provide some "formal sector-type" benefits to workers such as provident fund schemes are poor indicators of actual formality of employment, since they only deal with one aspect rather than the totality of work conditions. In any case, many workers who are registered under the schemes do not get the benefits or even know about them. Registration also provides no other security of employment or protection to the worker. Once again, women workers are more likely not to get benefits from such schemes. Women workers, who are concentrated in informal activities, are often the worst affected by formalisation measures because of the gender blindness of many measures. We found that even well-meaning measures to improve conditions of working women (such as maternity benefit laws) can operate against their interests without associated moves to change material incentives for employers, context and attitudes.

A much more effective way to ensure good quality employment for women workers is for the government to lead the way in providing it. Unfortunately, official insensitivity is evident even in government employment, which includes many women who form the bedrock of major public health and nutrition programmes, but are not classified as employees but as "volunteers." They are effectively informal workers who get much less than minimum wages under poor and insecure conditions of work. Formalisation of employment cannot succeed when the government itself seeks to exploit women informal workers. Therefore, the government must expand numbers and ensure proper conditions for women in public employment as a way of also driving labour market changes more generally. The success of the public rural employment programme MNREGA in reducing rural gender wage gaps shows that public employment can be effective in this way.

A major feature of employment in India is the fluidity of the situation confronting workers, as they can move across unorganised/organised sectors without changing their basic situation. The high degree of slack in the Indian labour market enables employers to take advantage of excess labour supply by denying workers even in formal enterprises their legal rights. The lack of awareness of many laws and schemes, as well as the sheer difficulty of accessing entitlements, still operate against the interests of informal workers. This is especially the case for women workers, who are disproportionately unaware of their rights and entitlements. This is partly due to literacy and level of education, but there is also a casual and insensitive official approach to dealing with informal women workers. Measures aimed at improving the conditions of women workers cannot succeed in isolation and need to be combined with measures to rapidly raise literacy and educational attainment of women. Also, there is need for specific local level measures to increase awareness, rather than only national level campaigns through the media.

The situation in India is particularly dire because of the broader labour market context and the macroeconomic situation characterised by low (and now even negative) employment generation despite reasonably fast GDP growth. This is now greatly accentuated by the current economic slowdown. Clearly, targeted interventions alone will not work: macroeconomic policies designed to expand employment, including good quality public employment, are required. This requires a broader perspective in which the generation of good quality employment is made a macroeconomic goal and both fiscal and monetary policies (including particular types of public expenditure) are directed towards that goal.

Notes

1 Consider, for example, the software industry, which is generally seen as a shining example of hyper-modernity, an outlier of high productivity that is somehow separate from the vast sea of low productivity work that surrounds it. In actual fact, the ability of this industry to be competitive globally relies crucially on the very cheap supporting services in the form of logistics, security, transportation, cleaning and catering that are provided

by companies or individuals that use workers on informal contracts that are well beyond the pale of labour protection. Similarly, the ability to hire highly skilled professionals in this industry at what are clearly salaries below global averages is dependent upon such workers' ability to access goods and services provided cheaply by India's informal workers.

2 For example, the eligibility criteria for the Janani Suraksha Yojana (one of the schemes enlisted under UWSSA) is as follows: (1) in low-performing states: All pregnant women delivering in government health centres, such as Sub Centers (SCs)/Primary Health Centers (PHCs)/Community Health Centers (CHCs)/First Referral Units (FRUs)/ general wards of district or state hospitals (2) in high-performing states: All BPL/ Scheduled Caste/Scheduled Tribe (SC/ST) women delivering in a government health centres, such as SC/PHC/CHC/FRU/general wards of district or state hospital (c) in all states: BPL/SC/ST women in accredited private institutions.

3 Response given to Enquiry under the Right to Information Act filed by study team.

4 Response to RTI filed by Indian Express.

5 Response to RTI filed by study team.

6 The survey was conducted through face-to-face interviews with workers. In a few cases, the survey was conducted over telephone when face-to-face interviews were not possible. Field investigators were asked to additionally note some comments based on respondent's reactions to questions and field observations during interviews.

7 Amongst the five women availing social security from government sources, two street vendor women received old age pensions, one home-based worker had availed maternity benefits, and one street vendor and one home-based women worker received widow pensions.

References

Arora, A., 2010. Economic Dualism, Openness and Employment in Manufacturing Industry in India. M.Phil. Thesis. Jawaharlal Nehru University, New Delhi, India.

Bairagya, I., 2010. Liberalization, Informal Sector and Formal-Informal Sectors' Relationship: A Study of India. Paper presented at 31st General Conference of the International Association for Research in Income and Wealth, St. Gallen, Switzerland.

Chakraborty, S., 2018. Gender Wage Differences in the Indian Labour Market, 1993–94 to 2011–12. Ph.D. Thesis. Jawaharlal Nehru University, New Delhi, India.

Chandraskhar, C. P., Ghosh, J., 2009. The costs of coupling: the global crisis and the Indian economy. *Cambridge J. Econ. Symp. Financial Crisis* 33, 725–739. 10.1093/cje/bep034.

Damodaran, S., 2010. *Global Production, Employment Conditions and Decent Work: Evidence from India's Informal Sector.* International Labour Office, New Delhi. Available at: https://www.ilo.org/legacy/english/protection/travail/pdf/rdwppt27b.pdf.

Desai, S., Dubey, A., 2011. Caste in the 21st century india, competing narratives. Econ. Polit. Wkly XLVI (11), 40–49.

Deshpande, A., 2020. The Covid-19 Pandemic and Lockdown: First Effects on Gender Gaps in Employment and Domestic Work in India. Working Papers 30. Ashoka University, Department of Economics, Sonipat, Haryana, revised Jun. 2020.

Ghosh, J., 2009. Never Done and Poorly Paid: Women's Work in Globalising India. Women Unlimited, New Delhi.

Ghosh, J., 2015. Growth, industrialisation and inequality in India. *J. Asia Pac. Econ.* 20 (1), 42–56, 10.1080/13547860.2014.974316.

Ghosh, J., Chandrasekhar, C. P., Patnaik, P., 2017. *Demoteisation Decoded: A Critique of India's Currency Experiment.* Routledge (Taylor and Francis), New Delhi.

Harriss-White, B., 2005. *India's Market Economy.* Three Essays Collective, Delhi.

Himanshu, 2011. Employment trends in India: a re-examination. *Econ. Polit. Wkly* XLVI (37). https://www.epw.in/journal/2011/37/special-articles/employment-trends-india-re-examination.html.

Human Rights Watch, 2007. *India: Hidden Apartheid: Caste Discrimination against India's "Untouchables"*. Shadow Report to the UN Committee on the Elimination of Racial Discrimination. http://www.chrgj.org/docs/IndiaCERDShadowReport.pdf.

Kannan, K. P., Raveendran, G., 2009. Growth sans employment: a quarter century of jobless growth in Indian organised manufacturing. *Econ. Polit. Wkly.* https://www.epw.in/journal/2019/44/insight/jobless-job-loss-growth.html.

Kesar, S., 2017. Subcontracting Linkages in the Informal Economy in India: Analysis and Implication for Inclusive Growth. 5th Conference of the Regulating for Decent Work Network at the International Labour Office, Geneva, Switzerland, 3–5 July 2017.

Mitra, S., 2017. *The Dynamics of Non-Farm Employment of Women: An Empirical Analysis, 1993–2012*. Ph.D. thesis. Jawaharlal Nehru University, New Delhi.

Mukherjee, A., 2012. Exploring inter-state variations of rural women's paid and unpaid work in India. *Indian J. Lab. Econ.* 55 (3).

National Sample Survey Organisation, 2001. *Employment and Unemployment Situation in India, 1999–2000, Fifth Quinquennial Survey, Parts I and II*. National Sample Survey Organisation: Ministry of Statistics & Programme Implementation, Government of India, New Delhi.

National Sample Survey Organisation, 2001a. *Non-Agricultural Enterprises in the Informal Sector in India, 1999–2000 - Key Results*. Report No. 456. National Sample Survey Organisation, Ministry of Statistics and Programme Implementation, Government of India, New Delhi.

National Sample Survey Organisation, 2001b. *Informal Sector in India, 1999–2000 - Salient Features*. Report No. 459. National Sample Survey Organisation, Ministry of Statistics and Programme Implementation, Government of India, New Delhi.

National Sample Survey Organisation, 2002. *Unorganised Manufacturing Sector in India 2000–01 - Key Results*. Report No. 477. National Sample Survey Organisation, Ministry of Statistics and Programme Implementation, Government of India, New Delhi.

National Sample Survey Organisation, 2002. *Unorganised Manufacturing Sector in India 2000–01 – Characteristics of Enterprises*. Report No. 478. National Sample Survey Organisation, Ministry of Statistics and Programme Implementation, Government of India, New Delhi.

National Sample Survey Organisation, 2006. *Employment and Unemployment Situation in India 2004–05, Parts I and II*. National Sample Survey Organisation, Ministry of Statistics and Programme Implementation, Government of India, National Sample Survey Office, New Delhi.

National Sample Survey Organisation, 2007. *Operational Characteristics of Unorganised Manufacturing Enterprises in India*. Report No. 524, NSS 67th Round. National Sample Survey Organisation, Ministry of Statistics and Programme Implementation, Government of India, New Delhi.

National Sample Survey Organisation, 2011. *Key Indicators of Employment and Unemployment) in India, 2009–10*. NSS 66th Round. National Sample Survey Organisation, Ministry of Statistics and Programme Implementation, Government of India, New Delhi.

National Sample Survey Organisation, 2012. *Key Results of Survey on Unincorporated Non-Agricultural Enterprises (Excluding Construction) in India*. NSS 67th Round. National

Sample Survey Organisation, Ministry of Statistics and Programme Implementation, Government of India.

National Sample Survey Organisation, 2012a. *Operational Characteristics of Unincorporated Non-Agricultural Enterprises (Excluding Construction) in India.* Report No. 546, NSS 67th Round. National Sample Survey Organisation, Ministry of Statistics and Programme Implementation, Government of India, New Delhi.

National Sample Survey Organisation, 2012a. *Operational Characteristics of Unincorporated Non-Agricultural Enterprises (Excluding Construction) in India.* Report No. 546, NSS 67th Round. National Sample Survey Organisation, Ministry of Statistics and Programme Implementation, Government of India, New Delhi.

National Sample Survey Organisation, 2013. *Key Indicators of Employment and Unemployment) in India, 2011–12.* NSS 68th Round. National Sample Survey Organisation, Ministry of Statistics and Programme Implementation, Government of India, New Delhi.

National Sample Survey Organisation, 2019. *Periodic Labour Force Survey 2017–18.* National Sample Survey Organisation, Ministry of Statistics and Programme Implementation, Government of India, New Delhi.

Sahu, P. P., 2010. Subcontracting in India's unorganised manufacturing sector: a mode of adoption or exploitation? *J. South Asian Dev.* 5(1), 53–83.

Shah, G., Mander, H., Thorat, S., Deshpande, S., Baviskar, A., 2006. *Untouchability in Rural India.* Sage Publications, New Delhi.

Srivastava, N., Srivastava, R., 2010. Women, work and employment outcomes in rural india. *Econ. Polit. Wkly.* https://www.epw.in/journal/2010/28/special-articles/women-work-and-employment-outcomes-rural-india.html.

Sundaram, A., Ahsan, R. N., Mitra, D., 2012. Complementarity between formal and informal manufacturing in India. *Reforms and Economic Transformation in India,* 49–85.

Thorat, A., 2010. Ethnicity, caste and religion: implications for poverty outcomes. *Econ. Polit. Wkly* 45, 47–53.

Thorat, S., Negi, P., Mahamallik, M., Senapati, C., 2009. *Dalits in India: Search for a Common Destiny.* Sage Publications, New Delhi.

Vaaneman, R., Dubey, A., 2011. Horizontal and Vertical Inequalities in India, Indian Human Development Survey Working Paper No. 16.

Vyas, M., 2020. India has a jobs bloodbath as unemployment rate shoots up to 27.1%. *Business Standard.*

3

GROWING INFORMALITY AND WOMEN'S WORK IN SOUTH AFRICA

Hameda Deedat

I Introduction

The South African labour market landscape is rapidly changing from a once highly formalised labour market to one that is informalised. Key industries such as mining, manufacturing, retail and the services sector are both shedding jobs and transforming to rapid informalisation of formalised work, characterised by the accompanying precarity and downward variation, and even deindustrialisation as some proponents argue. As the formal market both sheds jobs and reconfigures, its inability to absorb the increasing number of unemployed skilled and unskilled becomes more evident.

This transformation is characterised by informalisation of employment in both the traditionally formal sectors of the South African economy, that is, manufacturing, retail, nursing, transport, security, cleaning, refuse removal, agriculture amongst others. Simultaneously, expansion within sectors of the informal economy such as street vending, waste pickers, domestic workers, transport (Uber and Taxify services) online services and artisans such as carpenters, painters, mechanics and so on are on the increase. This dual economy is not surprising, given the high levels of income disparity between the rich and the poor in the country. South Africa has been identified as the most unequal country in the world as measured by the Gini Coefficient. Nevertheless, South Africa has recently been reclassified as a developed country, despite the poverty, high levels of food insecurity, malnutrition, lack of access to water and sanitation, healthcare, education services, high levels of unemployment and poor quality of life for the majority of South Africans. According to the recent STATSA data, the informal economy has started to play an increasingly important role in the overall growth, whereas the formal economy appears to be shrinking and shedding jobs; the informal economy is growing and increasing job opportunities.

Another significant factor (which is not given specific attention in this chapter) is the influx of migrants and refugees from neighbouring African countries as a result of war, poverty and climate disasters, into South Africa, in the attempt to seek employment. Many informal economy workers were once employed in the formal economy and organised by trade unions. Many have held on to the traditions of organising; hence, as early as the 2000s, they began organising themselves. One of the first organisations organising informal traders and street vendors (Self-Employed Workers Union or SEWU) was formed by Pat Horn. It no longer exists but has evolved into Streetnet, which has become an international network of street workers and is still currently active. It drew inspiration and modalities from the Self-Employed Workers Association, the formidable association of informal women workers in India.

The aim of this chapter is to share insights on South Africa's trajectory from formalisation to greater informality with a gendered perspective; and to consider how the South African government has sought to bring in processes to formalise the informal economy to address the challenges brought about by this shift. The chapter will tease out the gendered impacts of these processes on workers and patriarchal relations, identifying and assessing the initiators and drivers. The legal and policy frameworks will also be interrogated to evaluate their intent and extent to which they have facilitated meaningful benefits particularly for women workers in the informal economy. These points are illustrated with reference to case studies of women informal workers in the municipal waste/refuse sector, street vending, informal mining, domestic work and agriculture. The chapter concludes by linking this analysis to policy implications and recommendations for future work.

II Trends in aggregate employment

In 2018, South Africa recorded the second economic recession since the early 1990s. This recession spanned the first two quarters of 2018, during which the economy shrunk by 2.7 per cent and then 0.5 per cent. There was some recovery thereafter, with positive growth rates of 2.6 per cent and 0.8 per cent in the latter two quarters of 2018 (QLFS, 2018). However, the labour market continued to exhibit extreme slack, with falling rates of employment of the working age population (15-64 years), from 46.3 per cent in 2009 to 43.3 per cent in 2018. In the fourth quarter of 2018, of the working age population of 38.1 million people, the employed were 16.5 million, openly unemployed were 6.1 million and those classified as "not economically active" (including those engaged in unpaid work within homes) were 15.4 million. Of this last category, as many as 2.8 million were "discouraged workers" who were no longer seeking employment, and their number had increased by 108,000 compared to the previous quarter. This is not surprising in view of the persistently high rates of open unemployment, which remained in the range of 26–28 per cent over the previous few years. The total number of unemployed people increased from 4 million in the last quarter of 2008 to 6.1 million in the last quarter of 2018. Within that, the share of the long-term unemployed increased from 62 per cent to 71 per cent.

Women (29 per cent) showed a higher unemployment rate than men (25 per cent), and if discouraged workers are included, the expanded unemployment rate for women was as high as 41 per cent, compared to 33 per cent for men. Both race and gender were differentiating factors for unemployment, with black women (33 per cent) showing the highest rates of open unemployment as well as expanded unemployment (46 per cent). Unemployment rates were higher for the less educated, and also for younger people: 33 per cent of those aged 25–34 years were unemployed, compared to 15 per cent of the 45–54 years group. Among the young, education was not a solution: rates of educated unemployment were very high. The strong tendency for youth unemployment is reflected in the large numbers of young people classified as Not in Employment, Education or Training (NEET), who amounted to 31 per cent of the age cohort 15–24 years in 2018. A greater proportion of females age 15–24 years (33 per cent) were likely to be NEET, compared to males (29 per cent). When slightly older people are included, the NEET numbers are even more striking: in the age group 15–34 years, 43 per cent of young women and 35 per cent of young men were NEET.

Among the employed, there is a significant degree of diversification across sectors, as indicated in Figure 3.1. While South Africa is often considered as a primary producing economy, mining and agriculture together account for 11 per cent of GDP and only 9 per cent of employment. However, man of the services that dominate in aggregate employment are likely to be relatively low-paying and more informal in nature. Thus, trade (including retail trade that includes street vendors and others) and domestic workers together account for 28 per cent of total employment.

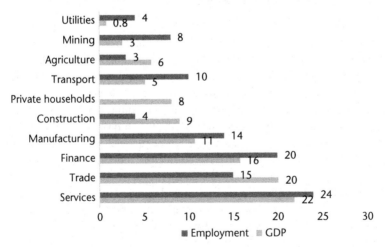

Sectoral shares in GDP and employment in 2018 (%)

FIGURE 3.1 Sectoral shares in GDP and Employment (2018)

Source: https://www.slideshare.net/StatsSA/quarterly-labour-force-survey, accessed on 19 June 2020.

The formal sector in South Africa is still the main employer of the workforce, accounting for 65 per cent of total employment. However, it is worth noting that between 2008 and 2017, the informal sector, however, grew by 18 per cent, compared to 12 per cent growth registered in the formal sector (Hassan et al., 2018). Furthermore, there is a correlation between increased employment on the one hand and growth of the informal sector on the other (Hassan et al., 2018), such that new jobs are more likely to be informal. This has also been associated with corresponding changes in trade union participation: only 29 per cent of workers are unionised, which is alarming for South Africa noting its history of a strong labour movement and highly organised labour force (Statistics South Africa, 2017).

Women are more likely to be informal workers and fewer of them tend to have the benefits normally associated with formality, as shown in Figure 3.2. Furthermore, informal work is not uniform, and although men and women both do informal work, women are particularly vulnerable. Home-based workers who are women are paid on a piece rate while men who are more likely the ones employing these women and are thus more likely to be employers (Chen, 2018; Rogan, 2018).

In developing countries with large informal sectors, informal enterprises usually operate quite openly outside of the government's regulatory sphere. Using the Streetnet, WIEGO, and the International Labour Organization (ILO) definitions, this chapter considers the following workers as informal: self-employed workers in small unregistered enterprises; unpaid but contributing family workers; wage workers without worker benefits or social protection including unprotected employees of informal enterprises, unprotected employees of formal firms, unprotected domestic workers, casual or day labourers and sub-contracted workers (called home workers if they work from their home). In the next section, I consider the conditions of informal women workers in some sectors and assess policy approaches to formalisation and their outcomes.

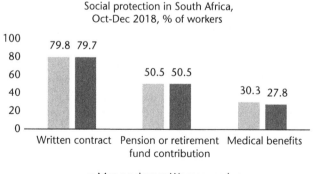

FIGURE 3.2 Social protection indicators in South Africa, 2018
Source: StatsAfrica, QLFS, 2018 Q4.

III Some sectoral experiences

Street vendors

Street vendors are a mixed group of workers largely dominated by women who operate in public spaces and are generally categorised as "self-employed." Many do not have employers, despite effectively being engaged in activities as intermediaries for corporations. For example, street vendors, who distribute shampoo, phone SIM cards, prepaid airtime, etc., are not considered to be employees of the company concerned. As a result of the "workplace" being the street, vendors and other market workers are also affected by a multiplicity of actors: various government departments that regulate their use of public spaces, associations regulating the operations of local markets and the private suppliers of goods. Being on the street or in designated public spaces for trading leaves street vendors vulnerable to challenges based on public infrastructure policies and other byelaws. At times, these result in marketplace evictions, relocation and displacement. Being an informal worker also implies little or no protection through either the labour or company laws of South Africa. The most visible impact is the extent to which access to public space for vending, storing or producing (e.g. cooking) goods for sale is impacted or hindered by new or existing legislation. Access to these spaces is central to the livelihoods of street vendors, determining whether they can gain access to their clientele in these spaces. Through processes of formalisation, local governments have administered and rationed access to these spaces to competing vendors. Vendors are then forced to conform or face the wrath of the law, either through fines or having their stalls demolished if they fail to comply. Formalisation for such informal street vendors, who are mainly women, therefore, means direct exposure to bureaucratic processes: for trading licenses, paying market fees, being relocated to zoning/rezoning areas, access to or being relocated away from transportation; even as they face inadequate provisions for their safety in public spaces (Kohn, 2017).

This is why recognition and collective bargaining rights have been central to street vendors' demands. Women vendors have raised some of the gendered implications of unilateral decisions made by municipalities and how it affects them. In the attempt to "clean up" cities and formalise street vendors, municipalities use their mechanisms of control to rezone trading spaces, which affects their movement and place of work without giving due consideration to transport challenges to and from the newly designated areas. Officials also disregard hygiene issues and do not consider the proximity of the new trading spaces to public taps and toilets. In instances where the new trading zone is further away from public transport, the market for trading either shrinks or becomes unsustainable, with major impacts on their incomes and the well-being of their households and dependants. Safety also becomes an issue when the access to transport becomes inaccessible, especially at night.

Various studies (e.g. Informal Economy Monitoring Study [IEMS]) have found that the working environment for street vendors is generally unpredictable, and even directly hostile, such that the policy and regulatory environment have inhibited the livelihood of informal workers. The lack of legal recognition and protection means that informal workers often face demands for bribes, confiscation of goods and equipment, evictions and other forms of harassment, often in the name of "cleaning the city." As a result, vendors are less inclined to invest in improved technologies or enhanced stock. Street vendors without secure vending sites and storage facilities cannot invest in expensive or heavy equipment. This lack of a secure workplace storage space, along with the high costs for permits and rent, and high costs of transport, limits investments in both technology and stock building, and thereby limits the scope of their activities and hamper the progress that street vendors could make.

Waste pickers and reclaimers

There are an estimated 200,000 waste pickers in South Africa, but because they are dominantly informal workers, the exact number is not known. While they are amongst the most disadvantaged and least protected of all workers, they perform valuable services for the population and economy, given the amount of waste generated in cities and towns and the importance of recycling activities in general. The activities of informal waste pickers and recyclers also provide substantial savings to municipal corporations: according to the South African Council for Scientific and Industrial Research, reclaimers recycle between 80 and 90 per cent of plastic and packaging in South Africa, thereby saving authorities up to 750 million Rand ($53 million) per year.

There have been various efforts to formalise waste picking and recycling by different municipal authorities, by bringing in formal recycling companies to replace the small-scale individual operators who tend to work in informal groups, or attempting to formalise these groups. For example, the Waste Management Strategy of the city of Johannesburg sought to create formal employment in the waste sector. At the time, there were 192 "reclaimers" (waste pickers") working on the landfill sites, who had won the right to do so as a result of a major struggle with the city administration. The reclaimers had worked as informal workers on the landfill sites since 1992 and survived the attempted eviction by Pikitup, an outsourcing company contracted to the city of Johannesburg to do waste (refuse) management. As part of the city's integrated waste management strategy, they decided to encourage more than a 1000 waste pickers (reclaimers) to become formalised and organised into cooperatives and tender to provide services to the city. As part of the support programme Sort at the Source (S@S), reclaimers were sent on workshops, employed formally under the Extended Public Works Programme, paid a stipend and given protective clothing—all as an attempt to formalise them. As a cooperative, they were encouraged to compete with the private sector; to change their modus operandi of being informal workers and to operate as businesses; to change their identity to "entrepreneurs" with the potential to become employers themselves. Formalisation created a different sense of value and identity for the reclaimers and as part of the S@S project, the economic value of their work was recognised and work security improved; they were even provided with protective clothing which improved their health and safety and were offered the option of having a health insurance.

However, a study by Dladla (2018) showed that despite this well-meaning attempt to formalise this informal activity, most of the reclaimers were unable to actively benefit from this "opportunity." Key to the failure was the model which turned informal workers who were organised under African Reclaimers Association (ARO), and who worked as a team, into competitors. They were asked to register as cooperatives and start competing with one another and with Pikitup to work on the landfill sites that had for years been their workplaces. As informal workers, they remained organised under ARO and through them joined WIEGO. One of the key roles WIEGO then played was to facilitate and mediate the role between the workers and the city. This was critical as the city was only prepared to recognise the contribution made and the value of these workers through the "formalised" cooperative initiative. This intervention forced the city to acknowledge the invaluable contributions of reclaimers within the informal economy, which in turn empowered the reclaimers to see and recognise their own value. This demonstrated that attempts at formalisation that are out of sync with informal economy workers and their specific needs, such as the city's top-down approach to integration and an externally driven and determined training and capacity-building process, are unlikely to succeed.

Research by Samson (2015) and Sekhwala (2017) has drawn attention to the legal and policy framework that waste reclaimers operate in, which can act as hindrance for reclaimers in the waste sector. There are several such examples: the National Environmental Management Waste Bill 2001 and 2001a; the National Environmental Management Waste Act 2008; the DEA Reduction, Reduce, Recycle and Recover Policy 2012; the DEA National Management Waste Strategy 1999; the White paper on Integrated Pollution and Waste Management; and the two policies already mentioned, the City of Johannesburg Integrated Waste Management Plan 2011; and the S@S Business Plan for Pikitup.

A study on waste reclaimers in the Durban metro (Chan, 2018) showed how these policies impacted on the workers. In Durban, solid waste management is still a public sector function through the Department of Durban Solid Waste (DSW). Reclaimers start out early in the morning and work both streets and landfill sites. For those working the streets, it is imperative that they get to the bins and recyclable material before the municipal recycle truck does. One group of waste reclaimers pickers reported that "(t)he DSW often comes early and takes all the waste including cardboard, so it is important for us that we arrive before the DSW." However, there are times when the municipal pick up is made earlier, having an adverse effect on reclaimer's ability to access the solid waste they collect. An additional complication arose from the formal mobile waste dealers who drove around the market area looking for recyclable waste to buy, either from the wandering waste pickers or directly from shopkeepers. The Durban waste pickers used trolleys to haul their waste around the market area and were unable to compete with those with cars or trucks. Incidents of official harassment also abounded, with reclaimers for metal waste in Durban pointing to being constantly harassed by police, including confiscation of essential tools required for their work. Since these tools are the same as those used by house burglars, they tend to be suspect and face police brutality.

The number of women involved in waste picking is growing (Vanqa-Mgijima, 2015) and they face additional constraints beyond those faced by men. While both men and women are engaged in risky and often hazardous work without protective equipment or clothing, women sorters are often even more exposed than mere collectors. While most waste pickers are paid relatively little by middlemen, who engage in resale at much higher prices, because of discrimination women do not always get access to the recyclables with the highest value, thereby reducing their income from such activity. Often, waste pickers from townships are barred from other areas where there are more valuable forms of waste. Also, the job exposes women to crime and sexual violence because of the long and irregular hours they are forced to work.

Domestic workers

We no longer sing, "My Mama was a kitchen girl" (SADSAWU interview).
"When he is inside the house he can shout, and you feel … you are not dressed, you are not a human … So I don't know, now I don't want her [his] money. I want justice only. Because he already … accuse me of stealing. What I want, I just want justice only." Christine Wiro, domestic worker who claims she was assaulted by ANC MP Mduduzi Manana (Eye Witness News 8/5/2018)

According to Rees (2018), there are over a million domestic workers in South Africa of which the overwhelming majority (96 per cent) are women. A third of all domestic workers are under the age of 40, the rest are older. In terms of education, numeracy and literacy levels were low with the majority being without formal schooling. In terms of formal conditions of employment such as written contracts, which were introduced several years ago in a bid to formalise and improve the social protection of domestic workers, 77 per cent did not have a written employment contracts while less than 4 per cent had limited duration contracts (QLFS of 2017). A total of 42 per cent of all domestic workers reported that they were permanently employed. Added benefits such as retirement or medical aid benefits were the exception, with less than a quarter of workers having taken annual leave in 2018, despite this right being legislated under the Basic Conditions of Employment Act and the sectoral determination for the sector. Even more disconcerting is that three quarters of all domestic worker employers did not have UIF (unemployment benefits) despite it being a legal requirement.

Less than 1 per cent of these informal workers are organised. Those who are organised belong to a union called the South African Domestic Workers Union (SADSAWU). Those domestic workers who have belonged to a union for decades attribute their salary increases to the union, as a result of negotiations or collective bargaining. Since 2018, domestic workers have fallen under the new legislation of the National Minimum Wage Act 2018. The minimum hourly rate is now set at R15 which is a slight increase from R13.05, and there are regional variations which, depending on the cost of living, vary across the country. In a bid to improve the social protection and rights of domestic workers almost 20 years ago, a submission was made to the September Commission highlighting the plight and challenges facing domestic workers. Unfortunately, despite legislative changes as a way of regulating the working conditions, the aspirations are yet to be realised.

A new trend emerging in Cape Town province is that of placement agencies starting to operate in the sector and broker between workers and employers. The placement agencies engage the union as an advisory body and also advocate for decent working conditions, but the effects of this are yet to be seen. That this new process has not necessarily improved conditions facing domestic workers is evident from the demands being raised by SADSAWU. Domestic workers have made several demands that they want formalisation to achieve: freedom from harassment or abuse by recruiters or employers; freedom from exploitation by agencies and intermediaries; implementation of the Domestic Workers' Convention and accompanying Recommendations as a minimum set of conditions; the right to a living wage and working conditions such as time off and leave, overtime pay, sick leave, health insurance and pensions; the right to have workplaces (effectively private homes) taxed, inspected and controlled; decent living conditions where live-in arrangements are part of the employment contract; access to education, recreation and leisure time; no child labour (including when disguised as family labour); migrant workers' contracts concluded before leaving home countries; and full and equal rights for migrant domestic workers.

The very nature of these demands demonstrates vividly not only that these conditions are not being met, but also that formalisation requirements are sector specific and have very different implications when the workplace is within private households. In addition, the patriarchal nature of domestic work that places domestic workers at the mercy of their employers (male and female) has not been addressed through the gains made thus far, as issues of abuse, sexual harassment, rape and forced family or child labour continue to permeate this sector. This situation has worsened in South Africa particularly with the entry of undocumented workers, who are often well qualified but driven by circumstances into this market. Their myriad vulnerabilities have played into the hands of employers who in the face of an abundant workforce are flouting the law and gains made by South African domestic workers, by pegging worker against worker in a bid to drive wages lower. WIEGO has tried to organise domestic workers to mitigate this situation, but with limited success. Hence, there is a lot of uncertainty about whether the benefits to be derived through formalisation would actually be realised by domestic workers.

Informal artisanal women workers in the mining sector

Valiana and Ndebele (2018) have provided a unique study focused on informal women workers in mining, a traditionally male-dominated sector. The presence of women workers in informal mining sectors (as underground mine workers as well as artisanal mining on remains of diamond mines) provides a complex picture of unexpected benefits along with vulnerability. Prior to this research, there was very little data on women artisanal miners in South Africa. This study of informal women artisanal diamond miners in Kimberley in the Northern Cape is not a representative sample of all women artisanal miners in South Africa, it provides a picture of an important sample. The common experience of mining work among the women considered in this study was overwhelmingly positive. The study focused on women miners living in informal settlements around the mines, which typically did not have water, electricity and sanitation facilities. At the time of the research, there were approximately 4,000 informal miners, many of whom were women. Many of the women had taken to artisanal mining to replace or supplement their traditionally undervalued, female work. They saw artisanal mining as a means to escape the gender discrimination experienced in various facets of life, in both the productive and social reproductive spaces. This opportunity brought with it hope of attaining degrees of freedom and respect especially in the workplace. It also offered the prospect of financial rewards, which for most of the women was the main attraction of the mines. Despite the nature of the work, the women interviewed described their work positively, emphasizing the ability to choose one's hours of work flexibly, allowing for breaks and being able to determine the pace of work. The experience of working in the soil was also a source of enjoyment and one they embraced openly as they honed their skills in understanding and detecting the variety of soils and differentiating the ones most likely to contain diamonds.

Valiani and Ndabele (2018) describe this as a "combination of materiality and belief without excessive materialism" and pointed out that it is quite unique and perhaps even an exclusive work experience among women artisanal mine workers. The research also found that while most female artisanal miners did not find diamonds regularly, they remained driven to continue in this work. While access to the mining camps presented no challenge, the necessary tools were required: having a shovel, a pick, two buckets, some bags for sorting and two sieves were imperative to the trade. Therefore, the main barrier to entry was possession of or access to the required tools. As a result, theft of tools was quite rife and was easy to carry out, because of the temporary nature of the work and the informal structures in which people lived. Interestingly none of the women reported harassment, safety issues or violence against them accompanying the theft. Male co-workers were the ones who by and large owned the tools and many women described how the tools were used as a currency for abuse against women. Transactional sex in exchange for access to tools was very common and many women workers had entered into these arrangements to improve their chances of finding a diamond.

Several of the women workers referred to this as "financial abuse" and highlighted how men miners were able to exploit and manipulate this vulnerability. All the respondents indicated uniformity across the work tasks; however, the social reproductive sphere remained "the woman's job" despite them having toiled as hard as the male counterparts. They continued to carry the burden of care work in addition to the other work.

A further drawback was the issue of the black market. Women workers were most vulnerable when it came to selling their finds, since the negotiators were mainly men who were the go-betweens. Being undercut by the middlemen was experienced by all workers, but women were more disadvantaged than men. The lack of work permits exacerbated this, with the black market being the only option for sale. The opportunity to sell to the South African Diamond Exchange and Export Centre (referred to by participants as "the Board"), where prices were more favourable was possible but was the exception rather than the norm, since most workers did not have permits. While "legality" was a major challenge faced by both male and female artisanal miners, male mining workers were more likely to have permits. In response to this challenge, the women miners were attempting to form cooperatives to be eligible for permits, though this initiative was only incipient at the time of the research.

This shows that underground mining and artisanal mining today, like asbestos mining in the past, represent a way out of unemployment and/or typically undervalued, female work. Gendered power imbalances, discrimination and violence against women are persistent, but nevertheless were significantly less in artisanal mining. Furthermore, the ample supply of land and relatively open access to it were key structural conditions that created positive experiences for women workers in the informal artisanal diamond mines and allowed for their inclusion. Such work had the added benefit of worker-selected production teams, worker-determined pace of production, team-controlled earnings and the potential for cooperative structures for legal and administrative purposes. The informal mining sector unlike those in the formal economy has gone beyond the benefits of mere mineral extraction and presents the possibility to adapt production of various ecologically and socially sound goods including the mining of waste in more beneficial ways. Nevertheless, in spite of the financial gain and flexibility, and prospects of earning more, women mine workers endured continuous hardships, ranging from the impact of direct contact with asbestos, gender-biased technologies and standards confronting underground miners, harsh living conditions and constant threats from authorities faced by artisanal miners. Additionally, the suboptimal use of women's informal labour has led to the destruction of community wealth and stunted social reproduction.

Informal artisanal miners are not organised and there are few regulations on activity in this sector apart from those linked to the actual sales of the diamonds. However, it is quite a significant market and space for labour market activities and while there are similarities to other informal sectors, there are also some quite diverse characteristics and features. Like the other examples presented here, this highlights the need for processes of formalisation of the informal economy to recognise the context, specificities and more critically the varying gendered dimensions which prevail in each activity, thereby requiring a nuanced and sector-specific approach. However, for formalisation to translate into something meaningful, informal economy workers need to be organised. The next section focuses on ILO Recommendation 204, and how it provides insights on how this could be achieved.

IV ILO Recommendation 204 and its relevance for South Africa

In June 2015, the ILO Recommendation 204 on the Transition from the Informal to the Formal Economy was adopted by the International Labour Conference of the ILO. This was significant in several ways. Prior to this, informal workers were identified as "employers" and could not access the ILO processes. The key objective of the Recommendation is to address the issue of transition from informal to formal economy and expand the full scope of informal workers (Pat Horn interview, June 2018). Central to the Recommendation is the acknowledgement that workers enter the informal economy due to a lack of opportunities in the formal economy, and or an absence of any other means of livelihood and thus having little or no choice.

This process was immensely important for South Africa since the government, South African trade unions and organisations such as Wiego and Streetnet were supportive and became active participants in this process. Recommendation 204 is not at odds with the South African national policy and legislative landscape, which is increasingly being redefined and reshaped to adapt to the reconfiguration of the labour market. The point of departure in South Africa is that the nature of work and the formal economy itself is becoming highly informal and transitions from the informal to formal is necessarily the answer. Several demands made by WIEGO and others were captured in the framing of Recommendation 204:

- Avoiding destruction of livelihoods in the process of formalisation, which was captured in the preamble as "ensuring the preservation and improvement of existing livelihoods during the transition."
- Informal initiatives were seen as attempts by economic units to earn an income as opposed to being seen as "enterprises."
- Informal economy workers are now workers as per Recommendation 204, and recognised and captured in STATS data as own-account workers rather than as employers.
- The regulated use of public space is now recognised for generation of livelihoods in the informal economy, which is an essential victory for street vendors.
- The need for regulated access to natural resources used in informal economy livelihoods is recognised.

- Instead of the previous ILO language of "social enterprises," the Recommendation talks of cooperatives and the social and solidarity economy, a significant advance.
- Collective bargaining and direct representation were recognised as necessary and integral parts of transitioning from informal to formal.

However, one lacuna is with respect to local government: Recommendation 204 fails to underline the specific role and responsibilities of local government in providing an enabling environment for decent work in relation to many categories of workers in the informal economy. This can inadvertently become a major deterrent to achieve formalisation in the formal economy, thereby making the transition less likely.

Despite this limitation, there are many ways in which it could provide the framework for facilitating the formalisation of informal economy workers in South Africa, even without achieving a full transition. It allows for flexibility in interpretation and application across various informal activities. For example, even though sex work in the case of South Africa is not legalised, the Recommendation technically could include them. Sections of the Recommendation that acknowledge the right to work, rights at work, in law and practice, and covers vulnerable categories including women, young people, migrants, older people, indigenous and tribal peoples, persons living with HIV or affected by HIV or AIDS, persons with disabilities, domestic workers and subsistence farmers all could be utilised in favour of informal workers. The aim is to ensure appropriate coverage and protection of all categories of workers and economic units. The Recommendation also cautioned against measures which penalise the workers for their lack of formality and points to the need for labour inspection to extend coverage to informal economy workers "to all workplaces in the informal economy *in order to protect workers.*" In terms of social protection, the Recommendation is very sensitive to the specific needs of women workers in the informal economy, extending social insurance coverage and making it more accessible, extending maternity protection and access to affordable quality childcare. Since Recommendation 204 has been recognised in South Africa and is discussed at NEDLAC, it can be a useful tool in initiating favourable formalisation processes. Nevertheless, it will be workers in the informal economy and their organisations that will lead the way for implementation.

V The gendered impact of the COVID-19 pandemic on informal workers

The nationwide lockdown—as a containment measure for the pandemic, which required everyone except for those employed in essential services to stay at home—shared a significant gender bias with other countries engaging in similar policies. This was reflected in the complete lack of recognition of the triple burden that women in both formal and informal economies were forced to bear under the lockdown: the social reproductive responsibilities that women carry out, the risks to health and safety for women workers in essential services in the formal economy and those informally employed; and the added burden created by the closure of schools and day-cares, which added childcare and home schooling to the re- sponsibilities on the already overstretched shoulders of women. Even the re- cognition of essential services was restricted to formal economic activities. There was also increasing evidence of greater gender-based violence within homes.

Even before the pandemic, by the first quarter of 2020, the unemployment rate had increased to 33 per cent from 29 per cent in 2019 (QLFS 2020 Q1). This was coupled with high levels of deindustrialisation, as many manufacturing industries such as steel suffered. As formal employment becomes even more precarious and less available, more or job seekers are turning to the informal economy. Unfortunately, this has not prompted the government to adopt ILO Recommendation 204. This may be because the emphasis was more in the interest of workers in the informal economy than creating the opportunity for informal economy workers to be incorporated into the tax revenue stream for governments (national and local), so the initial zeal for formalisation lost its appeal. Consequently, there has been adverse effects for the large number of informal workers under COVID-19. Due to this lack of adoption of Recommendation 204, government departments such as the Department of Labour and Employment and the Department of Social Development have no formal record of the number of workers in the informal economy, the sectors in which they trade, the pro- portion who solely rely on this form of income as their main or only source of livelihood, the number of dependants being supported by the informal worker, their conditions of work and key sources of information linked to their trade such as access to transport, their place of work, the value chain they are located in etc., and the most critical the number of whom are women.

The lack of this critical information led to the initial stages of the lockdown disregarding some of the key functions performed by informal workers as essential. For example, subsistence farmers, who are by and large informal and who were supplying food to their local community, or cooking for school-feeding schemes, or small-scale suppliers of organic produce such as spinach for example to Pick and Pay, were prevented from doing so. As a consequence, informal farmers suffered a severe blow to their livelihoods, impacted both those dependent on their income and poor communities who could not afford to buy from large retailers or super- markets. In the second phase of lockdown, informal traders particularly those selling food were allowed to trade, largely because of pressure from civil society groups.

Similarly, removal services provided by the local municipality were declared as an essential service and workers were allowed to work and were provided with person protective equipment (PPE). Unfortunately, PPE was not provided for the 6,000 informal reclaimers who are members of African Reclaimers Organisation (ARO; affiliated to WIEGO), and the thousands more who are unorganised, pointing to the invisibility of their valuable contribution to government officials. Had these workers been registered on the system as workers (as per Recommendation 204) and acknowledged for the essential services they provide, they would not only have been allowed to continue to work, but local municipalities would have been able to issue them with formal work, permits, provide them with the necessary PPE and facilitating the distribution of food parcels to reclaimers. As noted earlier, a large number of reclaimers are women and as primary care givers had the double burden of caring for their children while trying to eke out a living on the rubbish dumps. Some women were forced to take their small children with them to the landfill sites or to the suburbs on bin day, as they rummaged through household refuse. Others had to leave their children unattended or pay someone, (which was illegal) under the lockdown regulations. Both reclaimers and street traders felt the full breadth of the law and were harassed, victimised, had their goods confiscated (recycled waste) and were even arrested for trying to earn something to feed their families. The desperation which drove them to place themselves at risk was lost on the law enforcement.

Domestic workers suffered a similar fate. Without warning, planning or recourse, they too found themselves unable to return to work with no buffer. The presence of both the police and army made movement without a permit difficult and many employers who themselves faced loss in wages or short time could no longer employ their domestic worker. The virus itself that posed a health threat and required physical distancing implied that domestic workers by virtue of the nature or function of their work were unable to work. Once again many domestic workers are not formally organised, do not receive the National Minimum Wage and are not able to draw upon unemployment insurance. Similarly, there is no database for domestic workers and as a result despite their circumstances, access to food parcels as relief could not be facilitated. Anecdotal evidence suggests, however, that as South Africa moved into level 4 and more people were allowed to return to work, and taxis had extended hours of operation, domestic workers returned to work without PPE and without employers seeking permits for them. Many domestic workers would have returned to work to provide childcare for children they otherwise looked after, or those children who would otherwise have been at school, while many left their own children unattended, with school work compromised and unsupervised.

A survey carried out by WIEGO between the 23rd March and 8th April 2020 covered mainly domestic workers, home-based workers, street vendors and market traders and waste pickers: predominantly women who are vulnerable, earn low wages or are in self-employment. For many of them, the pandemic and lockdown have resulted in a permanent loss of income. Some of the common challenges by informal women workers in different sectors are as follows: physical distancing is impossible in over-crowded urban neighbourhoods and informal settlements. Informal workers have limited access to information on the virus and how it spreads and have been the target of misinformation campaigns. They often lack access to soap and water to wash their hands. Many of them require protective gear to undertake their essential work and daily activities but are not provided these and cannot afford to purchase them, especially in the face of price-gouging and stockpiling by the middle and upper classes. Meagre daily incomes have meant that they could not stockpile food and other necessities ahead of the lockdown.

Harassment by police of informal workers was common across all regions resulting in the confiscation of goods, fines or physical violence and abuse. Migrants returning to rural areas are losing their incomes and housing and have become targets of violence. Women informal workers across all sectors are finding it more difficult to work due to childcare responsibilities as schools and childcare centres are closed. Many do not have digital bank accounts and/or access to mobile money transfers; restrictions on mobility makes it difficult for informal workers to collect income support. Lockdown measures have increased the threat of domestic violence. The sense of isolation as support systems have broken down has increased the mental health challenges of informal women workers.

What is evident is that the pandemic and lockdown have underlined the brutal fact that women informal workers in particular have no cushion to fall back on. As a result, in times of crisis such as the pandemic, not only do they bear the brunt of economic disruptions, but they are forced into bearing potentially unbearable multiple burdens at great risk to their own physical and health security and mental and emotional health.

VI Conclusion

Despite Recommendation 204, substantive engagements and legal and policy frameworks remain a contested terrain. For the ILO, the aim is to transition workers from the informal economy to the formal, while for workers and their respective organisations, the formal economy is not necessarily where they would want to be. This chapter does not engage the debates on the rationale behind formalisation or the drives for transitioning the informal economy to the formal. Nevertheless, it is clear that under the current neoliberal macroeconomic frameworks, worker rights, collective bargaining freedom of association, the right to strike, "employee status" workplaces, etc., are all in flux. If we add the Fourth Industrial Revolution to this analysis coupled with the new forms of work "future of work" and the demand for the social wage and new forms of worker ownership, the trajectory envisioned for transitioning back to the formal may need an urgent review. The formal economy, work and workplaces as we know it are changing and then informal spaces of work could inevitably become the "formal."

Any analysis that locates women at the centre and considers how economic decisions can perpetuate patriarchal relations must recognise that the macroeconomic system is inherently biased and skewed against women; therefore, mechanisms to advance women's rights also need to dismantle the patriarchal system. The informal economy space allows one to envision these possibilities and so this chapter concludes with inputs from informal economy workers on the WIEGO platform, who express what formalisation means for them. They provide pragmatic, yet very specific, issues of contestation, demands and the envisioning of what is possible.

All informal women workers on the platform demanded the following: first, recognition as workers who make a valuable contribution to the economy and society as part of the economically active population; second, the right not to be subjected to punitive regulations, policies or practices; and third, the right to enjoy specific promotional and protective measures, including protection against exploitation by intermediaries.

Home-based workers have the following demand, which could differ in degree across self-employed and sub-contracted workers: freedom from forced relocations and zoning restrictions; social protection, including maternity grants; childcare facilities to enable workers to work undisturbed; protection from being subjected to poor-quality raw materials, arbitrary cancellation of work orders, arbitrary rejection of goods or delayed payments; the right to basic infrastructure services—water, electricity, sanitation—at their homes, which are their workplaces; access to markets for their goods and services; the right to fair prices in markets and fair piece-rates; the right to secure, transparent contracts, whether as work orders or commercial transactions; occupational health and safety training, business skills training; no double taxation; and land/space/venues for working collectively.

Street vendors demand: freedom from harassment, confiscation of goods, evictions, arbitrary warrants and convictions, arbitrary relocations, unofficial payments and/or bribes; freedom from fear of authorities and *mafia* elements; freedom from exploitation by intermediaries who take high fees; the right to have natural markets of street vendors recognized and built into urban zoning and land allocation plans; the right to vend in public spaces under fair and reasonable conditions (which balance competing rights of different users of public spaces) and to maintain natural markets; the right to fair and transparent allocation of permits and licenses; the right to appropriate sites near customer traffic; if relocated, provision of suitable alternative sites near customer traffic; the right to better services and infrastructure at their vending sites, including shelter, water, sanitation and storage facilities; provision of infrastructure, including special infrastructure for vendors with disabilities; provision of protection centres to keep children out of child labour; education on trading bylaws and local government systems; access to user-friendly service-providers; simplified taxation systems; and simplified regulations for informal cross-border traders.

Waste reclaimers demand: freedom from harassment, bribes and evictions by city authorities; the right to access recyclable waste without restrictions; access to markets; provision of infrastructure; recognition for their economic contribution and environmental service to communities; the right to access recreational community facilities; provision of protection centres to keep children out of child labour; freedom from fear of authorities and *mafia* elements; freedom from exploitation by intermediaries who take high fees; the right to fair and transparent price-setting in the recycling chain; inclusion in modern waste management systems, and access to equipment and infrastructure for collecting, sorting and storage; the right of their organizations to bid for solid waste management contracts; cooperatives and Social Solidarity Economy system; recognition of their labour as service providers and right to be paid for their service; the right to ensure solid waste collection is not private but managed by mixed systems between governments and waste pickers' associations, including both cooperatives and unions; an end to the use of incineration and harmful landfill disposals technologies; and promotion of segregation, recycling and composting as ways to secure workers' income.

These demands may be sector-specific but they are based on a fundamental common understanding: "All informal workers – whether wage workers or self-employed workers – in all sectors must have access to basic organizing and labour rights, voice and bargaining power, legal identity and standing, economic rights and social rights, including social protection. Further, it is imperative that informal workers across sectors and in all global regions have input into what formalization, in fair terms, will require" (Horn, 2017).

Neoliberal capitalism can be attributed for the climate crisis, huge inequity between the rich and the poor and putting people before profits at all costs, but as a feminist, the ongoing perpetuation for the feminisation of poverty, inequality and the most recent feminisation of COVID-19 can leave no doubt about the patriarchal nature of capital. But in every crisis, one has to grab the opportunity, and COVID-19 with all its havoc has demonstrated the perverse and inhumane nature of patriarchal capitalism and as such lends itself to advocates to demand a better system, where women and issues of gender are given due consideration. If the informal is to be the "norm," then what COVID-19 vividly illustrates is the absence of mechanisms to deal with it both in times of crises and otherwise. Recommendation 204 has gone a long way in its attempt to conscientise governments to recognise the important role of the informal economy and the need to recognise workers in the informal economy as workers. This requires the implementation of mechanisms of formalisation that are not about only controlling the informal economy or collecting more revenue, but also to understanding the nature of the informal economy, the labour force, its diverse needs and the significant role it plays vis-à-vis the economy and citizens. The lack of this information has hurt both the South African economy and its people, and the poor and vulnerable of which women are the majority. Had South Africa made concerted efforts to formalise, and had it done so with a strong gendered grounding and orientation, it would have gone a long way in mitigating some of the difficult conditions that poor, vulnerable and largely unemployed or informally employed women currently face. It would then not have needed a crisis of health and economic devastation to highlight the essential role that women play in the informal economy.

References

Bonner, C., Carré, F., 2013. Global Networking: Informal Worker's Build Solidarity, Power and Representation through Networks and Alliances. WIEGO Working Paper (Organizing and Representation) No. 31.

Budlender, D., Buwembo, P., Shabalala, N., 2001. The informal economy: statistical data and research findings, country case study: South Africa. Paper produced for Women in Informal Employment Globalising and Organising.

Carre F., 2013. Defining and Categorising Organisations of Informal Workers in Developing and Developed Countries. WIEGO Brief No. 8, 1–16.

Carre, F. et al., 2017. Considerations for Revisions of International Classifications of the Status of Employment (ICES-93). WIEGO Statistical Brief No. 17, 1–18.

Chen, M. , 2012. The Informal Economy: Definitions, Themes and Policies. WIEGO Working Paper, 1 August 2012, P1–26, UK.

Chen, M., 2018. "Working with the informal economy: solutions for formalization" formalization from perspective of informal worker a PowerPoint presentation given at the public seminar on June 6, 2018 in London. The event was co-organized by WIEGO and by the Open Society Foundation.

Dladla, N., 2018. The construct of state practice: excavating municipal relations with waste pickers in the city of Johannesburg.

Eye Witness News. Article 8 May 2018.

Hassan, E. et al., 2018. Unpublished research report on worker education, compiled by NALEDI, funded by the Human Resource Development Council, on behalf of the Worker Education Committee.

Horn, P., 2014. WIEGO Network Platform. Transition from the informal to the formal economy in the interests of workers in the informal economy.

International Labour Organisation, 2015. Newsletter, ILO adopts historic labour standard to tackle the informal economy.

Kohn L., 2017. Using Administrative Law to Secure Livelihoods – Lessons from SA. WIEGO Technical Brief (LAW No. 10). Johannesburg, 99–135.

Pillay, V., 2017. Amplifying voice and validity: waste pickers in Johannesburg, South Afr. Lab. Bull. 41 (4), 1–3.

Rees R., 2018. Unpublished report for the COSATU Campaigns and organising Committee and the International department on organising Informal Economy Workers.

Robbins et al., 2015, WIEGO Working Paper No. 34.

Rogan M., 2018. How a pyramid sketch redefined the informal economy -and the new data that is putting that 20-year-old idea to the test. WIGO Blog. wieg.org/blog/how/py.

Rogan M., 2019. Informal Workers in Urban South Africa: A Statistical Snapshot. Statistical Brief No. 19.

Samson, M., 2010. Reclaiming reusable and recyclable materials in Africa – critical review of English language literature. WIEGO Working Paper (Urban Policies) No.

Samson, M., 2015. Forging a New Conceptualization of "The Public" in Waste Management. WIEGO Working Paper No. 32.

Samson, M. et al., 2019. The political work of waste picker integration: chapter forthcoming in the informal economy revisited: looking back, thinking forward.

Sekhwala, M., 2017. The policy and practice of reclaimer integration in the City of Johannesburg.

Skinner, C., 2008. Street trade in Africa: A review. WIEGO Working Paper (Urban Policies) No.

Statistics South Africa, 2017–2020. Quarter Labour Force Surveys for years 2018–2019.

Statistics South Africa, 2020. https://www.slideshare.net/StatsSA/quarterly-labour-force-survey.

Valiana, S., Ndebele, N., 2018. A feminist perspective on women and mining in South Africa.

Valinai, S., Ndabele, N., 2018. The future of mining in South Africa: a feminist perspective on mining in South Africa. In *Sunsets and Sunrises: Debating the Future of Mining in South Africa*. MISTRA, South Africa.

Valodia, I., Heintz, J., 2008. Informality in Africa: A Review. WIEGO Working Paper No. 3.

Vanqa-Mgijima, N., 2015. Struggling for unity: women waste pickers in South Africa. https://globalrec.org/2015/04/15/struggling-for-unity-women-waste-pickers-in-south-africa/.

WIEGO, 2014. Informal Economy Monitoring Studies, IEMS April 2014 report.

WIEGO Report, 2020. The impact of public health measures on informal economy workers livelihoods March/April 2020.

Wills, G., 2009. South Africa's Informal Economy: A Statistical Profile. WIEGO Working Paper (Statistics) No. 6.

Yu, D., 2011. Informal Employment in South Africa. WIEGO Publication, Johannesburg.

4

DOES FORMALISATION IMPROVE WOMEN'S WORK CONDITIONS?

A review of the regulatory regime for contract farming and domestic trade in Ghana

Dzodzi Tsikata and Promise Eweh

I Introduction[1]

Based on his research in Ghana, Keith Hart, who is credited with coining the term "informal sector," observed in the 1970s that contrary to predictions, the informal sector, a set of complex arrangements for making a living in developing economies, was not going to shrink and disappear with economic growth and modernisation (Hart, 1973). Five decades later at lower middle-income status, Ghana's economy continues to be dominated by informal work and enterprises, with a diminishing proportion of the workforce engaged in formal work.

The informal economy is both rural and urban. The rural informal economy has a substantial proportion of Ghana's self-employed workers, mainly in (1) agriculture, (2) fishing and fish processing and (3) rural agro-based processing activities and forest products work. The urban informal economy is made up of (1) services, (2) construction and (3) industry, which consists of manufacturing and extractive industries. Work in the informal economy is generally gender segmented both in rural and urban areas. In rural areas, agriculture involves both men and women, albeit in different activities and spheres, while fishing is male dominated and fish processing is mostly done by women. Agro-processing work is dominated by women, while forest products workers are mostly male. In urban areas, services are dominated by women, and construction, manufacturing and extractive industries by men. In addition, the labour forms identified in the informal economy, that is, wage work (casual, permanent), self-employment, communal labour, family and child labour, and apprenticeships are also gender segmented. Gender segmentation is important because of specificities in the experiences of policies and livelihood outcomes among the different segments.

The structure of the economy and its labour relations have been reinforced by economic liberalisation policies since the 1980s that have sought to limit the role of government in the economy, to promote the private sector, to loosen the regulation of economic activities and labour relations and to promote free markets in goods and services. Well-known policies in this regard included the privatisation of state-owned mines, commercial enterprises and manufacturing industries accompanied by massive labour retrenchments that also affected civil service employment. These policies affected general confidence in the ability of the formal economy to absorb the growing labour force.

From the mid-1990s, the post-colonial state's hostility and ambivalence toward the informal economy was tempered with a new pragmatism about realising its potential for tax revenue and job creation through a myriad of measures broadly labelled as formalisation. The Ghanaian state's current position on the formalisation of the informal economy is contained in a new national development policy titled "An Agenda for Jobs: Creating Prosperity and Equal Opportunity for All." The policy aims amongst other things to "facilitate the transition of the informal economy to formality as a means of removing decent work deficits. Over the medium term, the policy objectives are to: improve human capital development and management and create decent jobs" (National Development Planning Commission, 2017, 75). The proposals set forth in the policy for achieving formalisation include identification of persons, properties and increasing access to financial institutions. These provisions are concerned with the regulation and taxation of economic activities and transactions, as well as improving the ability of businesses to access certain services. On the contrary, another set of interventions, proposed to achieve human capital development and create decent jobs, includes measures such as: "strengthening the linkages between social protection and employment services," "strengthening measures to prevent informalisation/casualisation of jobs in the formal economy" and "enforcing laws regarding social security" among others (National Development Planning Commission, 2017, 75). Thus, the policy has two sets of measures for formalisation, one focusing on the identification of enterprises and persons, and the other, concerned with creating the appropriate conditions for decent work. The outcomes of formalisation will depend on which of these two approaches are prioritised, and the amount of time and resources that will be dedicated to policy implementation. This policy and past efforts to formalise the informal economy through regulation have not received sufficient attention in the literature. In this chapter, we contribute to addressing this gap by exploring the implications of "regulation" of different aspects of informality, particularly the quality of employment and to what extent such regulation creates formal employment. In other words, does regulation lead to the formalisation of employment? This focus is important because "regulation" remains so central to definition of the informal economy. Yet, it has not been examined in its own right and it is often assumed that it will automatically be associated with formalisation of employment.

This chapter examines efforts to regulate the informal economy and how they have been experienced by enterprises and workers in Ghana, with particular reference to two sub-sectors that are an important source of women's work, contract farming and domestic trading. The study is guided by three broad areas of inquiry: (1) the context of formalisation, which consists of the labour market situation, the gendered patterns of employment and work and government policies towards the informal economy; (2) policies specifically directed towards reducing informality, of either enterprises or workers and 3) the nature of regulation in the two sectors. The two sectors have been selected for their importance for women's employment in rural and urban Ghana. As well, they have been indirectly targeted by formalisation drives. In the case of contract farmers, it is through donor project conditionalities, while for traders, it has been through longstanding efforts to register them for market tolls and taxation.

This chapter is mostly based on secondary data (e.g. existing large sample surveys, enterprise and economic census data, national income and labour force and employment data) to the extent available. Official data on policies and regulatory changes have also been used. The examination of contract farming is based largely on material from four recent studies on contract farming. The chapter is divided into five sections. This introduction is followed by a discussion of Ghana's economy, highlighting how both internal and external factors have contributed to economic growth and/or stagnation in different periods. The section shows that Ghana's labour force has expanded rapidly with very high levels of participation in economic activities, with almost equal rates for males and females, especially in recent decades. However, the majority of employed persons are engaged in the informal economy, and the gender analysis of this pattern indicates that women are more likely, than men, to be involved in the informal economy. In Sections three and four, we analyse the relationship between regulation and formalisation of employment by examining contract farming and domestic trading on questions such as (1) the nature of employment and enterprises in Ghana, (2) approaches to, sources, forms and mechanisms of regulation and (3) implications for formalisation, conditions of work and the quality of livelihoods. Section five concludes the chapter.

Our findings show that non-state actors with links to the Ghanaian state are heavily involved in regulating these two sectors. However, regulation has very little impact on the formalisation of employment. In the case of contract farming, regulation involves agro-processing companies which supply farmers with inputs in return for agricultural produce at the end of the farming season. The presence of these companies in rural communities may generate employment; however, the majority of employed persons (particularly women) are engaged as casual labour. Furthermore, agro-processing companies fail to pay attention to the labour conditions of household members and hired labour, who perform majority of the tasks on farms. The only practice with some semblance of formalisation relates to restrictions on the use of children and pregnant women as labour. However, these practices were primarily driven by global certification initiatives and were only prominent among firms which were export oriented. In contrast, regulation of trade is primarily undertaken by local governments. However, these institutions prioritise the regulation of economic activities over labour conditions and employment relationships. While a large share of local government revenue is generated from taxes on trading activities, traders often complained about the poor quality of market and related infrastructure. Critically, due to current approaches and poor implementation of social policy by the state, many traders, as well as farmers, are left without benefits such as medical care and social security.

II The socio-economic and policy context of regulation

Trends in economic growth

Ghana's economic growth in the decade and a half after independence showed a strong similarity to patterns of growth observed in other African countries. The period 1961-74 was one of generally modest growth with negative growth recorded in only 1966 (−4.3 per cent) and 1972 (−2.5%). In contrast, growth between 1975 and 1983 was mostly negative; 1975 is the most notable year during this period, recording a negative growth of 12.4 per cent. There were only two years of positive growth, namely, 1977 (2.3 per cent) and 1978 (8.5 per cent). The poor growth in this latter period was attributed to a general decline in the production of both agricultural and non-agricultural commodities. In addition to poor growth, deterioration in several indicators of well-being began to be observed in Ghana as well as other African countries.

In response to the decline in economic and human development, the Government of Ghana, with support from the International Monetary Fund (IMF) and World Bank implemented a Structural Adjustment Programme (SAP) in the 1980s. Economic growth under the SAP was anchored on increased production and export of agricultural commodities, forest and mineral resources. These measures resulted in appreciable growth of the Ghanaian economy. However, other indicators such as the balance of payments deficit saw very little improvement (Bank of Ghana, 2005; Whitfield, 2005). In addition, the reforms have generally been criticised for massive job losses, poor housing and reduced demand for critical social services (Graham, 1988).

In the 2000s, a newly elected government opted for the Highly Indebted Poor Country (HIPC) initiative, and later qualified for the Multilateral Debt Relief Initiative (MDRI). Together, these two initiatives sought to cancel all debts owed by low-income countries such as Ghana to the IMF, the World Bank and the African Development Bank. In the short term, debt relief under HIPC and MDRI significantly altered Ghana's debt situation and the debt service-to-revenue ratio, which originally stood at nearly 80 per cent in 2000, reduced to 7.6 per cent in 2003 (Bank of Ghana, 2005, 14-15). This resulted in increased spending in the social sector and was associated with improvement in enrolment at the basic school level (including for girls) and increased access to healthcare and potable water (Bank of Ghana, 2005, 19-25). The tenure of the government (2000-08) also saw the introduction of many pro-poor programmes such as the Metro Mass Transit (2002), the National Health Insurance Scheme (NHIS, 2003), the Ghana School

Feeding Programme (2005) and the Livelihood Empowerment against Poverty (2008) among others. Undeniably, these programmes and interventions pursued by the government had a positive impact on the wellbeing of the beneficiaries.

In recent years, Ghana's economy and its prospects for growth, poverty reduction and development have been at the centre of attention once more. In 2011, GDP growth was estimated at 14 per cent and the country was declared the "fastest growing economy in Sub-Saharan Africa" (World Bank, 2011). More importantly, the Ghana Statistical Service (GSS), upon a revision of its methods for the computation of GDP, concluded in 2010 that GDP per capita exceeded $1,300; an estimate which was far off the $750 that was expected under the old series (Jerven, 2012). This resulted in the classification of Ghana as a lower-middle income country.

These new developments occurred within the context of significant increases in productivity and favourable prices for Ghana's primary export commodities. Cocoa production had, for instance, seen marked increases since 1983 and this became particularly beneficial as prices paid for the commodity also began to improve from the 1990s (Kolavalli and Vigneri, 2011, 208). This pattern also applied to gold which was pre-eminent in the minerals sector in terms of its output and foreign exchange earnings. In addition, the discovery of oil in 2007 and its production from 2010 onwards played a contributory role in the temporary improvements.

However, economic growth began to take a downward turn immediately after it peaked in 2011. GDP growth fell to 9 per cent in 2012 and further to 7 per cent in 2013; this downward trend continued into 2015 until 2016 when growth started to pick up again. Like other periods of poor growth, this decline was attributed to a combination of internal and external factors. Critical among these was a prolonged nationwide power-rationing exercise between 2012 and 2015 (Abeberese et al., 2017). Adding to the negative consequences of the energy crisis was the introduction of a new pay policy namely, the Single Spine Salary Policy for public sector workers. The policy was associated with large increases in salaries and arrears paid to public employees, resulting in a doubling of government expenditure on salaries (International Monetary Fund, 2015, 5). The influence of oil production—which in part accounted for the phenomenal growth in 2011—began to wane as prices for the commodity followed a downward spiral from June 2014. By August 2015, oil was trading at US$50.60 per barrel and prices have not revived to the levels that they were in June 2014 (US$111.8) (Institute for Fiscal Studies, 2015, 1).

Finally, while a substantial amount of debt owed by Ghana was cancelled in 2006, the country returned to borrowing in 2007. Ghana's classification as a lower-middle income country negatively affected concessional borrowing and the country now relied on new economic powers such as China to secure credit. In addition, newer and alternative means of acquiring credit such as the issuance of bonds have also featured prominently over the past decade. Beginning from 2007, Ghana has issued bonds on five different occasions to raise capital for development

(Haque et al., 2017). Consequently, public debt has swelled and surpassed the amount of debt that was recorded after the initial relief granted under HIPC and the MDRI. According to the IMF's *World Economic Outlook Database*, Ghana's "gross debt" as a percentage of GDP was estimated at nearly 72 per cent in 2017 compared to 26 per cent in 2006.

Changes in the structure of the economy

Trends in the relative contribution of the three key sectors (agriculture, industry and services) to GDP signals a significant change in the structure of the Ghanaian economy. Perhaps, the most important change relates to the diminishing role of the agricultural sector. Agriculture's contribution to GDP has reduced consistently and substantially over the decades. In 1980, the sector's contribution to GDP was estimated at 60 per cent; this reduced to 39 per cent in 2000, and further to 21 per cent in 2015. In contrast, changes in the industrial sector have been uneven. In 1985, industry accounted for 18 per cent of GDP; this increased to about 28 per cent in 1993 and rates similar to this were observed from that period onwards until 2006 where the sector's share of GDP reduced to 21 per cent. By 2010, the industrial sector's contribution to GDP was almost at the level as it was in 1985, but again an increment to previous levels began to be observed from 2011. The continuous decline of agriculture has been accompanied by the exponential growth in the services sector's contribution to GDP in the past one and a half decade. As a result, the services sector has emerged as the most important contributor to GDP, with its share increasing from 32 per cent to 49 per cent between 2005 and 2010, and to 53 per cent in 2015.

Labour market context

Several indicators point to changes in the labour market. The labour force has, for instance, seen phenomenal increases over the decades with the largest of these occurring between 1984 and 2000. During this period, the labour force increased by more than 2.5 million people. In 2018, 6,740,000 men were in the labour force compared to 5,871,000 women (ILOSTAT, 2020). Put together these men and women comprise 41 per cent of the total population. Related to this is the labour force participation rate (LFPR),[2] which is generally higher for men compared with women, although gaps in participation have narrowed significantly since 1970, a pattern which could be attributed to improvement in the collection and reporting of employment data. In the most recent national labour force survey conducted in 2015, the LFPR for men was 79 per cent compared to 72 per cent for women (Ghana Statistical Service, 2016, 23). In spite of the improvements in data collection and reporting, LFPRs show that involvement in economic activities is higher among men than women. However, part of this disparity is due to the non-recognition of women's reproductive work, which results in their reduced numbers in the labour force and eventually the LFPR.

The majority of the Ghanaian working population are actually employed. Information on employment dating back to the 1960s show that the employment rate has mostly been around 94 per cent. The only exceptions are 1991/92 (81 per cent), 1998/99 (82 per cent) and 2000 (90 per cent). However, even these "poor performing" years, particularly the first two, indicate that only two out of ten people who were eligible and seeking work were unable to find jobs. A slightly higher proportion of the female working population were employed compared to their male counterparts in 1960, 1970 and 1984. However, this pattern changed in subsequent years as the figures reported for men were slightly higher than those reported for women. Thus, differences in the rate of employment between males and females are not significant, as has been observed for other measures of economic participation.

In Ghana and many parts of Africa, figures on employment are typically high even during periods of economic decline. This is generally due to the definition and methods of data collection and analyses of the employment situation. For example, in the third round of the Ghana Living Standards Survey (GLSS), persons aged 15 years and older were classified as employed if "they had done any work during the past 12 months for which they received a wage or other payment" (Ghana Statistical Service, 1995, 32). In subsequent rounds of the GLSS, a 7-day reference was used instead of the 12-month period used in the third round of the GLSS. Due to these technicalities, figures on employment are generally high while those on unemployment are always low. As a result, general measures of employment and unemployment are of little importance even within policy circles. Beneath the high rates of employment and the corresponding low figures reported for unemployment lie a reality that is obscured by statistical measures.

Thus, while findings from the latest round of the GLSS show that only 7 per cent of the Ghanaian working population were unemployed, the same report found that 23 per cent of households were poor (Ghana Statistical Service, 2018). However, the poverty rate was higher in households where the head was a self-employed worker in the agriculture sector (43 per cent) compared to households headed by unemployed (29 per cent) or inactive persons (27 per cent).

The high poverty rate observed—especially among employed persons—is also a partial reflection of employment relationships. This is because majority of employed persons are involved in vulnerable employment. According to the Labour Force Survey, only 20 per cent of employed persons were paid employees (Ghana Statistical Service, 2016). On the contrary, own account and contributing family workers (those in vulnerable employment) comprise nearly 75 per cent of all employed persons. Unlike data on employment rate which show very little difference in participation between males and females, indicators of quality of employment emphasize that employment is gendered. Thus, the Labour Force Survey reported that 27 per cent of men were engaged as paid employees compared to 14 per cent of women. Furthermore, 60 per cent of men were own account workers compared to 68 per cent of women, while only 5 per cent of men were contributing family labour compared to 12 per cent of women.

Another issue which high employment rates are insensitive to is the burgeoning informal economy which continues to absorb the majority of working people, including those who by legal definition are considered not fit to work. People working in the informal economy can only get by with the earnings they derive from participating in it, but they cannot also "afford to be openly unemployed" (International Labour Organization, 2002, 29). As Hart (1973, 83) has clearly pointed out, "the truly 'unemployed' are those who will not accept income opportunities open to them for which they are qualified, and this often means rejecting informal means of making a living."

Informal employment

Informality is arguably the most visible aspect of employment and the Ghanaian economy as a whole. While the term "informal sector" was used by the GSS in previous publications, a more elaborate definition of the concept, which could have provided additional information on how data on the phenomenon was compiled was largely absent in these reports. However, in the 2015 labour force report, the GSS defined "Informal employment…as employment in an establishment where workers were not entitled to paid holidays or leave, sick or maternity leave and where there was no verbal or written contract at the time a person started to work. Any one of the three conditions had to be fulfilled in order for a person to be classified as working in informal employment" (Ghana Statistical Service, 2016, 83). Quite surprisingly, this definition does not include the entitlement to social security, which is integral to the definition of informality in other countries, as is the case in Thailand (Vechbanyongratana et al., 2020, in this volume). In spite of this, the proportion of employed persons involved in informal employment is very high.

Table 4.1 provides data on participation of employed persons in different employment relations. By far, the most dominant of these is private informal employment which comprises 84 per cent and 86 per cent of those who were employed in 2000 and 2010, respectively. While the data show that participation by both males and females in the private informal sector is high, the participation of females is higher than for males. Furthermore, data from the 2015 labour force survey show that majority of persons in informal employment are either own-account workers (65 per cent) or contributing family labour (9 per cent), and the rates were higher for women than men in both categories (Ghana Statistical Service, 2016, 34). The challenge with the classification and data provided in Table 4.1 is that it assumes that informal employment is only associated with the private sector, and that public institutions do not engage in practices such as subcontracting and casual employment.

Honorati and de Silva (2016) have compared wage workers in the Ghanaian public and private sectors in terms of their ability to enjoy several of the benefits that are associated with formal employment. Generally, their findings point to large disparities in access to these benefits by wage workers in the public and

TABLE 4.1 Informal employment in Ghana (2000, 2010)

Employment sector	2000			2010		
	Both sexes	Male	Female	Both sexes	Male	Female
Public	6.4	8.3	4.5	6.2	8.1	4.5
Private Formal	8.5	10.9	6.0	6.8	9.7	4.1
Private Informal	83.9	79.1	88.8	86.2	81.2	91.0
Semi Public/Parastatal	0.8	1.2	0.4	0.1	0.2	0.1
NGO (Local & International)	0.4	0.5	0.2	0.5	0.7	0.3
International Organizations★	–	–	–	0.05	0.1	0.03
Other★★	0.1	0.1	0.1	–	–	–
All Sectors	100	100	100	100	100	100
N	7,428,374	3,748,887	3,679,487	10,243,447	5,005,522	5,237,925

Source: Ghana Statistical Service (2013, 268)

private sectors—a large share of workers in the public wage sector have a written contract and are entitled to pension, subsidized medical care and social security while majority of their colleagues in the private sector do not. A similar analysis using data from GLSS 6 on workers in agriculture and domestic trading[3]—two sectors which are dominated by self-employed persons and comprise the most important sources of informal employment in Ghana found that 33 per cent of sales and services workers have a written contract while the corresponding figure for workers in agriculture is only 10 per cent. The proportion of sales and services workers with a written contract is slightly higher than what is reported by Honorati and de Silva (2016) for wage earners in the private sector (slightly below 30 per cent). However, the latter figure is significantly larger than the proportion of workers in agriculture without a written contract, a difference of almost 20 percentage points. Furthermore, our data show that the proportion of workers without a contract (whether written or oral) is highest among workers in agriculture (45 per cent). The rate is also high among sales and services workers (27 per cent) although it is lower than the figure reported for craft and related trades workers (32 per cent) and those involved in elementary occupations (28 per cent). Similarly, agriculture dominates in terms of the proportion of workers without social security (91 per cent). This is followed by craft and related trades workers (89 per cent), elementary occupations (81 per cent) and Plant and machine operators, and assemblers (80 per cent). Among services and sales workers, the figure is 74 per cent. Again, in comparing our data with those of Honorati and de Silva (2016, 43), we find that the proportion of sales and services workers without social security is similar to what is reported for the private wage sector,[4] while agriculture lags behind since only 9 per cent of workers are entitled to social security. Lack of trade unions in workplaces is highest among craft and related trades workers (90 per cent), followed by agriculture (83 per cent), elementary occupations (82 per cent) and sales and services workers (77 per cent).

Access to subsidized medical care comprises a major problem for workers in all occupations. Perhaps, the only exception is armed forces occupations where 22 per cent reported not having access to medical care. Even among managers, the rate is as high as 50 per cent. Lack of access to medical care, was highest among workers in agriculture (92 per cent) and craft and related trades (91 per cent). The rate was also high among sales and services workers (82 per cent) although this is slightly lower than the figures reported for other occupations. These figures, particularly those reported for workers who are more likely to be formally employed (managers, professionals, etc.) should be treated with extreme caution. This is because many workers in informal employment are more likely to report the payment of premiums as a barrier which prevents them from benefiting from services provided under the NHIS. But this need not be the case for majority of workers in formal employment as a large share of the premium required for NHIS are "deducted at source." Thus, the high figures reported by workers in managerial and professional occupations either point to lack of enrolment due to inefficiencies associated with registration or a general lack of confidence in public health services provision.

III Contract farming and informality in agriculture

Situating contract farming

Almost all of the agrarian labour in Ghana is informal. Only 1 per cent of rural women and 3 per cent of men were paid agricultural workers (Food and Agriculture Organization, 2012), and it is unclear whether they were casual or permanent workers. In any case, the majority of persons in agriculture are either self-employed, or contributing family labour. This pattern has important gender dimensions: men are more likely to be self-employed in agriculture compared with women while the converse is the case for unpaid household labour (Ghana Statistical Service, 2016, 100).

Although the concept of the informal economy has now incorporated agricultural-related activities, the measurement of informality continues to emphasise participation in "non-agricultural" employment. This continuous neglect of agriculture-related activities in the measurement of the informal economy is problematic from a policy point of view. In Ghana, poverty, food insecurity and low wages are more likely to be reported for geographic areas where agriculture is the mainstay of the employed population (Food and Agriculture Organization, 2012, 7, 16-18). The recognition and critical analyses of informality in agriculture is thus crucial for achieving decent work objectives.

The stated aims of agriculture policies in Ghana are to address issues of poverty, food security and employment through linkages between agriculture and industry and private sector participation, among others. An important challenge that most policies seek to address is the removal of bottlenecks in agricultural production and marketing across the entire sector. This is clearly evident in the cocoa sub-sector where price incentives and the supply of free seedlings have been used to boost production. As such, policy documents emphasise the need to increase access to inputs, credit and extension services and resolve marketing challenges. For example, the Fertiliser Subsidy Programme which started in 2008 seeks to increase farmers' access to fertiliser in order to increase production and improve food security. Similarly, the Ghana Commercial Agriculture Project (GCAP) which is being funded by the World Bank and the United States Agency for International Development (USAID) seeks to "increase access to land, private sector finance, input and output markets by smallholder farms…" (World Bank, 2018, 8).

Agriculture policies generally assume that activities to increase production will result in the creation of job opportunities for the economically active population. Again, it is suggested that addressing low productivity issues would not only improve farmers' incomes and their food security but allow for re-investment in the farm and non-farm sector. This continuous investment then results in increased demand for farm workers and enables those who provide services to farmers to keep their jobs. A case in point is the Planting for Food and Jobs programme whose primary objective is to "motivate the farmers to adopt certified seeds and fertilizers through a private sector led marketing framework, by raising the incentives and complimentary service provisions on the usage of inputs, good agronomic practices, marketing of outputs over an E-Agriculture platform" (Ministry of Food and Agriculture, 2017, 3). Between 2017 and 2020, a total of 4,635,268 jobs are expected to be created under the programme (Ministry of Food and Agriculture, 2017, 32).

Putting aside the issue of how such an exact figure was arrived at and how this will be verified during implementation, it is noteworthy that the programme does not emphasise the types of employment that will be created and it is not likely that majority of these jobs, even if created, will be decent jobs.

Modernisation of agriculture also comprises a critical theme in national and agriculture policies. This is very much anchored in the productivity-centred approach which was highlighted earlier. One of the key proposed strategies for boosting productivity is increasing the participation of farmers in out-grower and contract farming schemes. This should be seen as an integral part of the global business models and "innovations" which structure the nature and organisation of work in the Global South in both manufacturing and agriculture. In agriculture, this specifically takes the form of contract farming, which refers to an arrangement between agribusiness firms and producers (large-, medium- or small-scale farmers). Through this arrangement, the agribusiness provides farmers with credit, inputs and services in return for the right to purchase produce from producers at the end of the production season at prices determined largely by the agribusiness firm. In addition, agribusinesses enforce standards that relate to the quality of produce that become the basis for rejecting produce regarded as sub-standard. There are different variants of contract farming. In most cases, farmers operate on their own land, but there are instances in which the agribusiness, besides supplying inputs and extension services, also provide producers with land. In such cases, the most important factor that farmers contribute to the production process is their labour. In other models, farmers assume nearly all the risks that are associated with production, and the contract is centred on the marketing of produce after harvesting has been undertaken. Amanor (1999, 27) comments that "Contract arrangements are attractive to agribusiness as they enable them to treat farmers as the equivalent of employees without all the social security and welfare obligations associated with employees." While contract farming is not the dominant mode of production in Ghana and many areas in the Global South, it is an important arrangement for agri-food chains that source produce from Africa and the rest of world. It is therefore crucial to understanding informal employment as it embodies the employment relationships associated with low-wages and lack of decent working opportunities in manufacturing. Smith (2016, 71) notes that:

> The two forms of TNC [Transnational Corporations] exploitation of low-wage labor seen in manufacturing industry—in-house and arm's length—are

also evident in agriculture. Nestlé's 800,000 contract farmers display many similarities to the arm's-length relations in manufacturing value chains; while, in contrast, plantation capitalism in old and new forms correspond to FDI [Foreign Direct Investment], in that they involve direct ownership of capital in the low-wage economy.

Contract farming is endorsed by the government of Ghana and the global policy community; it has become an important model for the penetration of agribusiness into farming communities where women are heavily involved in agriculture. It is often favoured over large-scale commercial agriculture due to its expected contributions to employment creation, incomes and food security. A sole focus on these "beneficial" outcomes, however, fails to highlight that these arrangements often target certain classes of rural households which are perceived as capable of meeting the demands of agribusiness. In addition, contract farming does not seek to reform power relations between household heads and members, and between households and hired agricultural labour. Rather, its success depends on continuous reliance on power relations, leading to labour exploitation and distribution of incomes in favour of those with more control over resources.

Contract farming in Ghana: from public private partnership to private sector leadership

Out-grower schemes and contract farming are not new in Ghana. They can be traced to the Government of Ghana's Special Agricultural Schemes (SAS) programme which was implemented in the 1970s involving partnerships between the Ghanaian state, donor institutions such as the World Bank and Transnational Corporations. The schemes within the SAS such as the Ghana Oil Palm Development Company (GOPDC), Twifo Oil Palm Plantation (TOPP) and the Ghana Sugar Estates Limited (GHASEL), largely produced oil palm, and in the case of GHASEL, sugar, with some combining production from estates with output from smallholder farmers. In the 1990s, contract farming became associated with the production of horticultural crops as part of a drive to diversify exports and increase foreign exchange.

The need to regulate contract farming is a fairly recent development and did not comprise a core objective of the projects that were implemented under SAS. The participation of farmers in the SAS projects was based on selection criteria which determined the groups of farmers who would be involved and those who would be excluded. In the case of GOPDC, the farms of out-growers and smallholders were required to be within a 25-km radius of the nucleus estate and 400 m of road access. Farmers also entered into contracts with GOPDC for a period of 25 years, the length of time required for the maturation of the palm fruit. Again, farmers were only considered for inclusion if they had registered the land they intended to use. They must be aged between 25 and 50 years and be married with children. The maximum land size that was required to participate in the

GOPDC scheme was 8 ha. However, 20 ha was allowed for men with at least two wives and many children. A sound financial background confirmed by a bank was a key consideration. For its part, GOPDC provided credit and inputs to the participants. It also paid an allowance of 80 per cent of labour costs which included family labour for five years until the oil palm started to yield fruits. However, the cost of labour was covered by the farmer until a certification was undertaken to confirm the extent of work done in maintaining the farm.

The TOPP project was managed by the state-owned Central Regional Development Corporation, the majority shareholder of TOPP Ltd. A similar farm size limit was required by both TOPP and GHASEL. Since GHASEL's out-grower scheme was between farmers and the funding agency (African Development Bank), both had their own regulations. ADB funding to new farms was limited to 10 ha while old out-growers had a limit of 40 ha. The funding to farmers was not less than five years. If a farmer had to increase the acreage annually, this was not supposed to exceed 20 per cent of the existing acreage. This limit was intended to prevent the use of hired labour. Both GOPDC and GHASEL emphasised family labour use, and this was explicit in the criteria of selection in the GOPDC scheme.

In all the out-grower and contract-farming schemes of the SAS projects, the provision of inputs and seedlings is linked to standardising production where farmers are obliged to use chemicals and seedlings provided by the firms. In terms of marketing, farmers have to follow laid down procedures of harvesting crops, transportation and other related marketing regulations such as exclusive sale of the products to the firms.

Many of these companies were sold to foreign agribusinesses from the 1980s when under the conditions of Ghana's economic liberalisation, it was no longer considered appropriate for the state to own and manage enterprises. The period also coincided with an expansion of the private sector's involvement in contract farming that was focused on new export commodities that had hitherto been grown by small-scale farmers for local consumption.

With the more recent global debates about the effects of large-scale land acquisitions by agribusinesses, contract farming has been proposed as an inclusive alternative and a win-win approach to agricultural development. Institutional proponents such as the FAO, World Bank and others argue that contract farming would link farmers to credit and input markets and also markets for their produce and transfer technology and knowledge to farmers. Besides the positive appraisals, some of these institutions have also provided substantial funding for the implementation of contract farming projects. For instance, the GCAP funded by the World Bank-International Development Association and USAID in Ghana is centred on 31 nucleus farmers who work with 9,400 outgrowers. The World Bank, Agence Française de Développement, Germany's Reconstruction Credit Institute (KfW) and the Government of Ghana provided funding to the Ghana Rubber Estate, the country's leading rubber producer for the Rubber Out-growers Plantation Project (ROPP) in 1995. The project resulted in the cultivation of 30,000 hectares of rubber produced by 8,500 outgrowers who produce an average of 19,000 tons of dry rubber annually. As part of the ROPP, 30 per cent of women were targeted for rubber production. Today, many crops are produced under contract farming arrangements—oil palm, fruits, cassava, chili, maize for export and for domestic processing.

In the segment that follows, we present four cases which illustrate the current regulatory regime for contract farming in Ghana. Products from all the four firms are sold on the domestic market but there are also two firms (Blue Skies and Serendipalm) whose products are sold on the foreign market, including in the United States and in Europe.

Four private sector led cases of contract farming

Blue Skies Ghana Limited[5]

Blue Skies Ghana Limited is a subsidiary of Blue Skies Holdings Ltd (UK). Besides Ghana, Blue Skies Holdings has subsidiaries in Brazil, Egypt, and South Africa. In Ghana, the company is located in Ankwa Doboro in the Nsawam-Adoagyiri Municipality of the Eastern Region, 1 of the 216 districts in the country. Blue Skies processes horticultural crops (mango, pineapple, papaya and coconut) for sale on both European and domestic markets. Blue Skies has two nuclei: an 1,800-acre pineapple farm and a 100-acre mango farm. In addition, the Company procures produce from 150 contract farmers in Ghana and an unknown number of farmers from Côte d'Ivoire, Senegal and Togo. About 4,000 workers, 60 per cent of these women, are employed during the peak production period in June.

Blue Skies has signed onto several initiatives and is certified by organisations including GlobalGAP, Fairtrade, International Food Standard, and Linking Environment and Farming (LEAF) amongst others. These initiatives are concerned with production and quality standards, and to some extent with labour conditions. For instance, "GlobalGAP standards...are primarily designed to reassure consumers about how food is produced on the farm by minimising detrimental environmental impacts of farming operations, reducing the use of chemical inputs and ensuring a responsible approach to staff health and safety" (Blue Skies, 2009, 27) while LEAF is also concerned with "environmental sustainability and increased biodiversity through the enhanced availability and diversity of our raw materials" (ibid, 27). The Fairtrade certification is primarily concerned with labour issues and it prohibits the use of child labour.

Blue Skies operates a flexible contract farming scheme. However, its suppliers must adhere to the GlobalGAP standards. Although no legal contract has been signed between the company and suppliers, in principle, farmers have to abide by rules established by the company. These include the provision of a toilet facility and on-farm shelter for workers, and storage of chemicals on farms in a manner that ensures the safety of workers.

Caltech Ventures Limited (Caltech)[6]

Caltech Ventures is located in Hodzo in the Ho municipality of Ghana and is one of the largest cassava processing companies in the country. Its main products are ethanol and "high quality cassava flour" which are used in the brewing and other industries of Ghana. Kasapreko Company Limited, a leading producer of alcoholic beverages in Ghana, owns 40 per cent of Caltech. Caltech has acquired 3,000 ha of land in the Ho municipality for a period of 99 years. A total of 40 per cent of this land (1,200 ha) is dedicated to the company's nucleus while 80 ha has been given out to contract farmers. The company also engages a group of 200 contract farmers who operate on their own lands, and 35 per cent of these are women.

Besides contract farmers, there are other groups of workers who are involved in various operations of the company. These include labourers who are engaged on the company's nucleus farms, and those involved in processing and harvesting. These activities are dominated by women: 77 per cent of workers on the company's nucleus farms are women and 80 per cent of those involved in processing are also women. No male is involved in harvesting. Thus, Caltech's activities have resulted in job creation for some residents in Hodzo and neighbouring localities. This has been beneficial to both women and men as the total number of jobs are almost equally shared between them. However, majority of the jobs are temporary, and the few permanent jobs, all eight management positions were occupied by men.

Besides operating within the Labour Act, Caltech is not known to have registered with any international regulatory body. Over the years, the labour regime at the company's factory and farms has changed considerably from a focus on direct employment of permanent workers to outsourcing of casual labour through labour contractors. This shift started in 2016 when the Company began producing ethanol which is now its main product. This new labour arrangement, which detaches workers from the company even as they still work for it, is a shift from formalisation to informalisation for some categories of workers.

Serendipalm Company Limited[7]

Serendipalm's prime business is the procurement and processing of organic oil palm, although it has recently ventured into organic cocoa production. Until its incorporation in 2010, Serendipalm operated as a non-governmental organisation which recruited women for employment at its processing facility through its partnership with a local women's organisation. The company is located in Asuom in the Kwaebibirem district of Ghana, one of the few districts in the country with a long experience of contract farming. Serendipalm's main buyers are Dr. Bronners (a producer of natural soaps in the United States), Rapunzel and GEPA (two manufacturers of food products in Germany).

Serendipalm engages 645 contract farmers, 283 (44 per cent) of whom are women. These farmers operate on smallholdings and depend primarily on family labour although they occasionally employ hired labour. In addition to contract farmers, Serendipalm has 257 employees who are engaged in a range of activities, 70 per cent of whom are women. Temporary employment at Serendipalm applies to three categories of workers namely, production-casual,[8] fruit cleaners and farm workers. With the exception of fruit cleaners who are all women, the other occupations are dominated by men. Permanent employment at the company also applies to three groups of workers—management (administrative and clerical staff), professionals (extension officers, etc.) and production management (a plant operator, etc.). These occupations are dominated by men and the only occupation where women appear to have some representation is production management where they comprise 36 per cent of the workers. All in all, 82 per cent of male employees are permanent workers while the corresponding figure for women is 16 per cent. In fact, majority of all women workers (81 per cent) are fruit cleaners—one of the groups of workers who are temporarily employed.

Serendipalm's products are certified by ECOCERT, a worldwide organic product certification body headquartered in France. Serendipalm is also a Fair-Trade certified Company. In Ghana, it works with The Oil Palm Research Institute, the Ghana Food and Drugs Authority and the Ghana Standards Authority. Its contract farmers are expected to follow a number of regulations which are production, labour and marketing related. The production-related regulations include avoiding the use of chemicals and plastics on farms, amongst others. With respect to labour, children and pregnant women are exempted from working on farms. Marketing is scheduled in clusters and farmers must inform the company of their readiness to sell on a specified date before harvesting. This enables the company to inspect the farm and determine whether the contract farmer has adhered to the production and harvesting standards or otherwise.

Building Businesses on Values, Integrity and Dignity (B-BOVID) Company Limited[9]

B-BOVID is located in the Ahanta West district of Ghana. This district is also home to two industrial oil palm production and processing companies, namely, Benso Oil Palm Plantation (BOPP) and Norpalm Ghana Limited. B-BOVID's productive activities encompass crops and livestock, but it is primarily concerned with palm oil and kernel processing.

The company operates a mixed agriculture model consisting of a nucleus farm, a contract-farming scheme with registered farmers, and purchases from independent farmers. In addition, it engages contractors who aggregate oil palm from farmers in various communities. Put together, this diverse group of farmers and aggregators comprise 2,500 persons. Only 10 per cent of the company's contract farmers are women. B-BOVID's arrangement with aggregators means that its relationship with farmers are mediated by brokers. In the areas from which the company obtains most of its raw materials, agriculture is organised around the household unit and hired labour is only used to carry out specific tasks. Thus, the company exercises little control over the workers who are employed by contract farmers.

B-BOVID has a total of 48 employees engaged in a range of activities at its factory. Only two of these are women. During the peak January–July season, it hires many casual workers, majority of whom are women or migrants from other regions of Ghana, who are laid off at the end of the season. The company provides these workers with letters that state the duration of engagement, work schedules and their salaries.

B-BOVID's contract regime operates at different levels. First of all, registered contract farmers are provided with passbooks to record their supplies, a practice similar to what occurs in the cocoa sector. The passbook system enables the company to pay its suppliers through the bank instead of by direct cash payments. Besides eliminating challenges associated with the payment of farmers, the passbook system was also intended to increase farmers' access to credit at the bank.

B-BOVID determines prices based on the particular variety of oil palm that its farmers produce. It has hired an expert who differentiates the variety of oil palm produced based on an oil extraction ratio calculation. The higher the oil content, the higher the market price per ton. Another innovation which farmers found interesting but is yet to materialise is a proposed price sharing model where representatives of the company and farmers negotiate prices for each variety of oil palm. The company also intends to intervene in the negotiation of prices by its farmer associations and contractors. Finally, a royalty reward is to be instituted for farmers.

B-BOVID operates through four marketing channels. These include indirect supplies to BOPP (its regional competitor) through Wilmar,[10] direct sales to other industrial buyers such as Avnash Industries and Unilever Ghana, and to market traders and medium-scale customers who sell in the West African region.

The regulatory regimes for contract farming schemes compared

The nature of regulation

The regulation of contract farming in Ghana involves several actors, with the most dominant ones being the state, agribusiness closely linked to international certification bodies and contract farmers themselves. International financial institutions (IFIs) and aid agencies including the World Bank have played a significant role in contract farming since the 1970s, and they continue to be critical actors. Their support, which normally involves the provision of loans, does not only facilitate access to credit needed by the Ghanaian state and agribusiness, but further symbolises institutional endorsement of contract farming. Global certification bodies, for their part, referee contract farming through monitoring and inspections. These various actors have collaborated in some cases and acted independently in others to create a regime for contract farming in Ghana.

State regulation: labour regulation

Contract farming linked to agribusiness is regulated from various sources. All companies in Ghana are required to operate within Ghana's Labour Act 2003 (Act 651). However, the applicability and enforcement of the Labour Act with respect to contract farming and agriculture in general is a challenge due to the informal nature of work in this sector. Government policy does little to formalise the informal nature of contract farming or regulate its labour relations. Instead, its approaches have had the effect of entrenching informal labour conditions especially the use of family labour.

Company regulation: production and labour regulations

At the business level, contract farming involves interactions between agribusiness firms and smallholder farmers, and it is at this level that the extent, processes and particular provisions of regulation are determined by agribusiness. There are significant differences in regulation between the two export-oriented firms (Blue Skies and Serendipalm) and the two firms whose products are sold on the domestic market (Caltech and B-BOVID). These differences are underpinned by the types of contracts or arrangements that firms have with contract farmers, and the relationships that firms have with international certification bodies.

Agribusiness firms have at their disposal three different arrangements which structure relationships with contract farmers. These are procurement, partial and total contracts (Singh, 2002). In the case of procurement contracts, firms are primarily concerned with the purchase of agricultural produce from farmers or their organisations. Partial and total contracts signify greater involvement of agribusiness in agricultural production with firms supplying only a limited number of inputs in the case of partial contracts. On the contrary, the company "supplies and manages all the inputs on the farm and the farmer becomes just a supplier of land and labor" (Singh, 2002, 1621) in the case of total contracts. While procurement contracts generally signify agreements about the sale of produce, companies still exert a significant amount of control over the production process. This takes the form of rejection of produce that is sub-standard and allocating quotas to farmers which implies that only a portion of the harvested produce is purchased. In addition, companies may choose to pay farmers lower rates for certain varieties of crops and harvest in clusters in order to control the quantity of product in the market. All the four cases analysed here generally combine partial contracts with procurement contracts as the dominant regime although some of Caltech's contract farmers produce on land that belong to the company.

Ultimately, the main goal of the different types of contracts is to ensure product standardisation. For farmers involved in contract farming with the two export-oriented companies, participation further requires compliance with the standards of international certification bodies. Farmers are expected to use specific planting materials or varieties as well as follow certain laid-down farming practices. While variations do exist, all four firms supply planting materials to farmers. In the case of Blue Skies, the export sector has already specified the preferred varieties, and farmers can only engage in trade with the company if they produce those varieties. Regarding practices, Serendipalm's organic farming model seeks to ensure that farmers do not use agrochemical products on their farms. Caltech, which processes cassava for local industrial use, also promotes its own internal practices including soil conservation, which is linked to product standardisation. Farmers who cultivate on the company's lands are not allowed to intercrop cassava with any other crop apart from leguminous crops and those who use their own lands are also advised to adhere to these rules although this is not strictly enforced. In general, the minimum land size required by any farmer who intends to produce cassava for Caltech is 5 acres, although this criterion for participation is no longer enforced by the company.

These standards about agricultural practices and use of specific planting materials are disincentives to some farmers as they are in direct opposition to 'traditional' farming practices. For instance, farmers are discouraged by Serendipalm's ban on agro-chemicals. With the increasing use of weedicides in the agricultural sector in Ghana due to the unavailability and high costs of labour, this is a serious constraint. Within this context, it is only the payment of a market premium and the slightly higher price paid for palm fruit by Serendipalm that has enabled the Company to stabilise its cohort of contract farmers in spite of their complaints about regulations. To address the labour question, the company has also introduced farmers to organic ways of weed control. It has also outsourced some of its service provision obligations to another company which rents equipment to farmers. This is intended to reduce the cost of labour. However, these incentives only seek to deal with the problem of labour availability while ignoring labour conditions which are equally important for achieving decent work. Similarly, contract farmers of Caltech Ventures Limited are unhappy with production regulations which forbid the inter-cropping of cassava with other crops. The restriction to the production of a specific variety of industrial cassava, which cannot be used for food is also a source of worry, because of its implications for food security. Compensation for these restrictions and regulations should reflect in high prices for produce. However, this is absent in this case. Caltech also has sometimes delayed payments and has been unable to fulfil its obligation of providing tractors for land preparation. As a result, many farmers have abandoned this scheme.

Labour regulation and the role of international certification bodies

It is in the area of labour regulation where the difference between export-oriented firms and those that produce for the local market is most significant. Blue Skies, the biggest firm and an export-oriented company, is the most regulated of the four cases. Its contract farmers work within the standards set by the various global certification bodies which the company has registered with. The regulations are concerned with labour conditions, safety, product quality and environmental sustainability. Additional certifications driven by the supermarkets that Blue Skies supplies are also in effect. For instance, the Waitrose Care Trace focuses on tracing the labour and quality conditions of products that end up in Waitrose shops. Similarly, Serendipalm, being an organic palm oil exporter and certified with ECOCERT and Fair-Trade International has extended its regulations to monitoring labour conditions on contract farms.

On the contrary, B–BOVID is not registered with an international certification body and sells most of its products on the local market. Thus, its practices regarding the regulation of labour are not as strict as those of Blue Skies and Serendipalm. Its only practice which has some semblance of formalisation relates to the issuance of passbooks for the payment of contract farmers through the banks. Although this is aspirational, the passbook system is also intended to help farmers' access credit from formal financial institutions. Similarly, contract farmers producing for Blue Skies receive their payments through banks and some farmers indicate that this has been helpful for accessing loans from banks. This is definitely an incentive for many farmers to join contract-farming schemes.

The four cases have shown varied forms of regulation based on the type of contract that firms have with farmers. The underlying rationale for regulation for all four cases is to achieve a reliable supply of quality products, irrespective of whether the crop in question is produced for the local or export market. However, export-oriented firms are also concerned with other issues that have little to do with product quality and secure markets. Consequently, Blue Skies and Serendipalm have limited labour conditions inscribed in their contract regime. The two firms pay regular visits to contract farmers to ensure that their practices are consistent with the regulations regarding the use of child and pregnant women's labour. Compliance with labour regulations are also monitored by officials of the international certification bodies' who visit farms from time to time. On the farms of contract farmers who produce for Blue Skies, there are visible structures to fulfil a labour regulation stipulating a place of rest for workers and a place to store chemicals to ensure the safety of workers.

The provisions, notwithstanding, the regulation of labour relations in contract farming is quite limited, and do not fulfil the basic requirements of decent work, as discussed in more detail below.

The labour relations of contract farming

In the four contract-farming cases, there is silence on arrangements to negotiate prices of inputs and produce, the wages of casual and permanent labour, the wage gap between women and men, working hours and leave periods among others. In many of the communities where agribusiness firms engage with contract farmers, the predominant practice is the use of informal labour practices (e.g. piecework on farms). For instance, communities have standard labour charges per task, charges per task for specific crops and charges per type of labour contract which is used as the gold standard. Thus, *by-day* labourers spraying a farm are aware of the amount they will receive as wages. Similarly, there is a standard rate for weeding an acre of land in every community. The pay gap between women and men is also embedded in the informal wage structure in these communities and contract farmers do not deviate from such wage structures.

Contract farming is based on agreements about supply of inputs and outputs between agribusiness firms and contract farmers. However, family and hired labour are an integral aspect of the production system that makes contract farming possible. In this connection, one of the main criticisms of contract farming is that one individual (for instance, the male household head) keeps a large share of the revenue earned from the sale of produce to the agribusiness firm. Thus, concerns about the welfare of contract farmers should consider the terms and conditions of family and hired labour. For example, the Fair-Trade regulations on fair wages, as applied by Serendipalm Limited, are limited to the company's relations with contract farmers and its wage workers, and do not apply to the hired and family labour used by contract farmers.

Enforcement of clearly stated regulations regarding the use of children and pregnant women as labour is determined by power relations between contract farmers and family or hired labour. For instance, some farmers are unhappy about Serendipalm's attempt to dictate labour use on their farms. In a focus group discussion with some farmers in March 2017, some participants asked, "how is it Serendipalm's concern if my pregnant wife helps me on the farm?" Others quizzed "didn't we work as children on our parents' farms? Why are they [Serendipalm] telling us not to go to farm with our children when labour costs are so high?" (DEMETER Project, 2017). On the contrary, given that a significant number of the contract farmers are women, it is not clear how the regulations which forbids pregnant women from farm labour are enforced.

Table 4.2 presents a summary of some of the global certification bodies for the four study cases studied.

Regulation of contract farming and its relationship with formalisation of employment

In general, the emphasis on partial and procurement contracts has improved the quality of products and immersed farmers in global production standards. It has also minimally brought consciousness to aspects of labour conditions on farms that are usually not considered in smallholder agriculture production. However, these are limited in scope and their enforcement, which is largely limited to the export-driven schemes, does not achieve decent work for contract farmers.

Contract farming in general leaves a lot to be desired. Exposure to global value chains increases the burdens and risks contract farmers carry without protection from the vicissitudes of the export commodities trade. Smallholder production is expected to meet specific standards and in cases where contracts include farmers' access to land, credit and inputs, firms reduce the cost of production and shift risks to farmers, including the demands of the global certification bodies. Crucially,

TABLE 4.2 Some global certification bodies with key influence on contract farming regulation in Ghana

Name of global certification	Key focus				
	Labour conditions and workers' rights	Food safety	Environmental	Trade	Other
Global G.A.P	Yes	Yes	Yes	No	No
LEAFLinking Environment and Farming	No	Yes	Yes	No	No
Care Trace	Yes	Yes	Yes	No	No
Ethical Trading Initiative	Yes	No	No	No	No
Fair Trade	Yes	No	Yes	No	Yes
International Food Standard (IFS)	No	Yes	No	No	No
Food BRC Global Standards	No	Yes	No	No	No
Business Social Compliance Initiative (BSCI)	Yes	No	No	No	No
ECOCERT	No	Yes	Yes	No	No

Source: Compiled by authors

gender segmentation of work is a common feature of contract-farming schemes, and this has an adverse effect on the benefits women can derive from contract farming as contract farmers, family and hired labour of contract farmers and casual employees of agribusiness.

The potential for formalisation of employment under contract farming is marginal if not insignificant. Contract-farming schemes have created extremely limited opportunities for permanent employment. In addition, regulations are silent on wage levels, as well as wage differences between women and men on contract farms and also at the level of the agribusiness firms. Typically, wages are determined by community standards, and not by contracting firms. Other silences include leave periods, overtime payments and the use of family labour on farms. In this process, it is observable that production and marketing are regulated and appear to be formalised, but not the labour conditions of contract farming. The contract farming case is thus a classic case of "false 'formalisation,' whereby (some) informal activities get subsumed by formal enterprises as part of their accumulation strategies" (Ghosh, n.d.). A few countries such as Brazil have started legal initiatives to formally introduce laws that could regulate contract farming (Watanabe et al., 2017). In Ghana, such legal avenues are not yet available and until then, firms and IFIs will directly and indirectly regulate contract farming schemes.

IV Domestic trading

Domestic trading comprises two broad types of activities: (1) trading activities operated by persons from both authorised (district markets and rented stalls) and unauthorised structures, and (2) street vending (Anyidoho and Steel, 2016, 5). Within these two broad types can be found a diverse set of activities and participants. For instance, street vending can range from highly mobile cold-water sellers to less mobile cooked food sellers who pack up their tabletops and cooking utensils at the end of each day. There are also market traders who, in a bid to increase interaction with buyers, might also engage in street vending. However, there are other groups of traders who do not fall neatly into any of the two broad categories. This includes women who combine household reproductive duties with trading, selling their wares in corner shops attached to residential accommodation or on tabletops in front of houses.

Domestic trading remains a crucial component of the Ghanaian economy in terms of the size of the working population that it employs. Results from several rounds (rounds 3-6) of the GLSS indicate that participation of the employed population in the sub-sector has generally been above 15 per cent. In 1991/92, participation in the sub-sector was estimated at 16 per cent (Ghana Statistical Service, 1995, 35) while the corresponding figure for 2012/13 was nearly 20 per cent of the employed population (Ghana Statistical Service, 2014, 51). Due to these relatively high rates of participation, domestic trading follows agriculture as the most important employer of the Ghanaian working population.

Markets are complex spaces in the range of activities and services they support and the hierarchies among different service providers. In addition to the traders, there are others who provide services to traders and buyers. These include city officials who manage markets, transportation services by truck, wheelbarrow and by head porterage; *susu* collectors who mediate between traders and the banks, security, childcare support services and those who keep the markets clean.

Identity is an important marker that structures participation in not only domestic trading, but also the informal economy in general. Often, an interplay between historical, political and economic factors amongst others results in a situation in which some social groups exercise enormous control within specific spaces in the informal economy. Thus, in his analysis of what he classifies as "Africa of the colonial trade economy," Amin speaks of a hierarchical trading structure "in which the Lebanese occupied the intermediate zones while the former African traders were crushed and had to occupy subordinate positions" (1972, 520). In *Landlords and Brokers*, Hill (1966) describes a Hausa and Muslim male-dominated cattle trading system with specialised roles such as that of the slaughterer "…who slaughters all the livestock in a manner accordant with Muslim law, for which he is rewarded with a fixed charge per head for different classes of stock" (1966, 366).

An important feature of market trading is that it is highly gender segmented. The participation of males notwithstanding, domestic trading in Ghana is generally regarded as the space of or for women. In 1991/92, 25 per cent of working women were engaged in trading compared to 5 per cent of men (Ghana Statistical Service, 1995, 35). Thus, in 1991/92, as well as in 1998/99 (Ghana Statistical Service, 2000, 32), the proportion of women engaged in trading activities exceeded that of men by 20 percentage points. This general pattern of women's predominance can also be observed for subsequent years, although the differences shrunk to 13 percentage points in 2005/06 (Ghana Statistical Service, 2008, 38) and to 18 percentage points in 2012/13 (Ghana Statistical Service, 2014, 51).

Further evidence of the predominance of women in domestic trading is presented in Table 4.5. The data show that a significantly large share of sales workers are women, with their participation accounting for as much as 89 per cent of sales workers in 1984. However, women sales workers as a proportion of total sales workers was estimated at 70.5 per cent in 2000, signifying a reduction of nearly 20 percentage points. This reduction logically leads us to conclude that a significant increase in male participation in domestic trading occurred between 1984 and 2000, a period coinciding with economic liberalisation and male labour retrenchment from the formal economy.

The results of a 2014 Integrated Business Establishment Survey (IBES) conducted by the Ghana Statistical Service (GSS) is significant in this regard. IBES was "the first non-household economic census covering all sectors" of the Ghanaian economy (Ghana Statistical Service, 2015a, iii). Data from this census supplements already existing evidence on the significance of trading and the dynamics of participation by males and females in the sector. A total of 290,274 wholesale and retail enterprises, comprising 45 per cent of all establishments, were covered in IBES. In addition, out of the "3,383,206 persons employed by all establishments," wholesale and retail trade emerged as the most significant provider of jobs. The sub-sector employed a total of 817,848 persons (24 per cent of workers in establishments) and was followed by education (14 per cent) and other services (13.7 per cent) (Ghana Statistical Service, 2015a, ix, 25-26). However, in contrast to previous evidence of a general predominance of women in trading, the results from IBES show that the proportion of women engaged in wholesale and retail trade (25 per cent) exceeded that of men (23 per cent) by only 2 percentage points. In fact, the actual number of men engaged in wholesale and retail trade (479,816) was significantly larger than the figure that was reported for women (338,032).

While this large and somewhat unexpected disparity in the participation of men and women in wholesale and retail trade may be accounted for by the conceptual and methodological approach that underpinned the IBES, it speaks to the gender segmentation of market trade. The IBES specifically targeted "establishments"[11] (Ghana Statistical Service, 2015b, 10) and their participants; thus, while it was a "census," it left out many workers in the informal economy who could not be identified with "establishments" such as "all mobile businesses e.g. hawkers", "traders in open spaces," "traders in homes where shops are NOT visible" and "all trading units which are mainly, retail shops selling on small tables under sheds. E.g. market sheds, and stalls without permanent occupants" (Ghana Statistical Service, 2015b, 3). The 2010 Population and Housing Census still maintains that women in sales and services greatly outnumber their male counterparts; 31 per cent of employed women were involved in services and sales work compared to 10 per cent of men (Ghana Statistical Service, 2013, 264). This finding, which has consistently been documented over the decades, in contrast to those of the IBES (bearing in mind that the latter did not cover sub-sectors that are arguably home to the majority of women traders), leads us to conclude that although women are much more visible as traders compared with men, they mainly dominate the over-crowded survival segments of the trading sector while their entry and participation in the smaller capital-intensive segments is restricted. As Chen has stated, "… around the world, men tend to be over-represented in the top segment [of the informal economy while] women tend to be over-represented in the bottom segments…" (Chen, 2007).

The gender segmentation of domestic trading is further complicated by hier-archies in the trading system structured by the control of capital and labour. There are wholesalers, combined wholesaler retailers and retailers. Among retailers, there are differences in the capital base, the nature of the goods they sell and the size of operations, which affects the nature of the workplace—whether it is a shop, a stall, in front of a shop or stall, in or outside the market, on the streets or at home. At all levels of the trading hierarchy, traders use hired labour or the labour of family members. Those hiring labour either have employees explicitly hired as such, or persons who are effectively but not juridically employees. For example, small-scale retailers who operate from a range of locations place young people by the roadside to sell goods at a commission. Some of these persons may be independent op-erators operating at a lower level of the retail chain. All of these labour relations are not subject to the Labour code unless they involve written contracts that can be enforced.

Several reasons are given for women's predominance in trading. It is argued that the participation of women in trading enables them to combine work of an "economic" nature with their gender-specific reproductive duties. Other stated factors include the low skill and capital requirements of trading and a supposedly strict separation in economic functions in which men are responsible for agri-cultural production or fishing whereas women are responsible for the marketing of produce (Ghana Statistical Service, 2005; Overa 2007). Studies of colonial policies have contested the choice and preference arguments by drawing attention to a common pattern across Africa of colonial policies that restricted the mobility of women and restructured African economies in ways that created the gender segmentation of work that has persisted into the post-colonial era (Akurang-Parry, 2010; Allman 1996Akyeampong and Agyei-Mensah, 2006; Allman, 1996; Pape, 2000; Tsikata, 2009). Historically, domestic trading, which now is unquestionably recognised as the space for women, had been the preserve of men. However, this changed during the colonial period as men became either associated with or di-rectly involved in mining and the production of primary export commodities. In the case of the Asante, Clark (1994, 6) comments that

> Asante men had moved out of market trading in many commodities now considered stereotypical for women around 1910, shortly after colonial conquest, and had moved into cocoa farming, which then brought them

higher incomes and better upward mobility prospects. Asante women and Northern men had expanded aggressively into the space they had left.

Regulation of domestic trading in Ghana

The regulation of trading in Ghana involves three main actors, namely, the state, local governments and traders' associations. Regulation here involves direct and indirect measures to achieve certain objectives such as revenue mobilisation for funding development initiatives and everyday operations of the districts, facilitation of trading activities and welfare. In this section, we discuss the three regulatory institutions in turn.

State regulatory actions: banking and financial sector reforms

The state and other international development agencies have long held the view that the lack of access to credit comprises a critical challenge (if not the most important challenge) to those who operate microenterprises, and participants in the informal economy in general (Egyir, 2010). Thus, there have been long-standing attempts to increase access to credit through the introduction of new systems, and the promotion of formal financial institutions as a more secure and viable alternative to informal institutions. In the 1980s, policy reforms in the banking and financial sectors—privatisation, granting of licenses to new banks, etc.—were undertaken as part of the economic liberalisation turn from the 1980s. This led to a rapid expansion of the formal financial sector. Among these were microfinance institutions, generally considered as institutions of and for the poor, women, rural dwellers and those involved in agriculture and trade. In 2017, a total of 34 banks, "68 Non-Bank Financial Institutions (NBFIs), 141 Rural and Community Banks (RCBs), 566 Microfinance Institutions (MFIs), 417 Forex Bureaux and three Credit Reference Bureaux were in operation" (Bank of Ghana, 2017, 19).

Some authors argue that the operation of formal financial institutions, specifically MFIs, have not only improved incomes and increased access to financial services, but that they have also provided other benefits outside of the financial sphere. Afrane and Ahiable (2011, 121) have for instance, identified non-monetary benefits such as "enhanced public respect and acceptance," "empowerment of women" and "reduced dependence on … husbands" amongst others. However, increasing interactions between microenterprises and financial institutions also has its downsides. Interests on loans can be high, posing serious challenges for repayment and sometimes resulting in the indebtedness of borrowers. In part, these problems stem from the fact that new and expanding MFIs prioritise their profit-making objectives ahead of the welfare concerns of their clientele (Anyidoho, 2016).

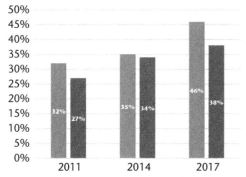

FIGURE 4.1 Access to a financial institution account
Source: Global Findex (2018)

Figures 4.1–4.6 provide data which allow for some assessment of the impacts of reforms on participation in the banking and financial sectors. In relying solely on such data, impacts of the reforms can only be described as limited, with notable differences between men and women in some cases. Certainly, some indicators have improved. For instance, with respect to a financial institution account, 46 per cent of males owned an account in 2017 compared to 38 per cent of women. Six years prior to this, the rates were 32 per cent and 27 per cent, respectively. Similar improvements can be observed for a mobile money account. Men's access to such accounts increased from 14 per cent to 44 per cent between 2014 and 2017. Correspondingly, the figures for women increased from 12 to 34 per cent during the same time period. However, even in these cases where improvements have been noticed, rates of access are still below 50 per cent. However, other indicators are clearly lagging behind. In 2017, 19 per cent of males saved at a financial institution while the figure for females was 14 per cent. Furthermore, borrowing from financial institutions was quite low, with no discernible differences between men and women (11 per cent against 10 per cent, respectively). Thus, the data point to the sustainability and continuous relevance of informal financial institutions and arrangements. Savings by men and women through these mediums are at rates similar to those reported for formal financial institutions (Figure 4.4), whereas borrowing from these sources are even higher (Figure 4.6).

New developments in the banking and financial sectors resulting from poor management on the part of banks, and inadequate regulation could erode public confidence in the sector. In 2018, seven banks which were on the verge of collapse were merged into one bank: The Consolidated Bank Ghana Limited. In August 2019, the licences of 23 financial institutions (mostly savings and loans companies) were revoked (Bank of Ghana, 2019). The Bank of Ghana has justified these actions as necessary to avert the crisis, minimise job losses and secure

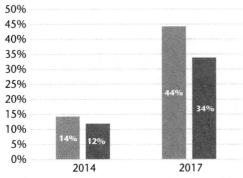

FIGURE 4.2 Access to a mobile money account
Source: Global Findex (2018)

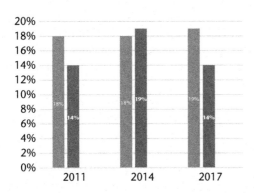

FIGURE 4.3 Savings at a financial institution
Source: Global Findex (2018)

depositors' savings. However, the measures have being criticised for being "spontaneous," lacking adequate stakeholder consultation and may result in loss of the indigenous element in the banking and financial sectors (Terkper, 2019).

Besides the reforms which have resulted in expansion of financial institutions, the Ghana government has also specifically rolled out programmes to extend credit to operators of microenterprises, particularly women. These include the Women's Development Fund which was set up in 2001 with a seed capital of $3 million and was administered by the Ministry of Women and Children's Affairs (now the Ministry of Gender, Children and Social Protection) (National Development Planning Commission, 2005, 144). Other programmes include the Micro and Small Loans Centre, a US$50 million "Micro Credit Fund...launched in

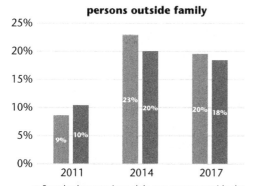

FIGURE 4.4   Saved with a savings club or persons outside family
Source: Global Findex (2018)

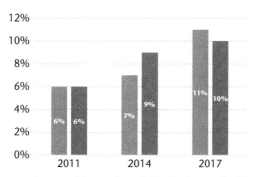

FIGURE 4.5   Borrowing from a financial institution
Source: Global Findex (2018)

September 2006" (National Development Planning Commission, 2007, 36) and the Skills Training and Employment Programme, amongst others. The requirements of these credit schemes include the opening of bank accounts, group formation and savings thresholds, amongst others. These could have the effect of formalising aspects of the operations of market trading enterprises.

Besides reforms in banking and the financial sectors, state regulation of trading has involved wide application of price controls by various governments, including colonial administrations. Experiences suggest that price controls imposed great difficulties on traders, and also had negative consequences for the urban poor and

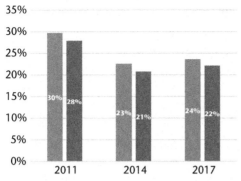

FIGURE 4.6 Borrowed from family or friends
Source: Global Findex (2018)

rural population. This is because of the extension to traders of agricultural produce, controls primarily targeted at traders of imported, manufactured and luxury items (Clark, 1988). Perhaps, the most extreme case of the use of price controls was that of the Armed Forces Revolutionary Council in the Makola and Kumasi Central Markets in 1979. Regarding the latter, Clark (1988) describes a situation in which military personnel relied on coercion and violence to arbitrarily determine the prices of commodities. The main goal of price controls is to set prices at levels affordable to the poor, and also counteract alleged price manipulations by traders. However, the enforcement of this measure in the Kumasi Central Market disrupted market activities and drastically reduced the quantity of goods available for sale. On the whole, price controls have been short-lived and ineffective (Darkwah, 2001). More successful have been those measures emanating from the SAP such as the introduction of a special tax on imported goods, changes in procedures regarding the importation and clearing of goods and currency devaluation (Darkwah, 2001). Many of these measures, including those that were expected to remove the obstacles, made trading more difficult for women involved in the import trade.

Local government regulatory approaches

Local government is perhaps more influential in regulating domestic trade than the central government. In a study in which traders were asked to identify and rank actors whose activities had an influence on trading, local government bodies "received the highest mentions on aggregate, indicating that these loomed large in the everyday lives of vendors" (Anyidoho and Steel, 2016, 13). In Ghana, local government units are collectively referred to as districts.[12]

Districts also differ from one another in terms of core economic activities, resource endowments and composition, amongst others. They are responsible for socio-economic and physical development, and the provision and maintenance of public infrastructure in all localities under their control. Due to these responsibilities, districts have extensive powers for regulating many aspects of social and economic lives, particularly the use of public spaces, and they are empowered to mobilise the "resources necessary for the overall development of the district" (Constitution of the Republic of Ghana, 1992, 139).

Financial resources for implementing activities and running the district administration normally come from three sources, namely, "decentralised transfers," "internally generated funds" and "donations and grants" (Local Governance Act, 2016Ghana Statistical Service 2016 64). Of these, internally generated funds (IGF) are the most reliable source of funds for most districts due to delays in disbursement of central government funds, which are generally regarded as inadequate for carrying out the development mandates of district assemblies. IGF is acquired from several sources including contributions from employees of the assembly. Local Governance Act 2016

However, a large share of revenue is generated from the granting of development permits, property rates, licenses, fees and taxes. For example, a "hawkers licence," is required by an operator who undertakes any hawking-related activity in a district while fees are charged for the use of facilities or services provided by the district (Local Governance Act, 2016, 69). This includes fees that are charged for the use of the district market. Finally, taxes are also charged for those involved in income-generating activities including "traders," and "cooked food sellers" (Local Governance Act, 2016, 121). Thus, trading—regardless of form—is one of the most taxed activities in many districts of Ghana. A study of two districts in the Central region found that "markets in the district capitals account for between 90 per cent and 98 per cent of total market revenue in both districts" (Owusu and Lund, 2004, 118). Similar findings about the importance of trade to revenue generation have been reported in other studies as well (Baah-Ennumh and Adom-Asamoah, 2012; Clark, 1994).

The segmentation of domestic trading has implications for revenue collection. In many of the large metropolitan and municipal areas in Ghana, it is those traders who lack sufficient capital and the right social networks who end up operating from unauthorised structures or as street vendors. The estimates vary for the latter with respect to gender composition, but studies suggest that majority of street vendors are women (Anyidoho and Steel, 2016, 7; Steel et al., 2014, 2). Even though these groups of traders also make significant contributions to the IGFs of districts, they are frequently targeted for evictions and decongestion. These involve the demolition of unauthorised structures (sometimes before the crack of dawn when most traders are still on their way to work), while street venders are normally prevented from selling in their most preferred locations by employed guards of district assemblies.

Confrontations with district assembly guards are quite regular and may in some areas comprise a part of the daily life of street vendors. This is because in many large towns and cities of Ghana, street vendors prefer to operate on streets and pavements in and around the central business districts, as well as bus terminals and open public spaces which generally attract both human and vehicular traffic to increase interaction and sales, as well as build a reliable customer base (Bob-Milliar and Obeng-Odoom, 2011; Solomon-Ayeh et al., 2011). On the contrary, there are buyers who are attracted to street vendors as they also prefer to reduce the distance, and the hassle of shopping in large markets. However, many of the spaces which street vendors prefer to operate from were originally designed and created for purposes other than trading. This creates competition and conflict between street vendors and other users of public spaces, particularly pedestrians. This situation often pits street venders against local government bodies with legal responsibility for the overall development of their areas. It appears that local governments in Ghana, particularly large metropolitan areas, are often judged more for their ability to deal with traffic management, congestion, sanitation and waste management than for their responsiveness to the needs of the informal economy or the well-being of traders in particular.

The two largest metropolitan areas in Ghana, namely, the Accra and Kumasi Metropolitan Assemblies, have responded to the competition and conflicts between street traders and other users of public spaces by resorting to a number of measures that are often draconian, ineffective and unsustainable. For instance, the Accra Metropolitan Assembly has banned selling on streets and pavements when this is the norm for street vendors. In spite of these measures, local governments continue to collect fees from hawkers until some need arises for the eviction and demolition of unauthorised structures. In 2007, the Tema Station Market which served hundreds of women traders was demolished by city authorities as part of efforts to beautify the city of Accra in preparation for Ghana's celebration of 50 years of independence (Tsikata, 2007). Demolitions are at the core of the regulation of street vending and other forms of trade, sometimes implemented in pursuit of some national goal of "modernisation," or "formalizing the use of public spaces" (Steel et al., 2014, 2). In the case of Kumasi, Solomon-Ayeh et al. (2011, 28) comment that "the bulldozer approach has been the main instrument of the Kumasi city authorities as they attempt to destroy structures of street vendors."

However, there are cases in which evictions and demolitions are carried out as part of the activities required for resolving the problem of lack of space or inadequate market infrastructure, which is believed to have led some traders to the street in the first place. A case in this regard relates to the relocation of street vendors to the 4,000 capacity Odawna Pedestrian Market in the Accra metropolis (Adaawen and Jorgensen, 2012). Some vendors were able to secure stalls in the new market, but many more were left with no option than to continue selling in the streets either because they could not afford the rent, or they lacked the connections that facilitated access to market stalls. Those who rented market stalls also complained about low profit margins, as well as design and construction issues (e.g. the narrow entrance) which made the market unattractive to many buyers. These issues, in addition to the market's propensity to flood resulted in "the abandoning of sheds and return to the streets" (Adaawen and Jorgensen, 2012, 57).

The powers of taxation and urban planning (which provide the justification for forced evictions and decongestion) as two dominant forms of the regulation of trade have historical antecedents. Taxation had been used by indigenous states in the pre-colonial period to raise revenues for achieving various state objectives. This power was usurped and utilised by the colonial administration, with market revenues comprising a large proportion of total revenue. In northern Ghana the colonial government established new markets, a move associated with the privileging of foreign merchants on the one hand, and the displacement of local markets and traders on the other hand. Violence remained central to such efforts (Plange, 1984). Similarly, new markets were established in various parts of southern Ghana. In some of these cases, the construction of markets was closely associated with the development of transport infrastructure, which itself, resulted from the expansion of the cocoa frontier (Amanor, 1994). Regardless of these different contexts and the forms of emergence, the role of markets as sources of revenue have remained crucial.

While local governments have been heavily reliant on trading for revenue generation, they have equally been hostile to traders. The antipathy of local governments (and sometimes the state) towards traders also has long historical antecedents. In the contemporary period, perhaps the most extreme form of this hostility was manifested in the destruction of major markets across Ghana in the late 1970s and early 1980s when market women were accused of contributing to the economic woes of the country through such measures as price manipulation (Schindler, 2010). Such demolitions continued to be a feature of the 1990s and beyond and were the subject of protests by women rights groups (Tsikata, 2007). However, traders who operate in markets and other locations approved by local authorities are normally insulated from actions that have disruptive effects on trading. Rather, the decongestions and relocations, accompanied by violence and the confiscation of goods, which have far more disastrous consequences, are experienced mainly by street vendors, who are more likely to be poor and female.

Traders associations

Traders' associations comprise one of the few actors which clearly represent the interests of traders in their dealings with local government. These associations draw on opportunities and strategies such as their representation in district assemblies or legal procedures to influence or challenge decisions that have a bearing on the welfare of their members. In some cases, association representatives may even take advantage of their relationships with politicians in the national government to steer the decisions of local governments in their favour (Bob-Milliar and Obeng-Odoom, 2011). However, traders' associations are probably less influential, and their abilities to influence the decisions of local governments limited or highly variable, depending on the circumstances. In 2007, for example, the United Petty Traders' Association in Kumasi failed to prevent the Kumasi Metropolitan Assembly from undertaking a planned decongestion exercise (Solomon-Ayeh et al., 2011), even after the association petitioned two national ministries six times within a period of six months. Bob-Milliar and Obeng-Odoom (2011, 273-6) argue that decongestion and forced evictions have political dimensions, drawing attention to the very high-level interventions to halt such processes when it affects the supporters of a particular political party.

Besides evictions, there are other matters that traders' associations engage with local governments about. One such issue is the rehabilitation or construction of new markets. This is a particularly important issue for associations because while fees and taxes generated from traders comprise a significant part of local government revenues, markets and related infrastructure are often considered substandard, not conducive to trading and raising questions about occupational and environmental health (Baah-Ennumh and Adom-Asamoah, 2012; Shepherd, 2005; Owusu and Lund, 2004).

Traders Associations are also involved in the organisation of trade, as well as attending to the day to day livelihoods and welfare needs of their members. Matters such as the determination of the quantity of produce that is available for sale in the market at any point in time are a major preoccupation for agricultural produce traders' associations. For example, one primary objective of the National Tomato Traders Association of Ghana "is to reduce price fluctuations and reduce the probability of traders being unable to sell their tomatoes at a price that covers their costs, or even at any price, particularly during the peak period when the prices typically fall significantly. Central to their activities is the control of tomato volumes entering the wholesale market" (Robinson and Kolavalli, 2010, 6). Similarly, the Ghana Agricultural Products Traders' Organisation, which is constituted by and represents many traders' associations such as the tomato association highlighted above "actively involves itself in promoting and regulating the buying and selling of different products and assists individual associations to manage supply in order to avoid periodic gluts and surpluses in the markets" (Shepherd, 2005, 19).

With regard to livelihoods and welfare, associations facilitate the extension of credit to members, resolve disputes and support members to perform social obligations such as funerals. Indeed, support with funerals is considered by some traders as the prime reason for the existence of these associations (Lyon, 2003, 16; Owusu and Lund, 2004, 122). The unexpected death of a spouse or other close family member often requires significant funding to organise the funeral and later assume certain responsibilities of the deceased. As this could substantially reduce savings the trader may have accumulated, the financial support provided by an association is regarded as a form of insurance to protect the bereaved from the loss of their trading capital because of social obligations (Lyon, 2003; Shepherd, 2005).

Traders' associations are also more successful than individual traders in the acquisition of group loans from microfinance institutions. That said, the credit issue is so fundamental that more effective specialised institutions are more prominent in addressing the credit needs of traders. For the large share of traders who are less likely to meet the requirements of formal financial institutions, these comprise a host of informal banking and insurance arrangements that enable them to share and manage shocks (Schindler, 2010; Wrigley-Asante, 2008). These include friends, family and money lenders, receiving goods from wholesalers on credit, and rotating savings and credit associations (ROSCA). ROSCAs, popularly known in Ghana as Susu groups, are composed of people who agree to contribute and share financial resources. Typically, all members of the group contribute money at specific time intervals and the lump sum collected at each round is given to one member at a time until every member has contributed to and benefitted from the process. Usually, the amount to be collected, and the procedure for distributing benefits is pre-determined by all members beforehand. The groups are formed by persons who share similar demographic or socio-economic characteristics; thus, it may be formed by those who sell similar products or occupy a particular section of the market or by traders who share a similar identity (Norwood, 2011). There are a number of lateral Susu groups operating at any point in time and some traders hope to maximise their opportunities for receiving support by belonging to more than one group, although this will automatically translate into additional responsibilities.

While they provide much needed credit to persons excluded from the formal financial system, informal arrangements have their problems. These range from the small amounts of credit provided, which are sometimes inadequate to meet the needs of some individuals, to issues of power relations and misappropriation of funds. More generally, Schindler (2010, 235) argues that while "informal credit is crucial to trading businesses and serves as the market women's main strategy for managing risks inherent in market trade," "the maintenance of informal credit networks is costly to traders and prevents them from growing out of poverty in the long term."

This discussion of the role of different actors involved in the regulation of domestic trade has found that various actors seek to achieve different objectives by pursuing different strategies. The state, through its policies, programmes and laws seeks to improve access to credit, and enhance entrepreneurship and skills development. However, its success in achieving this objective is limited. While the expansion of MFIs resulting from the increased participation of the private sector in the formal financial system may have resulted in improvements in access to credit, these institutions could also plunge borrowers into debt due to high interest rates. The collapse and inability of many of these institutions to provide services to their clientele in the last few years and an ongoing crisis in Ghana's entire banking and financial sector, are also likely to reduce the confidence and public support for such systems. Furthermore, informal banking and insurance arrangements continue to be sustainable and are sometimes the more reliable sources for traders.

Local government is a critical player in the regulation of trading, from which it generates a large share of the revenues used to finance local development. However, its spatial modernisation preoccupations and preferred use of instruments such as demolitions and forced evictions have proved unsustainable and cyclical. Traders associations are the most effective representatives and defenders of the interests of traders, using their representation in district assemblies as well as their relationships with politicians to steer decisions in favour of their members and providing them with much needed social insurance. All in all, regulation of domestic trading, particularly by the state and local governments, to a large extent have little to do with the formalisation of work. This accounts for the low enrolment in the formal social security system, and the insecurity of many persons employed in the informal economy.

Trading follows agriculture as the most important sector with regard to the size of the Ghanaian working population it engages. Unlike the contract farming case, trading does not fit neatly into any single one of the four trajectories of formalisation. There are some aspects of trading where the "false formalisation" case can be made. This would include medium-scale enterprises or wholesale agents who are linked to global value chains and in turn supply traders with the products they sell to their customers. Another dimension of "false formalisation" in trading relates to the intermediary roles of banking agents and how they serve as important links between market women and formal financial institutions. As a result, traders are a constant source of regular cash for many financial institutions, although this function is rarely acknowledged. In some of the contract farming cases discussed, there was some potential for minimal benefits such as restrictions on the use of children and pregnant women as labour due to the enforcement of international standards by agribusiness firms. In trading, these benefits—regardless of their importance to the broader goals of formalisation—are more likely to be absent due to limited direct interactions between traders and formal business entities. Many traders depend on other categories of workers (e.g. crop farmers, small manufacturers and consumers), who are themselves engaged in some form of informal work. Furthermore, traders sometimes find themselves at odds with these other workers because of objective contradictions in their positioning in relation to the prices of goods and services. Finally, very little has been done by the state and local governments by way of the regulation of labour relations within the trading system as their efforts have emphasized taxation and regulation of the activities of market traders in public spaces.

V Conclusion

With more than 90 per cent of persons of legal age in employment, unemployment does not appear to be a problematic issue in Ghana. On closer examination, however, it becomes clear that the majority of the 90 per cent are informal workers who are either self-employed or contributing family labour. They lack access to subsidized medical care, social security and other conditions associated with decent work. A total of 23 per cent of Ghanaian households are poor, and the rate is as high as 43 per cent for households where the head is involved in agriculture. High levels of poverty and lack of well-being in general are associated with the quality of work. Since the 1980s, the informal economy has expanded first due to massive public service labour retrenchments and later due to the failure of economic growth to translate into formal employment as growth was largely driven by sectors and strategies not capable of creating decent employment. Government priority in employment is by and large focused on job creation rather than improving the quality of existing jobs or ensuring that new jobs are decent. In addition, social security is increasingly divorced from work and work conditions through instruments such as NHIS, LEAP, School feeding programmes and capitation grants.

Our objective in this study has been to explore the implications of regulation for the formalisation of employment by focusing on contract farming and domestic trading. Generally, our findings show that regulation does not necessarily lead to formalisation; where it does lead to some formalisation, the particular type of formalisation pursued has not influenced conditions of work and livelihood outcomes. Also, formalisation efforts are mostly focused on enterprises, and where they focus on workers, efforts are limited to certification conditionalities, which are not always diligently enforced, or even if enforced fully, would not address the decent work deficits of informal work.

With respect to contract farming, non-state regulation in the form of global certification, or specific policies of agro-processing companies are more critical than state regulation. Also, regulation in contract farming has had gender-differentiated outcomes. Agro-companies mainly employ women as casual labourers, and less frequently, as contract farmers. At the household level, a preference for family labour in contract farming regimes ensures a labour subsidy to capital. Even more importantly, companies do not regulate the labour conditions of their own workers or those of their contract farmers except in very limited ways. In the case of domestic trading, the state has indirectly regulated this sector through its liberalisation of the banking and financial sector which resulted in the expansion of financial service providers. The impact of this intervention can at best be described as mixed as the roles performed by informal systems continue to be critical. Access to credit from financial institutions may prove difficult for many persons in the informal economy and repayment of loans may even be more problematic. While state efforts may be important, the main responsibility for regulating trade is performed by local governments. However, regulation mostly takes the form of taxation and the regulation of the activities of traders in public spaces. In addition, while incomes generated from taxation of trade are perhaps the most important source of revenue for many districts, traders complain about the poor state of market infrastructure and other municipal services. Regulation of contract farming and trading takes various forms and involves several actors. In spite of their differences, regulations have generally not resulted in the formalisation of employment in any of these two sectors.

VI Postscript

It may be too soon to predict the scale of devastation of COVID-19 impacts on the world of work, which was already in a state of flux because of widespread casualisation and precarity. Although Africa has the lowest figures for infections and deaths for any continent, its low testing capacity, as well as the frailties of its health and social security systems and its export primary commodity dependent economies, makes its situation one to watch carefully. With the world facing a second spike in infections, certainties about containment are fraying, and in Africa, it is still unclear if the first episode has peaked. In spite of the uncertainties and caveats, some glimpses of the future are available in early assessments of government responses. In Ghana as in many African countries where work is largely informal, the lack of a credible employment database is already hampering efforts to fashion and plan durable solutions.

With more than 16,431 confirmed cases (including deaths and recoveries) by 28 June 2020, Ghana has the highest number of cases in Africa after South Africa, Egypt and Nigeria. It is difficult to identify any aspect of social and economic lives which has been left untouched by the pandemic. Consequences have been particularly marked for Ghana due to the importance of primary export commodities such as crude oil, cocoa and other agricultural and mineral exports. Demand and prices for these commodities have reduced significantly and there has been a general reduction in domestic and international trades (Ministry of Finance, 2020, 9). Crude oil prices plummeted to below US$30 per barrel and the World Bank (2020, 3) noted that if prices should stay at "US$ 50.00 per barrel for 2020, government could lose about US$ 484 million in petroleum receipts." Consequently, a substantial reduction in import duties is expected and economic growth will very likely slowdown in contrast to previous optimistic projections.

Anti-COVID-19 measures for households, businesses and the general public

The government of Ghana has instituted several measures to manage the effects of the pandemic. Measures by the Bank of Ghana sought to improve the liquidity of commercial banks. The government also "waive[d] taxes on selected Third-Tier Pension withdrawals" (Ministry of Finance, 2020, 18) and extended the period for the filing of tax returns by companies. Critically, it established a Coronavirus Alleviation Programme (CAP) "to mitigate the impact of the coronavirus on businesses and households and ensure that economic activities are sustained, whiles minimizing job losses." CAP, which is to be implemented with GH¢1.25 billion (US$125,964,375) has a sub-component, the Business Support Scheme (CAPBuSS), which is expected to provide financial support to more than 230,000 micro-, small- and medium-scale enterprises (MSMEs). According to the National Board for Small Scale Industries (NBSSI), a total of 110,000 MSMEs, 62 per cent of them operated by women, had applied to be considered for participation in

CAPBuSS by 10th June 2020. The NBSSI also announced that it was taking steps to ensure that participants of the informal economy were not excluded from the programme.

Some of the CAP funds were allocated to distribute food to 400,000 people in areas which were earmarked for the "partial lockdown," and provide free water for all Ghanaians for three months (April, May and June; NBSSI 2020). The government also paid "GH¢300 million to the National Health Insurance Scheme (NHIA)…to provide liquidity to Health Care providers and the pharmaceutical industry…[and] arranged Life and Sickness Insurance for Health Care Professionals on the front line of the Health Care Pandemic" (Ministry of Finance, 2020, 18). In addition to CAP, the government established a COVID-19 Fund "to support the well-being of those who will be worst-hit by the novel Coronavirus pandemic" (Citi Business News, 2020). As well, a Ghana COVID-19 Emergency Preparedness and Response Project in which the World Bank released a total of US$100 million to "prevent, detect and respond to the threat posed by COVID-19 and strengthen national systems for public health preparedness in Ghana" was announced.

Ghana Government Response to COVID-19
General Measures:

- Restrictions Act, 2020 (Act 1012)
- Establishment of Emergency Communications System Instrument, 2020 (EI 63)
- Border Closure
- Ban on Public Gatherings
- School Closures
- Public Information Campaign

Measures Targeting the Health Sector

- Provision of Personal Protective Equipments (PPEs) to frontline health workers
- Insurance package for health personnel and allied professionals
- Three-month income tax exemption for health workers
- Allowance of 50 per cent on basic pay of frontline health workers for three months
- Allowance of GHS150 a day to contact tracers

Measures Targeting Households

- One hot meal a day during three-week lockdown

- Distribution of dry food packages during lockdown
- Water and Electricity subsidies for three months
- Additional support to beneficiaries of LEAP concessions (cash transfer programme for chronically poor households)

Measures Targeting Businesses

- Tax Reliefs – Ghana Revenue Authority (GRA)
- Liquidity Expansion – Bank of Ghana
- Business Support Scheme

Source: Oduro and Tsikata (2020)

Who are the beneficiaries of Government of Ghana COVID-19 responses?

Early assessments of the emergency feeding programme, which consisted of either the provision of one hot meal a day or dry foodstuffs during the three-week lockdown period and the three-month water and electricity subsidies for households point to challenges of implementation and unexamined assumptions about the living and working conditions of Ghanaians. It is unclear how the beneficiaries of emergency food were identified in the absence of a credible household register in all the districts of Ghana. It is also difficult to ascertain if the food reached the numbers announced, especially as media reports highlighted many logistical challenges. With respect to the water and electricity subsidies, the eligibility criteria of water and electricity bills and decision to transmit the subsidies through the billing system has meant that only households with their own utilities meters benefited. Analyses of existing data on bill paying by households has established clearly that although many poor Ghanaian households consume electricity, the majority of bill-paying households are in the fourth and fifth expenditure quintiles, and less than 20 per cent of those who pay bills are in the first and second expenditure quintiles (40 per cent of households). With respect to the water subsidy, only 10.6 per cent of households have pipe-borne water inside their dwellings, and even fewer of these are likely to own a water meter. This also has implications for the effectiveness of the hand-washing campaign, which was already threatened by the number of schools, health and other public facilities and markets without running water and sanitation facilities (Oduro and Tsikata, 2020).

As is the case with other countries, Ghana imposed restrictions on international travel and closed its air and land borders. A three-week "partial lockdown" was imposed in the cities of Accra and Kumasi between 30 March 2020 and 20 April 2020. Prior to this, a ban on public gatherings was imposed across the country on 16 March. Schools were closed and places of religious worship were expected to put gatherings on hold. These measures substantially reduced the movement of persons. While the number of trips in these two areas increased after the lifting of the lockdown, these are still below the number recorded before the ban on public gatherings.

As part of the process of lifting the lockdown, and easing restrictions on work, funerals and religious observances, the wearing of face masks in public places was made mandatory on 25 April 2020. However, it is proving difficult for people to comply strictly with the guidelines of the health ministry. For instance, the same mask is not to be used for more than 12 hours while some categories of workers including food vendors and sellers at markets are required to wear masks "at all times." The government has responded by passing an Executive Instrument (E.I. 164) signed into law on 15 June 2020, which provides that the failure to wear face masks in public constitutes an offence that carries a prison sentence of four to ten years or a fine of between GH¢12,000 and GH¢60,000, or both. The severity of these sanctions is problematic in the sense that given the wages and incomes of the majority of workers in Ghana, they will disproportionately affect poor people, particularly informal workers such as market women and the numerous men and women who operate in open workspaces and or are reliant on public transportation. Those with their own transportation, work in offices and other formal workplaces and live in planned neighbourhoods are less likely to experience the level of policing that the women in the markets and young street traders whose challenges with social distancing are already well-known, will face. This is worrying as these groups have routinely experienced state sponsored violence in the past. The laws passed to control the spread of COVID-19 do not enjoin respect for and protection of human rights of citizens. Fines above the pay grade of most of the population are a recipe for corruption and debt distress at time of livelihood crises.

Anti-COVID-19 measures and the case study groups

Homeless persons, persons with disabilities, institutionalised persons such as prisoners and children in orphanages, migrant workers, particularly the female head porters in southern Ghana marketplaces, workers in rural and urban informal employment and women are particularly vulnerable to the shocks associated with the COVID-19 pandemic. Our case study groups—market traders and contract farmers—are represented in this list of vulnerable persons, and while the impacts of the pandemic will be differentiated, it is becoming clear that informal employment will be a significant marker of vulnerability. For persons in agriculture and related rural livelihood activities, the risk of infection may be low since majority of confirmed cases are concentrated in the main cities and towns of Ghana. However, as the opportunities to earn incomes depend on trade with wholesalers and retailers from urban areas, there is likely to be a major disruption in rural livelihoods and wellbeing. There is as yet no information about how the pandemic has affected agricultural development programmes. However, the disruption in trade could affect farmers' access to inputs. The Minister of Agriculture has also noted that some of the countries from which Ghana imports food had imposed restrictions on food exports, and this has, without a doubt, contributed to the rise in staple food prices.

The disruption in trade on the local and international markets is very likely to adversely affect demand for the products of Blue Skies Ghana Limited and Serendipalm Company Limited— two of our four contract-farming cases, who export most of their products to Europe and the United States. According to Blue Skies, they are adapting to changes in the global environment by relying on the use of cargo planes. However, casualisation of employment ensures that businesses are able to respond to COVID-19 by closing operations as the demand for products tumble. Blue Skies recruits up to 4,000 seasonal workers in June, and the majority are women, and B-BOVID also employs many women as casual labour between January and July. These recruitments are likely to suffer if demand upstream reduces, and this would affect contract farmers as well. As contract farming depends on household and hired labour, many more workers will be adversely impacted by a downturn.

For women traders, who are mostly small retailers of foodstuffs and non-food consumer goods, and cooked food vendors, the lack of registration will be an obstacle to their access to state support and their recovery. Although the CAPBuSS programme lists agro-businesses—food and beverages, and commerce/trade among the sectors being targeted, and encourages women and persons with disability to apply, many cannot meet the requirements for qualification, which include a Business Registration Certificate from the Registrar-General's Department, NBSSI Certificate, Tax Identification Number from GRA and Annual Sales Information. Enterprises are even required to show evidence of how they have been impacted by the pandemic. While it remains to be seen who actually benefits from CAPBuSS, it is fair to assume that many market and itinerant traders and cooked meals vendors, who are mostly women, will be excluded.

Market traders are at high risk of infection because the poor infrastructure and the lack of water and sanitation make social distancing and handwashing difficult to comply with. However, as they do not enjoy fixed incomes, they have no other choice than to work. In Accra and the Ashanti region, a total of 352 markets were closed for fumigation on 23 March and 27 March, respectively. There was some distribution of face masks and hand sanitisers to market women. However, instead of recognising the structural challenges with implementing COVID-19 prevention measures in the markets, market traders are being severely criticised by the President, state officials and commentators for non-compliance as a result of recalcitrance and greed. This is in sharp contrast with the enthusiastic praise received by private businesses operating in malls for putting in place preventive and protective measures. Across the country, local authorities have temporarily closed some markets for the reason that the social distancing measures were not being observed, and the Minister of Local Government and Rural Development has expressed a willingness to resort to market closures to ensure compliance with regulations.

If we have learned anything, it is that the informal character of the economy and the realities of unplanned settlements and shared facilities were ignored in the design of responses. This has made it much more difficult to support the majority of working people whose livelihoods have been disrupted by the efforts to contain the spread of COVID-19. It has also created conditions for draconian policing instead of national mobilisation. Granted that it is easier to plan responses in contexts where all economic activities and households are registered and vital information about them known, the starting point of responses should be where things are, and not where we wish they were. As the disruptions created by COVID-19 are not likely to be short term, they require that the Ghanaian state address the data deficits that ensure that its responses at all times do not exclude the poorest of the poor, whether or not registered, and whether or not in possession of water and electricity meters. In the medium term, Ghana needs to use its resources to catalyse a process of economic and social reform that restructures its economy, and settlement patterns to make all its citizens visible and legible and able to both contribute towards national development and enjoy the full benefits of citizenship.

Notes

1 The authors are grateful to Dzifa Torvikey for research assistance on the contract farming case study, and for generously giving us access to her Ph.D. research on Caltech Company Ltd. They also acknowledge Bram Nana Safo's assistance with research. Fred Dzanku permitted the use of his unpublished research findings from the Agricultural Policy Research in Africa (APRA) Project and Kate Meagher drew attention to pertinent literature on informal work.

2 The LFPR "measures the proportion of the working age population which is economically active" (Ghana Statistical Service, 2016, 23).

3 Our analysis in this section is based on data that combines sales and services workers into one category. Workers in this category include: "personal services workers," "sales workers," "personal care workers" and "protective services workers" (International Labour Organization, 2012, 66). In spite of this limitation, we assume that the workers of this group share similar characteristics.

4 "By contrast, in the private wage sector, 30 percent of workers, or fewer, have access to any form of social security…"

5 The material used for this case study is drawn mainly from Torvikey et al. (2016) and Yaro et al. (2017).

6 The material used for this case study is drawn mainly from Torvikey, incomplete Ph.D. thesis

7 The material used for this case study is from Demeter Ghana Research Reports (2016; 2017).

8 These workers are mostly engaged at the oil processing facility during the peak production season.

9 The material used for this study is from Dzanku et al. (2017) and APRA Exploratory field qualitative interviews (2017).

10 Wilmar in turn owns shares of BOPP.

11 An establishment was "defined as a unit of production engaged in a single kind of activity under a single ownership at a single location" (Ghana Statistical Service, 2015a, 4). The GSS was guided by this definition, although it could not strictly apply it in all cases.

12 However, they are broadly categorised into metropolitan, municipal and district assemblies, depending on their population size and functions of the locality.

References

Abeberese, A. B., Ackah, C. G., Asuming, P. O., 2017. How did the 2012-2015 power crisis affect small and medium manufacturing firms in Ghana? Policy Brief No. 33305. International Growth Centre, Accra.

Adaawen, S. A., Jorgensen, S. H., 2012. Eking out a living: the livelihood implications of urban space regulation on street hawking in Accra, Ghana. Afr. Rev. Econ. Fin. 3 (2), 49–95.

Afrane, S., Ahiable, G., 2011. The informal economy and microfinance in Kumasi. In: Adarkwa, K. K. (Ed.), Future of the Tree: Towards Growth and Development of Kumasi. University Printing Press (UPK), Kwame Nkrumah University of Science and Technology, Kumasi, pp. 111–127.

Akurang-Parry, K. O., 2010. Transformations in the feminization of unfree domestic labor: a study of Abaawa or prepubescent female servitude in modern Ghana. Int. Labor Working-Class History 78 (1), 28–47.

Akyeampong, E., Agyei-Mensah, S., 2006. Itinerant gold mines? Mobility, sexuality and the spread of gonorrhoea and syphilis in 20th century Ghana. In: Oppong, C., Oppong, P.A., Odotei, I. (Eds.), Sex and Gender in an Era of AIDS: Ghana at the Turn of the Millennium. Sub-Saharan Publishers, Accra, pp. 41–58.

Allman, J., 1996. Rounding up spinsters: gender chaos and unmarried women in colonial Asante. J. Afr. History 37 (2), 195–214.

Amanor, K., 1999. Global Restructuring and Land Rights in Ghana: Forest Food Chains, Timber, and Rural Livelihoods. Research Report No. 108. Nordic Africa Institute, Uppsala.

Amanor, K. S., 1994. Ecological knowledge and the regional economy: environmental management in the Asesewa District of Ghana. Dev. Change 25, 41–67.

Amin, S., 1972. Underdevelopment and dependence in Black Africa—origins and contemporary forms. J. Mod. Afr. Stud. 10 (4), 503–524.

Anyidoho, N. A., Steel, W. F., 2016. Perceptions of Costs and Benefits of Informal-Formal Linkages: Market and Street Vendors in Accra, Ghana. WIEGO Working Paper No. 35. WIEGO, Cambridge.

Awadzi, E. A., 2018. Remarks by the Second Deputy Governor, Mrs. Elsie Addo Awadzi, At the Joy FM Financial Sector Forum on November 1, 2018. Retrieved from https://www.bis.org/review/r181220o.pdf

Baah-Ennumh, T., Adom-Asamoah, G., 2012. The role of market women in the informal urban economy in Kumasi. J. Sci. Technol. (Ghana) 32 (2), 56–67.

Bank of Ghana, 2005. The HIPC Initiative and Ghana's External Debts. Bank of Ghana, Accra.

Bank of Ghana, 2017. Annual Report. Bank of Ghana, Accra. Retrieved from https://www.bog.gov.gh/privatecontent/Publications/Annual_Reports/Annual Report 2017 12th July.pdf

Bank of Ghana, 2018. State of the Financial Sector in Ghana.

Bank of Ghana, 2019. Notice of Revocation of Licences of Insolvent Savings and Loans Companies and Finance Houses, and Appointment of a Receiver. Bank of Ghana, Accra.

Baumann, P., 2000. Equity and Efficiency in Contract Farming Schemes: The Experience of Agricultural tree Crops. Working Paper No. 139. Overseas Development Institute, London.

Blue Skies, 2009. Making fruit happy: blue skies sustainability report 2008/2009. Blue Skies Holdings Ltd, Northamptonshire. Retrieved from https://www.blueskies.com/happyfruit.pdf

Bob-Milliar, G. M., Obeng-Odoom, F., 2011. The informal economy is an employer, a nuisance, and a goldmine: multiple representations of and responses to informality in Accra, Ghana. Urban Anthropol. Stud. Cult. Syst. World Econ. Dev. 40 (3/4), 263–284.

Chen, M. A., 2007. Rethinking the Informal Economy: Linkages with the Formal Economy and the Formal Regulatory Environment. DESA Working Paper No. 46. Department of Economic and Social Affairs, New York.

Citi Business News, 2020. Nana Addo establishes COVID-19 Fund, offers his 3 months' salary as seed money. Published on March 28, 2020. *Retrieved on 16 June 2020 from* https://citibusinessnews.com/nana-addo-establishes-covid-19-fund-offers-his-3-months-salary-as-seed-money/

Clark, G., 1988. Price control of local foodstuffs in Kumasi, Ghana, 1979. In: Clark, G., (Ed.), Traders Versus the State: Anthropological Approaches to Unofficial Economies (1988). Westview Press, Boulder, pp. 57–79.

Clark, G., 1994. Onions Are My Husband: Survival and Accumulation by West African Market Women. The University of Chicago Press, Chicago and London.

Constitution of the republic of Ghana, 1992. Ghana Publishing Corporation, Accra.

Darkwah, A., 2001. Confronting the phantom in our midst: market women negotiate the Ghanaian trade policy framework. Soc. Pol. 2 (1), 1–7.

Dzanku, F.M., Hodey, L., Quarmine, W., Asante, K., 2017. Ghana Report of Pre-Survey Explorative Study for Work Stream 1 (Unpublished Report). Future Agricultures Consortium, APRA.

Egyir, I., 2010. Rural women and microfinance in Ghana: challenges and prospects. Joint 3rd African Association of Agricultural Economists (AAAE) and 48th Agricultural Economists Association of South Africa (AEASA) Conference, 1–14. Retrieved from http://ageconsearch.umn.edu/bitstream/95782/1/34. Rural women and microfinance in Ghana.pdf%5Cnhttp://ageconsearch.umn.edu

Food and Agriculture Organization, 2012. Gender Inequalities in Rural Employment in Ghana: An Overview. Food and Agriculture Organization, Rome.

Ghana Statistical Service, 1995. Ghana Living Standards Survey: Report of the Third Round (GLSS 3). Ghana Statistical Service, Accra.

Ghana Statistical Service, 2000. Ghana Living Standards Survey: Report of the Fourth Round (GLSS 4). Ghana Statistical Service, Accra.

Ghana Statistical Service, 2005. Population Data Analysis Reports. Socio-Economic and Demographic Trends Analysis. Vol. 1. Ghana Statistical Service, Accra.

Ghana Statistical Service, 2008. Ghana Living Standards Survey Report of the Fifth Round (GLSS 5). Ghana Statistical Service, Accra.

Ghana Statistical Service, 2013. Population & Housing Census: National Analytical Report. Ghana Statistical Service, Accra.

Ghana Statistical Service, 2014. Ghana Living Standards Survey (Round 6). Ghana Statistical Service, Accra.

Ghana Statistical Service, 2015a. Integrated Business Establishment Survey: National Employment Report. Ghana Statistical Service, Accra.

Ghana Statistical Service, 2015b. Integrated Business Establishment Survey: Summary Report. Ghana Statistical Service, Accra.

Ghana Statistical Service, 2016. 2015 Labour force report. Ghana Statistical Service, Accra.

Ghana Statistical Service, 2018. Ghana Living Standards Survey Round 7 Poverty Profile (2005 – 2017). Ghana Statistical Service, Accra.

Ghosh, J., 2020. Introduction to this volume.

Graham, Y., 1988. Ghana: the IMF's African success story, Race & Class 29 (1), 41–52.

Hall, R., Scoones, I., Tsikata, D., 2017. Plantations, outgrowers and commercial farming in Africa: agricultural commercialisation and implications for agrarian change. J. Peasant Stud. 44 (3), 515–537.

Haque, T., Bogoev, J., Smith, G., 2017. Push and Pull: Emerging Risks in Frontier Economy Access to International Capital Markets. The World Bank, Washington, DC MFM Discussion Paper No. 17.

Hart, K., 1973. Informal income opportunities and urban employment in Ghana. J. Mod. Afr. Stud. 11 (1), 61–89.

Hill, P., 1966. Landlords and brokers: a West African trading system (with a note on Kumasi Butchers). Cahiers d'études Africaines 6 (23), 349–366.

Honorati, M., de Silva, S. J., 2016. Expanding Job Opportunities in Ghana. World Bank, Washington, DC.

Institute for Fiscal Studies, 2015. Ghana: Impact of the Falling Crude Oil Prices. Occasional Paper No. 5. Institute of Fiscal Studies, Accra. Retrieved from http://ifsghana.org/wp-content/uploads/2015/12/Occasional-paper-No-5-Ghana-Impact-of-the-Falling-Crude-Oil-Prices-Sept-2015.pdf

International Labour Organization, 2002. Decent Work and the Informal Economy. Report VI. International Labour Organization, Geneva.

International Labour Organization, 2012. International Standard Classification of Occupations, vol. I. International Labour Organization, Geneva.

International Labour Organization, 2020. ILOSTAT database. Available from https://ilostat.ilo.org/data/

International Monetary Fund, 2015. IMF Country Report. Ghana. International Monetary Fund, Washington, DC.

Jerven, M., 2012. For richer, for poorer: GDP revisions and Africa's statistical tragedy. Afr. Affairs, 112, 138–147.

Kolavalli, S., Vigneri, M., 2011. Cocoa in Ghana: shaping the success of an economy. In: Chuhan-Pole, P., Angwafo, M. (Eds.), Yes Africa Can: Success Stories from a Dynamic Continent. The International Bank for Reconstruction and Development/The World Bank, Washington, DC, pp. 201–218.

Local Governance Act, 2016. Act 936. Ghana Publishing Company Limited, Accra.

Lyon, F., 2003. Trader associations and urban food systems in Ghana, institutionalist approaches to understanding urban collective action. Int. J. Urban Regional Res. 27 (1), 11–23.

Matenga, C. R., Hichaambwa, M., 2017. Impacts of land and agricultural commercialisation on local livelihoods in Zambia: evidence from three models. J. Peasant Stud. 44 (3), 574–593.

Minister for Finance, 2020. Statement to Parliament on Economic Impact of the Covid-19 Pandemic on the Economy of Ghana. Monday, 30th March, 2020. Submitted By Ken Ofori-Atta.

Ministry of Food and Agriculture, 2017. Planting for Food and Jobs: Strategic Plans for Implementation (2017-2020). Ministry of Food and Agriculture, Accra.

National Development Planning Commission, 2005. Ghana Poverty Reduction Strategy 2004 Annual Progress Report. National Development Planning Commission, Accra.

National Development Planning Commission, 2007. The Implementation of the Growth and Poverty Reduction Strategy (GPRS II) 2006-2009: 2006 Annual Progress Report. National Development Planning Commission, Accra.

National Development Planning Commission, 2017. An agenda for jobs: creating prosperity and equal opportunity for all (first step) 2018-2021. National Development Planning Commission, Accra.

NBSSI, 2020. Presidential Launch of Coronavirus Alleviation Programme (CAP) Business Support Scheme. Published on May 18, 2020. Retrieved on 16 June 2020 from https://nbssi.gov.gh/capsupport/presidential-launch-of-coronavirus-alleviation-programme-cap-business-support-scheme/

Norwood, C., 2011. Women, microcredit and family planning practices: a case study from rural Ghana. J. Asian African Stud. 46 (2), 169–183.

Oduro, A., Tsikata, D., 2020. Gender analysis of Ghana's COVID-19 response measures, Unpublished Report Prepared for NETRIGHT, Accra.

Overa, R., 2007. When men do women's work: structural adjustment, unemployment and changing gender relations in the informal economy of Accra, Ghana. J. Modern African Stud. 45 (4), 539–563.

Owusu, G., Lund, R., 2004. Markets and women's trade: exploring their role in district development in Ghana. Norwegian J. Geography 58 (3), 113–124.

Pape, J., 2000. Gender and Globalisation in South Africa: Some Preliminary Reflections on Working Women and Poverty. International Labour Resource and Information Group, Cape Town.

Plange, N. K., 1984. The colonial state in Northern Ghana: the political economy of pacification. Rev. African Polit. Econ. 11 (31), 29–43.

Robinson, E. J. Z., Kolavalli, S. L., 2010. The Case of Tomato in Ghana: Marketing. GSSP Working Paper No. 20. International Food Policy Research Institute, Accra.

Schindler, K., 2010. Credit for what? Informal credit as a coping strategy of market women in Northern Ghana. J. Dev. Stud. 46 (2), 234–253.

Shepherd, A. W., 2005. Associations of Market Traders. AGSF Occasional Paper 7. Food and Agriculture Organization, Rome.

Singh, S., 2002. Contracting out solutions: political economy of contract farming in the Indian Punjab. World Dev. 30 (9), 1621–1638.

Singh, S., 2003. Contract Farming in India: Impacts on Women and Child Workers. The Gatekeeper Series No. 111. International Institute for Environment, London.

Smalley, R. , 2013. Plantations, Contract Farming and Commercial Farming Areas in Africa: A Comparative Review. Working Paper No. 055.

Smith, J., 2016. Imperialism in the Century: Globalization, Super-Exploitation, and Capitalism's Final Crisis. Monthly Review Press, New York.

Solomon-Ayeh, B. E., King, R. S., Decardi-Nelson, I., 2011. Street vending and the use of urban public space in Kumasi, Ghana. The Ghana Surveyor 4 (1), 20–31.

Steel, W. F., Ujoranyi, T. D., Owusu, G., 2014. Why evictions do not deter street traders: Case study in Accra, Ghana. Ghana Soc. Sci. J. 11 (2), 52–76.

Terkper, S., 2019. Seth Terkper writes: banking sector reforms; high fiscal costs, lessons and alternatives. Retrieved from https://citinewsroom.com/2019/02/seth-terkper-writes-banking-sector-reforms-high-fiscal-costs-lessons-and-alternatives/

Teye, J., Yaro, J., Torvikey, G., 2016. Land and Agricultural Commercialisation in Ghana: Emerging Employment and Labour Relations. Paper prepared for presentation at the "2016 World Bank Conference on Land and Poverty," Washington, DC.

Torvikey, G. D., Yaro, J. A., Teye, J. K., 2016. Farm to factory gendered employment: the case of blue skies outgrower scheme in Ghana. Agrarian South: J. Polit. Econ. 5 (1), 77–97.

Tsikata, D., 2007. Women in Ghana at 50: still struggling to achieve full citizenship? Ghana Stud. 10 (2007), 163–206.

Tsikata, D., 2009. Informalization, the informal economy and urban women's livelihoods in Sub-Saharan Africa since the 1990s. In: Razavi, S. (Ed.), The Gendered impacts of liberalization: Towards "embedded liberalism"? Routledge, New York, pp. 131–162.

Vechbanyongratana, J., Yoon, Y., Kingsuwankul, S., Lekfuangfu, W. N., Pakampai, W., Tangtammaruk, P., 2020. Formalizing the informal economy in Thailand: a gender perspective.

Watanabe, K., Paiva, N. S., Lourenzani, A. E. B. S., 2017. Contract farming in Brazil – an approach to law and economics. Revista Direito GV 13, 95–122. doi: 10.1590/2317-6172201705.

Whitfield, L., 2005. Trustees of development from conditionality to governance: poverty reduction strategy papers in Ghana. J. Modern Afr. Stud. 43 (4), 641–664.

World Bank, 2011. Ghana looks to retool its economy as it reaches middle-income status. Retrieved July 15, 2018, from http://www.worldbank.org/en/news/feature/2011/07/18/ghana-looks-to-retool-its-economy-as-it-reaches-middle-income-status

World Bank, 2018. Project Paper on a Proposed Additional Financing and Restructuring in the Amount of SDR 34.8 Million (US$50 Million Equivalent) to the Republic of Ghana for a Ghana Commercial Agriculture Project. Report No. PAD2300.

World Bank, 2020. Ghana COVID-19 Emergency Preparedness and Response Project: Project Information Document (PID).

Wrigley-Asante, C., 2008. Men are poor but women are poorer: gendered poverty and survival strategies in the Dangme West District of Ghana. Norwegian J. Geography 62 (3), 161–170.

Yaro, J. A., Teye, J. K., Torvikey, G. D., 2017. Agricultural commercialisation models, agrarian dynamics and local development in Ghana. J. Peasant Stud. 44 (3), 538–554.

5

STRIVING FOR FORMALISATION

Gender and youth aspects of informal employment in Morocco

Mouna Cherkaoui and Taoufik Benkaraach

I Introduction

Informality is a complex phenomenon that is approached differently depending on whether one chooses to emphasise the informality of firms or to underline those that hold informal jobs. In this chapter, the emphasis is on informal employment, recognising that it can be found both in formal and informal enterprises.

Persons in informal employment include informal workers within and outside of the informal sector. The informally employed are those that hold a job that is not covered by national labour legislation such as minimum wages legislation, that does not provide social protection and entitlement to employment benefits such as sick leave or that is not the object of a contract. This makes the informally employed very vulnerable and reduces their ability to face numerous risks, including health and loss of employment risks. It also diminishes their aptitude to take advantage of the government programmes for social inclusion. Informal employment is often accepted as a last resort solution, when the workers loose hope of finding a formal job. Informal employment refers to different types of employees and employers: employees holding informal jobs in both formal and informal enterprises, employees informally employed by households as paid domestic workers, employers employed in their own informal sector enterprises, own-account workers, contributing family workers and members of informal producers' cooperatives. Informal employment includes wage and non-wage earners and full-time, temporary and part-time workers. It is measured in various ways. These comprise the share of unpaid employment, the share of self-employed as a share of total employment, the share of overall employment not contributing to social security and the share of employees without a contract.

As in many other developing economies, a large proportion of the Moroccan labour force holds informal jobs. The Moroccan labour market is segmented and wide differences in work conditions persist between public sector jobs, private sector formal jobs and private informal jobs. Within each group, there are wide divergences between men and women, between the young and the older people, between the educated and those with no or little education, between those living in rural areas and those in urban areas, between sectors of work etc. In Morocco, an Office for Economic Cooperation in the Mediterranean and the Middle East (OCEMO) survey on the expectations of young people in Morocco (2014) asserts that youth express a very strong expectation of better quality jobs. In total, 75 per cent of the young people surveyed say they want to access a job that opens rights to the social protection system.

This chapter will analyse the Moroccan labour market segmentation with an emphasis on differences between formal and informal employments of Moroccan men and women. It is argued that the Moroccan economy does not create enough employment opportunities for a growing labour force which pushes a large part of the job seekers into informal employment and that this is particularly true for women and the youth.

The chapter is organised as follows. Section II presents briefly the economic context in Morocco analysing the macroeconomic and labour market trends. The informal employment is studied using both the National Survey of the Informal Sector (NSIS) which covers only informal employment in the non-agricultural sector and the National Labour Force Surveys (NLFS) secondary data which deals with formal and informal employments in all sectors. Section III deals with policies and laws with respect to formalisation. It covers both the policies aiming at the formalisation of enterprises and the strategies, programmes and laws aiming at labour formalisation and adopted in Morocco in recent years. It reviews the National Employment Strategy (NES), the active employment programmes and specific laws focusing on the elements that denote a drive towards employment formalisation and that will impact formalisation cost. Section IV evaluates the impact and effectiveness of the various policies adopted. The active employment programmes outcome and the effects of two new laws (the domestic employment and the self-entrepreneurs' laws) are reviewed and analysed in light of their impact on formalisation. Because employment informality is particularly important for the youth, Section V uses the 2016 SAHWA survey data on young people's aged 15-29 to discuss men and women youth informal employment characteristics (considering the issues of values, gender, age, educational background, marital status and parental work status) and uses a logistic regression analysis to explore the effect of demographic and social factors on informal employment.

II Economic context

Macroeconomic trends

Both structural and sectoral reforms that give a greater role to market forces and that have as an ultimate objective to generate higher growth rates and increase job creation were adopted in Morocco. They led to some growth but could not create enough employment opportunities leading many job seekers into informal jobs. GDP in constant prices (national currency) annual growth rate in Morocco averaged 3.8 per cent from 2008 until 2018. The highest growth levels in the last decade were reached in 2008 with 5.92 per cent GDP growth and in 2011, with more than 5 per cent GDP growth. The lowest growth rates were registered in 2016 at 1.18 per cent. The growth was also below 3 per cent in 2014 and 2018. After 2008, the net debt started to increase again progressively and it remained around 65 per cent in 2016, 2017 and 2018. The budget deficit was equal to 3.7 per cent in 2018.

Growth is affected both by the drought and the economic situation of European countries. The drought impacts agricultural production which is still an important component of GDP despite a decline in its share of total production. The European economic situation affects Moroccan growth through its impact on Moroccan residents' remittances, foreign direct investments, exports and tourism. The impact of the 2008 crisis on the Moroccan economy highlighted its vulnerability to the economic situation in Europe and was analysed by a number of reports such as that of Institute Royal des Etudes Strategiques and the one by the Ministry in charge of Moroccan residing abroad.

Despite a stable macroeconomic environment, Moroccan growth is still considered by various observers as below the required level. Observers generally agree that growth in Morocco is not inclusive enough and concomitant with relatively high consumption inequalities and large regional disparities. Growth is still volatile; despite a reduction of volatility, there is highly dependence on agriculture and job creation is insufficient to create enough employment for a growing population. The overall unemployment rate increased between 2016 and 2017 from 9 per cent to 10.60 per cent and it declined between 2017 and 2018 from 10.6 per cent to 9.90 per cent. The youth unemployment rate already at 22.80 per cent in 2016 rose to 28 per cent in 2017 and declined slightly to 27.40 per cent in 2018.

TABLE 5.1 Real GDP growth, unemployment and youth unemployment in Morocco 2008-18

	Real GDP growth	Unemployment	Youth unemployment
2008	5.92	9.5	18.3
2009	4.24	9	17.9
2010	3.82	9.2	18.8
2011	5.25	8.5	18.2
2012	3.01	8.7	18.1
2013	4.54	9.5	19.6
2014	2.67	9.7	19.7
2015	4.55	9.2	20
2016	1.18	9	22.8
2017	4.09	10.6	28
2018	2.96	9.9	27.4

The economic reforms undertaken in Morocco include trade and financial liberalisation, fiscal reforms and sectoral policies. The economic liberalisation was accompanied by structural transformations of the economy with new sectors emerging such as agri-business, automotive, aeronautics and pharmaceuticals industries (Freund and Theodore, 2017).

Morocco in the last decade opened up to trade via tariff reforms and free trade agreements with various parts of the world and fostered economic liberalisation by reforming investment, competition policy and the exchange regime. Trade agreements concluded and implemented have a major impact on the economy. This openness resulted in an increase in the share of exports and imports as a percentage of GDP and in greater diversification in terms of markets and goods. In 2018, despite an increase in phosphate exports and automobile exports, the current account deficit as a percentage of GDP reached 5.9 per cent of GDP. This was due to an increase in imports (energy) and a decline in the remittances of Moroccans living abroad. In 2019, the current account deficit was expected to decrease.

Morocco also undertook to liberalise its financial sector. The reforms include consolidating the financial sector control and oversight framework, diversifying financial instruments, improving financial inclusion, positioning Casablanca Finance City as a regional and international financial hub and easing exchange control. The new status of Bank Al Maghrib (the Moroccan Central Bank) came into effect in July 2019. It aims to strengthen the independence of the Central Bank, increase its autonomy and expand its role. The exchange rate regime has also been relaxed. The Dirham can now fluctuate in both directions relative to its target rate and since January 2018, the band of fluctuation of the Dirham has been widened from ±0.3 per cent to ±2.5 per cent. Exchange rates have remained in the band of fluctuations without intervention of the central bank since March 2018.

The fiscal reform aims to insure the sustainability of public finances and debt. It gives priority to infrastructure, social development and social protection of vulnerable groups. In order to strengthen the efficiency and fairness of the tax system, the reforms seek a simplification of tax legislation, broadening the tax base, reducing marginal tax rates, improving compliance and reducing informality. A significant reform of the compensation was introduced since 2000. In 2015, the liquid petroleum products sector was liberalised. In 2019, only three products remain subsidised (butane gas, sugar and domestic wheat flour). In order to improve the coordination, effectiveness and targeting of social protection programmes, a social registry is being prepared. This unified national registry should facilitate the targeting of disadvantaged populations.

A number of structural reforms have helped improve the environment and the business climate. They focused on strengthening competition, modernising the legal and regulatory frameworks for businesses and fighting corruption. Morocco gained 55 rankings in the Doing Business indicators between 2011 (when it stood at 115 out of 183) and 2019 (the year where it is 60th out of 190). Improvements included starting a business, registering property, cross-border trade and resolving insolvency. A law passed in November 2018 also specifies that all the legal procedures for the creation of a business must be carried out electronically and an electronic platform for this purpose was created by the law in last January. The President and the Board of Directors of the Competition Council have been designated and the Council is now operational.

A number of sectoral policies in agriculture, industry, fisheries, tourism and digital transformation complemented the more global policies. The sectoral policies did not succeed in achieving their objectives in terms of job creation and the estimates regarding job creation of each sectoral policy given by their respective ministries are contradicted by the number of net job creation given by the statistical office.

Labour market trends

The labour market faces significant challenges: low labour force participation, underemployment, unemployment and informality affect both men and women but hurt particularly women and youth.

Labour market legislation

Several mechanisms aim to reduce distortions in the labour market. The most important is the labour code. The 2004 Labour Code introduced significant changes to individual labour relations (Kingdom of Morocco, 2004). These are as follows: the prohibition of forced labour, the elimination of all forms of discrimination between men and women in accordance with the principle of "equal work, equal pay," the increase in the age of admission to employment from 12 to 15, the prohibition of discrimination in employment, improvement of the legal and social situation of women, children at work and persons with disabilities, prohibition of unfair dismissal and determination of cases representing valid reasons for dismissal, the determination of the list of serious misconduct and the introduction of the obligation of the procedure of listening to the employee to enable him to defend himself in case of serious misconduct. The Labour Code provides in Sections 356 and 357 for the legal minimum wage, which may not be lower than the amounts fixed by regulation for agricultural and non-agricultural activities.

In addition to the labour code, the international conventions and charters ratified by the Kingdom are also a source of this law. In case of conflicts of laws, priority is given to the most advantageous provisions for employees. Morocco's labour regulations provide for different provisions for some sectors of activity. Employment in the public sector is governed by a 1958 decree specifying the general status of the civil service. Some sectors such as fisheries and public works have their own statuses.

The Labour Code does not cover domestic workers, who are covered by a law published in 2016 and implementing decrees published in 2017 that set out the model contract of employment and the list of prohibited tasks for domestic employees under 18 years of age. This law is discussed in more detail below. Workers in the informal sector are not covered by the provisions of the Labour Code. In the formal sector, hiring and firing procedures are relatively restrictive. Companies cannot terminate an employee's contract for economic reasons. The possibility of dismissing an employee exists only in the case where the worker commits a fault. The complexity and difficulty of dismissal has been advanced as one of the reasons for the low demand for labour.

The Moroccan system of labour inspection covers both the formal and informal employments. Labour inspectors are public officials who are responsible for monitoring the application of labour laws and regulations, providing information and technical advice to employers and employees, to bring to the attention of the governmental authority responsible for labour the shortcomings or overruns of legislative and regulatory provisions in force and to make attempts at conciliation in matters of individual and collective labour disputes. The labour inspectorate is part of the administrative structure of the deconcentrated and central services of the Ministry of Employment and Vocational Training. The Ministry of Labour is the central authority responsible for supervising the control of the labour inspectorate.

Employment in Morocco

The total population of Morocco reached 33.8 million individuals in 2016. Of these 10.6 million are employed, 1.1 million are unemployed and 22 million are inactive. This chapter focuses on the 10.6 million that are employed distinguishing the men and women formally employed from those in informal employment. Men represent the majority of the persons employed in Morocco; with 7.9 million men employed and only 2.7 million women in employment in 2016. The difference in the women and men employment is more striking in urban areas. A total of 5.4 million persons are employed in urban areas of which only 1 million are women, whereas 5.2 million persons are employed in rural areas of which 1.7 million are women.

There are striking differences between men and women. For the country as a whole, the employment rate reaches 64.5 per cent for men and only 21 per cent for women, a difference of 43.5 points. In urban areas, the difference is even larger and reaches 45.6 points with a men and women employment rate at, respectively, 58.5 per cent and 12.9 per cent. In the rural areas, it is lower and equal 40 points with men employment rate at 74 per cent and women employment rate at 34 per cent. The share of jobs that are held by women in 2016 was 25.9 per cent. It was higher in rural areas at 32.9 per cent and very low in urban areas at 19.2 per cent. This feminisation rate has steadily declined since 2006 when it was 28 per cent for the country as a whole (33.6 per cent in rural areas and 21.1 per cent in urban areas).

The employed are for a large part uneducated. In total, 60.4 per cent of the employed had no diploma in 2016. The uneducated represented 78.9 per cent of the labour force in rural areas and 42.5 per cent of the labour force in urban areas.

Young people represent a large part of the working population and in 2016, 41.7 per cent of the employment was detained by those aged 15-34. This rate was higher in rural areas at 46.4 per cent and lower in urban areas at 37.1 per cent. A significant share of youth is, however, neither in employment nor in education (NENE). In fact, 27.5 per cent of young people are not working and not being educated. The rate of youth NENE is almost four times higher for women (44 per cent) than for men (11.7 per cent).

The structure of employment by professional status shows that the employers represent a very small share of employment (2.4 per cent of individual are employers, 4 per cent in the urban areas and 0.7 per cent in rural areas). The employees account for 46.7 per cent of total employment, but this category is more present in the urban areas where it stands at 65.8 per cent of employment and modestly present in rural areas where the share of employees equal 26.9 per cent. The family help accounts for almost 20 per cent of employment and is mostly present in the rural areas (37.6 per cent) and relatively limited in urban areas (3 per cent). The self-employment is an important professional status overall (28.2 per cent) that is significant in both urban (23.9 per cent) and rural (32.6 per cent) areas.

The share of the employed labour force declined steadily in recent years. The share of persons in employment declined from 46.3 per cent in 2006 to 42 per cent in 2016. In the rural areas, the employment rate declined from 58.3 per cent in 2006 to 53.4 per cent in 2016. In urban areas, the employment rate dropped in recent years and reached 34.9 per cent in 2016.

The individuals working in the formal sector receive a wage that is at least equal to the minimum wage. The latter is set for the employees in the agricultural sector and for those in the industrial sector. It is regularly revised and has increased between 2010 and 2016 five times. It increased from 1,433 Moroccan dirhams in 2010 to 1,813 Moroccan dirhams in 2016 for agricultural workers and from 2032 Moroccan dirhams in 2010 to 2,571 Moroccan dirhams in 2016 for workers in the industry. In the public sector, wages are based on a collectively agreed wage structure for civil service positions. In the formal private sector, the wages are based on collective bargaining with social partners. In the informal sectors, wages are negotiated between the worker and the employer.

Wages in the private sector are freely determined but must comply with the legal requirements regarding minimum wages. According to a study by Angel-Urdinol et al. (2016), the labour regulations and particularly the minimum wage policy contribute to higher unemployment rates and limit formalisation in Morocco, especially for youth and women. We believe that a reduction of the minimum wage and payroll taxes would contribute to the formalisation of self-employed workers and to a decrease in unemployment.

Wage employment increased significantly overall and in both urban and rural areas between 2000 and 2016. Overall, wage employment increased from 37.7 per cent in 2000 to 46.7 per cent in 2016. The augmentation was from 61.6 per cent to 65.7 per cent in urban areas and from 17.2 to 26.9 per cent in rural areas.

Informal employment and surveys of informality

The Moroccan statistical office captures informality in two different ways. The first one is via a NSIS which surveys informal production units (IPUs) and which was conducted in 1999, 2007 and 2014. The second one is via the Labour Force Employment Survey conducted every year.

Informal employment in the NSIS

The NSIS defines the informal sector by the production units that do not keep accounts in accordance with the accounting regulation in force in Morocco. The NSIS distinguishes production units in the informal sector from "formal" economic units. This definition is adopted for the sake of consistency, in terms of the delimitation of economic agents and the comprehensiveness of economic aggregates. The complement of this sector is defined by all the units keeping accounts in accordance with the accounting regulations in force. Thus, all units not subject to this regulation belong to "households."

The 2013-14 NSIS covered the entire national territory (urban and rural) and all regions of the country and concerned all components of the informal sector. To account for seasonal variations, field data collection spanned a full year, from June 2013 to May 2014. The NSIS does not include the agricultural sector or the production of goods on their own account, and does not include domestic employment by households. The identification of IPU is conducted in two phases. First, a sample of IPUs is identified from the National Employment Survey and second, informal units are identified. In total, a representative sample of 10,085 IPUs was surveyed.

Over the period of the survey (June 2013–May 2014), the number of IPUs was estimated at 1.68 million units (Haut Commissariat au Plan). One of the main features of the informal sector is the dominance of one-person production units. In fact, three quarters of the units operating in the informal sector employ only one person and the average size of the informal units does not exceed 1.39 persons.

Micro units dominate all sectors of activity but units employing only one person represent 61 per cent of all units operating in the industrial sector, whereas they represent, respectively, 79.1 per cent, 77.8 per cent and 76.5 per cent of the total units in the construction, trade and services sectors. The resale sector remains the largest sector for these units; 50.6 per cent of informal units operate within commercial activity, 24.5 per cent of the IPU operate in the service sector and 16.2 per cent of IPU operate in the industry sector with a clear dominance of the textile, clothing, leather and footwear industries.

In 2014, the volume of employment in the non-agricultural informal sector was 2.3 million jobs with 1.6 million in urban areas and 631,671 in rural areas. In 2014, the contribution of informal sector employment to overall non-agricultural employment was 36.2 per cent.

Employment in the informal sector is not feminised. The share of women's informal employment in 2014 does not exceed 10.5 per cent compared to 17.4 per cent for overall non-agricultural employment. The strong presence of men is more marked in the construction sector where they represent 99.4 per cent of all workers and in the resale sector where they represent 93.3 per cent of workers. Women have a higher propensity to work in the industrial sector where they hold one in five jobs (20.1 per cent). For the services sector, they account for 13.7 per cent of total employment.

By age those that are informally employed are for a large part young individuals. Overall, 38.2 per cent of those working in the informal sector are less than 35 years old. The youth represent a larger share of informal employment in rural areas (41.9 per cent) compared to urban areas (36.9 per cent). The youth are more present in industry and public works at around 42 per cent than in trade and services at around 36 per cent.

Almost half of informal sector employment is concentrated in the trade sector (47 per cent), the rest of informal employment is distributed among services (24.1 per cent), industry (20.1 per cent) and construction (8.8 per cent).

The analysis of the structure of permanent employment of the informal sector by professional status indicates the predominance of self-employment. In total, 78.9 per cent of permanent workers in the informal sector are self-employed, 68 per cent are own account workers and 10.9 per cent are employers. The self-employed represent 77.4 per cent in urban areas and 83.0 per cent in rural areas. The number of wage earners was estimated at only 15.9 per cent of all permanent workers. The share of wage earners was higher in urban areas at 18.2 per cent compared to rural areas 9.7 per cent.

More than 50 per cent (58 per cent) of worker in informal non-agricultural employment work 48 hours or more per week. Only 11 per cent work less than 16 hours per week and 31.1 per cent work between 16 and 48 hours per week. A total of 65 per cent of workers work 21 days or more per month. Resale sector workers work more than the average workers which is at work for 48 hours per week. Their average weekly hours of work are 50.2 hours and their average monthly work is 23.2 days. The construction sector, on the contrary, is characterised by the shortest average number of hours of work. The building and civil engineering workers work an average of 43 hours a week and 18 days a month.

Informal employment in the NLFS

Informal employment in the NLFS is defined as the absence of affiliation to a social security system, the absence of a contract of employment, the absence of wages or a low quality of employment. Informal employment can prevail in the public sector (including government and local governments) or the private sector, in large or small firms.

Medical coverage

The NLFS provides data on the degree of work-related medical coverage of the Moroccan population. In 2016, 78.4 per cent of the employed aged 15 and more did not have medical coverage related to their job. The rate was similar for men and women and was equal to 78.2 per cent for men and 78.4 for men. In other words, less than a quarter of men and women employed had medical coverage related to their work. The availability of coverage depends on the professional status; 42 per cent of employees have medical coverage followed by employers at 26.2 per cent. It also varies by sector of activity; 38.5 per cent of those employed in the "industry including crafts" sector and 34.9 per cent among those in the "services" sector are covered. The rate is much lower in the "Housing and Public Works" sector at 11 per cent and in the "Agriculture, forestry and fisheries" at 5.7 per cent (Aaibid, 2018).

When one distinguishes between urban and rural areas, the absence of medical coverage is higher in rural areas where 92.8 per cent do not have access to work-related coverage and lower in urban areas at 64.6 per cent (In other words, less than 8 per cent of those working in rural areas and 35.4 per cent of those employed in urban areas had medical coverage in 2016.)

Retirement benefits

A study by the Haut-Commissariat au Plan (2019) based on employment surveys provides 2017 data on work-related retirement benefits. About one in five employees are covered by the pension system with large disparities depending on the place of residence, the sector of activity and the professional status; 20.9 per cent of employed individuals aged 15 and over are covered by a pension system. The rate of coverage by a pension system is similar for men and women with 20.5 per cent and 21.8 per cent covered, respectively. It is lower in rural areas (6 per cent) compared to urban areas (33 per cent).

The pension coverage increases with age. The share of the youth aged 15-29 that benefit from pension coverage is 13.2 per cent. The share of those aged 30 and over is 23.2 per cent. Pension coverage increases also for those that are more educated. Only 10.6 per cent of the non-degree holders are covered by pension, whereas 75.2 per cent of employees with a higher education degree are.

The sectors of "Industry including crafts" and "Services" have the highest pension coverage rates at 37.1 per cent and 32.9 per cent, respectively. The "Housing and Public Work" and "Agriculture, forestry and fishing" records the lowest pension coverage rates at 8.9 per cent and 4.5 per cent, respectively. According to professional status, nearly four in ten wage earners (39.5 per cent) and one in five employees (22.2 per cent) are affiliated to a pension system. The share of self-employed with pension coverage is only 2.4 per cent.

Contractual employment

According to the Haut-Commissariat au Plan (2019), more than six out of ten wage earners or 59.4 per cent do not have a contract that formalises their relationship with their employer. Of those that hold an employment contract (some 40 per cent of the employed), only 24 per cent have an indefinite-term contract, 8 per cent a fixed-term contract and 7.1 per cent of employees have a verbal contract. In 2018, the percentage of wage earners without a contract reached 79.7 per cent in rural areas compared to 52.1 per cent in urban areas. This share increases from 48.8 per cent among women to 62.1 per cent among men.

Young people and non-graduates remain the categories that are the most affected by non-contractual employment. Young people under the age of 25 are the most concerned by work without a contract, 88.8 per cent of them do not hold a contract. The share of employees aged 45 and over that are working without a contract is lower and reaches 54.3 per cent. The one that hold a higher education degree are the most likely to be protected against precarious employment. Only 22.8 per cent of those with higher education work without a contract against 79.2 per cent of those with no diploma.

Wage employment

According to the Haut-Commissariat au Plan (2019), about one in six (16.4 per cent) of the active workers are in unpaid work. This rate is higher in rural areas at 33 per cent and lower in urban areas at 3 per cent. Unpaid employment is particularly important among women. Almost 39.3 per cent of employed women worked without pay in 2018 compared to only 9.5 per cent of men. The unpaid work is even higher among rural women where 70.5 per cent of them work without remuneration. Unpaid employment is also more prevalent among youth; 45.5 per cent of young people under 25 are unpaid workers, whereas 11.2 per cent of adults aged 45 and over are unpaid workers. Holding a diploma protects somewhat from unpaid employment; 9.9 per cent of graduates are employed without pay when the share of non-graduates without pay is 21.2 per cent.

The share of paid employment has increased since 2014 especially in rural areas. It was equal to 77.5 per cent in 2014 and reached 83.4 per cent in 2016. The progress was particularly important in the rural areas where paid employment rose from 58.4 per cent in 2014 to 66.5 per cent in 2016. For those that receive wages, the prevalence of low wages in 2016 is 20.1 per cent. However, women are more likely to receive low wages. The prevalence of low wages is 18.8 per cent for men and 27.4 per cent for women. Those working in urban areas are surprisingly more likely to suffer from low wages and excessive work time.

III Policies with respect to formalisation

Policies towards the formalisation of enterprises

The informal sector (undeclared and unprotected economic activities) continues to play an important role in the Moroccan economy.[1] Public authorities, aware of the extent of the informal economy and its impact on state taxation, the competitiveness of formal enterprises and the quality and stability of employment, have raised the level of integration and formalisation of the informal economy as a national priority and strategic objective. Accompanying programmes do not only concern the formalisation of informal actors, but also the support and capacity building of the most fragile entities [self-entrepreneurs, very small enterprise and small and medium enterprises (SMEs)] to prevent their sliding towards the informal sector.

One of the first laws in favour of financial and economic inclusion and the integration of the informal sector is law 18-97 relating to microcredit (modified by law 85-18). This law aims, in addition to the restructuring and professionalisation of the microcredit sector, to improve the access of very small enterprises (VSE) to financing in order to facilitate their growth and sustainability. It also provides financial support to self-employed persons in the informal sector and to income-generating activities with a view to formalisation. The 13 microcredit associations are governed by the law of microcredit and play an important role in social and financial inclusion in both urban and rural areas. These associations are the bridge between national and international donors and beneficiaries of microcredits who are often in the informal sector and thus excluded from the banking sector. The microcredit associations are perceived, by a broad category of actors, as a way of moving from the informal to the formal sector. However, their low territorial coverage and lack of innovation does not sufficiently support the standard need for formalisation and limit their capacity to increase inclusion.

More recently, several other state and private initiatives have emerged as part of programmes to support entrepreneurship and the integration of the informal sector. The most important are those included in the strategic orientations of the industrial acceleration plan (2014-20). They include measures to help business creation and promote the status of self-entrepreneurs. The objective is the modernisation of microenterprise and the strengthening of their capacity. In this context, the status of self-entrepreneur (which will be discussed in more details below) aims to promote the spirit of entrepreneurship and the creation of formal jobs. The self-employed benefit from very simplified administrative procedures and are enrolled in the social security system provided for by the legislation and regulations in force. It is therefore an important initiative to mainstream informal employment in the formal sector and to promote economic and social inclusion. The "Dar AL Moukawil" web platform created in 2016 by the Attijariwafa Bank aims to support the initiative of self-entrepreneurship by making it easier for self-entrepreneurs and VSE to encourage their transition to the formal environment.

On the financing side, the state has put in place several financing instruments[2] for the integration of the informal sector, some of which are part of sectoral development plans. The objectives assigned to these state programmes are the sensitisation and the reinforcement of the communication, with the carriers of project and the promoters, on the public financial assistance intended for the self-entrepreneurs and the SMEs, with regard to financing, loan, grant or guarantee. Among the 11 structures identified in 2018, the most visible are the Central Guarantee Fund (CGF) and Morocco National Agency for the Promotion of Small and Medium Enterprises (NAPSME). The NAPSME was created in 2002 to support SMEs, this agency has expanded its support field since 2015[3] to integrate VSEs and auto-entrepreneurs. The CGF was established in 1949. It is an important state actor in the field of facilitation of investment financing and social development. Since 2009, it has been the reference institution in the national guarantee system for SMEs. One of the roles assigned to the CGF is to accompany the VSEs to avoid their sliding in the informal economy and to insure they remain formal.

Policies and laws towards worker's formalisation

The NES

The 2015-25 National employment Strategy (NES) of Morocco clearly identifies informality and gender discrimination as important aspects of the Moroccan labour market. NES targets workers in microenterprises and the informal economy, women subject to inactivity and discrimination in employment, young graduates exposed to long-term unemployment and young people who have dropped out of school early and face precarious work.

The main objective of the NES is to promote decent employment through productive and quality job creating growth, increasing the participation of young people and women in the labour market, strengthening equality in access to employment and the reduction of territorial disparities in employment. In order to concretely promote productive and decent employment in Morocco, the NES is structured around a set of objectives that include the extension of social protection to all workers and the reduction of gender inequalities through education and training.

In order to ensure social equity, NES advocates for greater inclusion of young people in employment and a reduction of gender discrimination. This requires a greater openness of the employment structures of large companies and SMEs to integrate young people with high qualifications, an upgrading of small enterprises which are the main employment area for early school leavers and the strengthening of employability and entrepreneurship programmes. The NES also advocates the correction of gender inequalities which requires improving women's employability, reducing gender discrimination, helping inactive women find jobs and improving industrial competitiveness, which is a significant factor in the employment of inactive women. The NES also recommends the reduction of territorial disparities of employment and the management of the migratory phenomenon for professional purposes.

A number of measures recommended by the NES aim at making labour formalisation less costly. Many of them led to specific programmes that will be discussed in the next section. The recommendations of the NES include the promotion of employment, human capital enhancement and insuring the effectiveness of active employment programmes. These measures are directed towards both the firm and the employees. They are, for the most part, directed towards reducing the cost of formalisation for either the firm, the employee or both. The employment promotion aims to support the microenterprises and the self-entrepreneurs through facilities provided to the firm. The human capital enhancement aspect targets the employees and aims at facilitating training, reducing the burden of job loss, improving intermediation and expanding medical and social security coverage. The strengthening of active promotion programmes affects both the firms and the employees by reinforcing intermediation and encouraging paid employment.

Within the job creation promotion objective, various initiatives are called for. They include support to the transition of VSEs to formality through fiscal incentives, support of the law on self-entrepreneurs and of the microenterprise development strategy and the establishment of a programme to upgrade small trades. To support the law of self-entrepreneur and the micro business, the NES recommends helping formal VSEs in their development and emergence through tax incentives, facilitation of procedures, financial measures and other forms of support. It also endorses the encouragement of "visible units" in the process of formalisation and restructuring so as to access the advantages reserved for formalised structures. In order to upgrade small trades, the NES calls for the creation of a mechanism to analyse and monitor productive practices towards the informal economy and to identify activities where innovations are available and can be disseminated and strengthened and for the provision of training of micro-entrepreneurs.

Under the enhancement of human capital, the NES calls for the qualification of the labour force and the enhancement of social protection of workers through the consolidation of the national social protection floor and the extension of social protection. To promote the female labour force, NES recommends mobilising the female labour force through the strengthening of training, setting up a specific programme supported by intermediation services and improving the conditions of women employment and combating gender discrimination.

To reform and extend social insurance schemes, the NES proposes to extend the scope of social security to uncovered populations. In particular, it calls for the provision of medical coverage for the population, extend access to a pension plan for all workers, extend family benefits to uncovered populations, extend the benefits of the National Social Security regime to the shipping and coastal fishing industry, as well as domestic workers, and expanding the scope of benefits, by consolidating the compensation system for job loss and unemployment insurance.

The NES aims to improve the effectiveness of active employment programmes by consolidating and developing employment promotion schemes and strengthening labour market intermediation by developing services for jobseekers and employers. In order to reinforce the incentives for salaried employment, the NES proposes to partially or totally reduce the social security contributions of certain companies, to improve the mechanism of the Integration Contract and to develop a support system for employment of people with special needs. The NES also aims at improving employability and proposes to consolidate and improve hiring training schemes and expand employability enhancement schemes to new categories. In order to support self-employment and local employment initiatives, the NES proposes to support integration through self-employment and support territorial initiatives to promote employment.

Active employment programmes

Active employment programmes take the form of two different schemes. The first one gives incentives to firms to hire job seekers through exemptions from tax and social charges or both and the second provides training that enhances job seekers' skills and improve their employability. To some extent, the first scheme reduces the cost of formality for firms hiring workers. The second, although emphasising the employee, reduces the cost of formal employment both to the firm and the employee.

A large number of active employment programmes have been introduced since 2005. These include programmes to encourage youth formal private sector employment. Many programmes aim at encouraging wage formal employment such as the IDMAJ and the TAHFIZ programmes. The TAEHIL programme is another programme introduced in 2006 with three components: qualifying training for reconversion, contractualised training for employment and the support system for emerging sectors. To encourage self-employment through the creation of microenterprises, the MOUKAWALATI programme was set up in 2006. Other employment programmes with more specific objectives were also introduced. IKRAM 1 and IKRAM 2, MINAJLIKI and WADIYATI are specifically geared towards women. ISTIAAB focuses on the integration of informal activities into the formal economy. MOUBADARA seeks to reinforce employment in the social economy. Finally, TAATIR seeks to requalify those that have been unemployed for a long period of time.

To promote wage employment, the Ministry of labour first introduced in 2006 the IDMAJ programme and then the TAHFIZ programme in 2015. The IDMAJ programme includes three components: the social security coverage by the state and the professional integration contract. It aims to facilitate the transition of youth from school to work through placements in firms. The IDMAJ programme gives the youth graduating from the university, the vocational training or who have just finished high school the opportunity to acquire a first work experience within a private enterprise and it provides the enterprise the opportunity to hire young graduates without supporting all the wage costs. Social security coverage was introduced in 2011. It ensures social coverage for beneficiaries of training-insertion contracts by the state. If the beneficiary is recruited under a contract of indefinite duration, the state pays the employer's share for one year. Individual private enterprises and legal persons operating engaged in a craft, agricultural, commercial, industrial, service or property development activity as well as associations, affiliated to the National Social Security Fund/Caisse Nationale de Sécurité Sociale (CNSS) and who recruit bachelors and graduates of higher education or vocational training enrolled in National Agency for Employment and Skills/Agence Nationale de Promotion de l'Emploi et des Compétences (ANAPEC), are exempt from the contributions to the CNSS and from the vocational training and income tax during the duration of the internship. The professional integration contract was also introduced in 2011. It aims to promote decent employment, by allowing job seekers for more than one year who hold university degrees regardless of their training field and to the holders of a diploma encountering specific difficulties, to integrate the job market and to gain access to a first job. The objective is to allow job seekers, registered at ANAPEC and holding at least a secondary education, vocational training or higher education, to acquire the necessary skills to fill an identified job and, therefore, improve their employability. The state assists firms and local, regional or sectoral professional associations under private law by contributing to the financing of training. An integration allowance of 25,000 dirhams is paid by the state to the firm if a contract of indefinite duration is signed at the end of the internship period.

The TAHFIZ programme, introduced in 2015, aims to encourage firms and associations to hire job seekers on permanent contracts. The firms and associations created between 2015 and the end of 2019 and hiring job seekers on permanent employment contract within 24 month following the date at which they have been created can benefit from public support. This support takes the form of an exemption of social security contributions and an exemption from income tax for 24 months, for a gross salary of up to 10,000 dirhams per month. The benefits are granted within the limit of ten employees (since January 2018) recruited by the firm or association.

The TAEHIL programme, introduced in 2006, aims to increase employability through contractual training for job seekers registered with ANAPEC and having at least been in high school or having graduated from vocational training or university and who have been selected to be recruited by a firm or association. The job seeker acquires training required for an existing job and the firm or association is able to recruit profiles that it has difficulty finding. It is declined under two components: contractual training for employment or retraining and training for emerging sectors. This programme includes tailor-made training courses to help job seekers acquire the skills they need to take on some identified jobs, skills training or retraining to facilitate the integration of young people with integration difficulties by acquiring skills and adapting their profiles to the needs of the job market and training focused on emerging sectors.

The MOUKAWALATI programme aims to help graduates aged 29-45 with projects costing less than 250,000 dirhams. The programme supports entrepreneurs with business creation projects and also aims at ensuring the sustainability of the regional economic fabric through a monitoring system of newly created companies during the start-up period. Project holders are graduates or those with at least a basic education certificate, who have received qualifying training from one of the specialised training institutions. The state provides a guarantee of 85 per cent of the project loans and gives an interest-free advance representing 10 per cent of the investment and up to a limit of 15,000 dirhams repayable over six years including three grace periods.

Women and active employment programmes

A government national plan for gender equality called Ikram has been adopted by the government. It is declined in two phases. The first phase of the plan (Ikram 1) lasted between 2012 and 2016 and the second one (Ikram 2) is to be conducted between 2017 and 2021. These plans for gender equality are the framework of the different initiatives aiming at gender equality. The objectives of Ikram 1 were to combat all forms of discrimination and violence against women, to fight women poverty and precariousness, to promote the rights of older women and women with disabilities, to promote equitable access to decision-making positions and equal opportunities in the labour market. Ikram 2 emphasises women economic empowerment in order to promote women's rights and equal opportunities for men and women in the labour market.

Wad3éyati is a project aiming at gender equality in the workplace. It is a project funded by the Office of Trade and Labour Affairs of the Department of United States Work (USDOL). The project spans over the 2013-16 period. The overall objective of the project is to help improve the equality of men and women in the workplace in Morocco in terms of hiring, promoting and training in companies and communities targeted. It also aims to improve the conditions for women's access and retention at work. The objectives of the project are to provide support to enterprises in order to improve gender equality in the workplace with respect to hiring, promotion and training and to facilitate women's economic participation by improving infrastructure in selected communities.

Laws aiming at formalisation in specific sectors

1. The domestic employment law

The Moroccan Law on domestic workers, Law 19-12, sets the conditions of work and employment of domestic workers and was adopted in August 2016 and entered into force in August 2017. An application Decree of the Law (Decree n° 2-17-356) was adopted in September 2017. It completes the list of jobs in which it is forbidden to employ domestic workers between 16 and 18 years of age. Another Decree (Decree n° 2-17 355) published in August 2017 specifies the model of the contract of employment of the domestic worker.

The number of domestic workers in Morocco is not known with precision. Some institutions estimate the domestic population between 100,000 and 200,000 employees, others speak of a million or even 2 million domestic employees. Morocco has more than 7 million households and the use of domestic workers does not apply only to wealthy families. Domestic employment in Morocco is highly feminised.

The Labour Code, which came into force in 2004, does not cover domestic workers. Entry into force of Law 19-12 in October 2018, published in the Official Bulletin in August 2016. The law deals with domestic workers but also drivers, caretakers, gardeners, etc. The three decrees of application published in the Official Bulletin in October 2017 provide that their entry into force will take place one year after their publication. They set the model of employment contract and the list of tasks prohibited to those under 18 years.

An employment contract must be signed and legalised by both parties in triplicate, including one for the labour inspector. For workers under 18, a written authorisation from the guardian must accompany the contract. The work of persons between the ages of 16 and 18 is authorised by law for a transitional period of five years. The contract must specify if it is a fixed-term contract or one with unlimited duration. It also must state the nature of the work (cleaning, childcare, home help for the elderly, sick or disabled, driver, gardener, caretaker, etc.) and it must stipulate the trial period which is fixed at 15 days for both types of contacts. It must give the number of weekly hours of work which according to the law have to be limited to 48 hours per week maximum for the over 18 years of age, and to 40 hours per week maximum for those whose age varies between 16 and 18 years. The contract has to state the salary which must be equal to at least 60 per cent of the minimum wage (which is 13.46 dirhams per hour). That's about 1,550 dirhams per month for a full-time employee.

Under the law, the domestic employee is entitled to a minimum of 24 continuous hours weekly rest every week. In the case of an employee who continues to work after a period of pregnancy, a daily rest of one hour for 12 consecutive months is added to the weekly rest. The employee is also entitled to annual leave after six months of work and to holidays and leave for family reasons. The annual leave is calculated at the rate of one and a half days per month worked.

In the event of dismissal, the worker is entitled to compensation if he has worked for at least one continuous year on behalf of the same employer. The amount of the indemnity increases according to the duration of the work on behalf of the same employer, which is equivalent to: 96 hours of remuneration, for the duration of the actual work recorded during the first five years; 144 hours of remuneration, for the actual working hours recorded during the period from the 6th to the 10th year and 192 hours of pay, for the actual working time recorded during the period from 11th to 15th year.

Sanctions are provided if the employer does not respect the signed contract. If the employee is deprived of his/her leave and rest periods, the employer risks paying a fine ranging from 500 to 2,000 dirhams. Any breach of the employment contract gives rise to a fine of 3,000 to 5,000 dirhams for the employer. The contract must clearly include the employee's declaration of willingness to perform domestic duties on behalf of the employer. The employer faces a fine of 25,000-30,000 dirhams if he forces a person to work for him and a prison sentence of one to three months if there is a second offence.

A number of tasks deemed dangerous are prohibited to persons under 18 years of age. For example, it is prohibited that a domestic employee under 18 handle household products and other detergents containing hazardous chemicals, use electrical or cutting equipment, iron the clothes; provide care and handle medicated products, to remain close to a family member suffering from a contagious disease, drive any machine, even those that do not require a license, handle chemicals, insecticides and other products considered dangerous and keep the house. Failure to comply with these provisions exposes the employer to 25,000-30,000 dirhams of fine. In the event of a second offence, the penalties are either doubled or converted to prison term (one to three months).

2 The law on self-entrepreneurs

The Moroccan Law no. 114-13 dealing with the status of the self-entrepreneur was adopted in March 2015. It is accompanied by three application decrees. These are Decree No. 2-15-263 of April 2015 fixing the list of professions excluded from the statute of the auto-entrepreneur, Decree No. 2-15-257 fixing the composition and functioning of the national committee of the auto-entrepreneur, Decree n°2-15-258 of 10/04/15 relating to the modalities of registration in the national register of the self-entrepreneur and Ministerial Decree no. 151809 and 151810 June 2015 dealing with the time taken to examine applications for registration and the models of registration forms. Other legislative document dealing with this statute include article 5 of the Budget Law No. 43-06 for fiscal year 2007 establishing the General Tax Code and Article 6-I of the Budget law for the year 2015.

The creation of a legal and fiscal statute dedicated to self-entrepreneurs aims to reduce informal activities, develop the entrepreneurial spirit and facilitate access to the labour market through employment. The status of self-entrepreneur is open to any individual exercising an industrial, commercial or craft activity or service provider, whose annual turnover received does not exceed 500,000 dirhams for industrial, commercial and craft activities and 200,000 for service providers (the turnover should not exceed the above threshold for two consecutive years). It is accessible to both self-employed entrepreneurs who belong to the social security system and to self-employed persons registered in the national register of the self-entrepreneur.

The law gives a number of advantages to self-entrepreneurs. To begin with, they are exempt from the obligation to register in the commercial register and from the requirement to keep an extensive accounting. They have the possibility of domiciling their business in their residence or in premises operated jointly by several companies, they obtain social coverage from the date of registration to the National Register of the Auto-entrepreneur (NRAE) and they receive a number of fiscal advantages. For the self-entrepreneur, the value added tax does not apply. The income tax is only applicable to the turnover received but at very low rate (Direction Générale de l'Impôt 2018, Regime Fiscal de l'Auto-entrepreneur, Direction générale des Impots Edition 2018) 1 per cent on the amount not exceeding 500,000 dirhams for commercial, industrial and artisanal activities and 2 per cent on the amount not exceeding 200,000 dirhams for services). The self-entrepreneur is also exempt from business tax for five years from the date of the beginning of activity. The net capital gains are taxable according to the terms and the rates of the general tax code. The amount of tax payable by self-employed taxpayers is paid at the level of one of Barid Bank's branches before the end of the month following the quarter in which the turnover has been cashed.

The self-entrepreneurs also benefit from procedures that are significantly simplified. The self-entrepreneur needs to register at the NRAE. The registration procedure only includes three steps. The self-entrepreneur needs to complete the registration request via the NRAE portal, remove and sign the application and deposit it at Barid Al Maghrib's partner bank counter (within 30 days of the application on the portal). Once registered with the NRAE, the self-entrepreneur is given a common company identifier, the tax identifier and the identification number to the business tax.

The radiation or the write-off from the self-entrepreneur scheme is also kept very simple. It occurs on request of the interested party and deposited at the Barid Al Maghrib counter, in case of non-declaration of turnover, in case of transformation to another regime or status or in the event of non-payment of social and tax contributions.

Other policies of formalisation

Health insurance

The compulsory health insurance scheme (AMO) covers all or part of the costs of illness, accidents and maternity for insured persons and their family members. The Compulsory Health Insurance Plan is financed by the levy of contributions on income. Basic medical coverage applies to employees and pensioners in the public sector [National Fund of Social Welfare Organizations (CNOPS: Caisse Nationale des Organismes de Prevoyance Sociale)] and of the private sectors (CNSS). Since 2012, the medical assistance scheme called RAMED benefits poor and vulnerable people.

The CNOPS manages the compulsory health insurance (AMO) for the public sector in accordance with the provisions of Law 65-00. The CNSS (Caisse

Nationale de Securité Sociale) is a public institution that manages the mandatory social security scheme for all private sector formal employees in Morocco. The CNSS is under the administrative supervision of the Ministry of Employment. It is responsible for family allowances, short-term benefits (daily benefits in case of sickness or accidents, occupational diseases, daily allowances in case of maternity and allowance in the event of death) and long-term benefits (pensions and disability and survivor's pensions).

This Medical Assistance Plan (Regime d'Assistance Medicale: RAMED) is based on the principles of social assistance and national solidarity for the benefit of the poor. It allows an economically disadvantaged population to benefit from basic medical coverage that provides free medical care and services available in public hospitals, health centres and health services under the state both in the event of illness, emergency or during hospitalisation. In this context, mechanisms for allocating this right are well defined to identify beneficiaries and effectively target the neediest households. Eligibility is achieved through the granting of a family card with a three-year eligibility period giving entitlement to healthcare according to a well-defined basket of care.

To be eligible for RAMED, applicants must meet certain conditions. They must not benefit from any compulsory health insurance scheme either as insured persons or as entitled persons and must be recognised on the basis of some pre-established eligibility criteria based on the place of residence (urban or rural) that they do not have sufficient resources to meet the costs of care. In urban areas, they must have an annual income of less than 5,650 dirhams per person in the household, after weighting of the declared income, including transfers, by household socio-economic variables and having a score of socio-economic conditions (based on living conditions of the household) below a certain threshold. In rural areas, applicants must have a patrimonial score, calculated on the basis of all the elements constituting their assets, below a certain threshold per person in the household and also have a score of household living conditions below a certain level. These criteria define whether the candidate is poor or vulnerable. "Poor" households receive the RAMED card free of charge, while "vulnerable" households must pay an annual contribution of 120 dirhams per person, within the limit of 600 dirhams per household and per year.

In 2013, one year after its launch, RAMED covered nearly 3,320,000 people and more than 6,540,000 in 2014, a doubling from one year to the next. As of 30 November 2016, the cumulative number of registered persons has grown to more than 10 million since the beginning of the process, more than 4 million households, including 6,345,525 people with active cards (Observatoire National du Développement Humain, 2017). Moving away from the informal sector and to a formal sector that pays minimum wages or even below minimum wages (for domestic employees for example) implies giving up the RAMED because eligibility would be lost based on income.

The pension system

The pension system covers the risks of loss of income due to old age, disability that is not caused by an accident at work and death. The pension system in Morocco is characterised by its fragmentation with several schemes for different categories of workers and with different methods of financing, calculation of benefits and conditions of grant. The pension scheme for civil and military officials is administered by the Moroccan Pensioners' Fund. Pensions for private sector workers are managed by the CNSS, a public institution under the supervision of the Ministry of Employment and Social Affairs. The Collective Retirement Allowance Plan manages pensions for non-state employees and local authorities and all employees of public institutions subject to financial control of the State. The Moroccan Inter-Professional Retirement Fund, managed by an employers' association, is an optional pension plan open to CNSS members.

Family allowances are exclusively financed by the employer. Family allowances are paid by the state and form part of the remuneration for public sector employees, corresponding to 8.1 per cent of the salary of the public sector employees. The CNSS pays family allowances for private sector employees.

Benefits for loss of employment

The unemployed can receive a loss of employment benefit (IPE) for up to six months and trainings support by ANAPEC and the OFPPT (Office de la Formation Professionnelle et de la Promotion du Travail) to help them re-enter the labour market. The loss of employment compensation was instituted in 2014. The purpose of this compensation for loss of employment (IPE) is to allow a person insured by the CNSS to be compensated for six months for loss of employment. It corresponds to 70 per cent of the salary obtained by the insured during the last 36 months of his activity. The monthly amount of compensation cannot exceed the amount of the legal minimum wage.

IV The impact and effectiveness of formalisation policies

The impact of active employment programmes

There are some 20,000 beneficiaries of the TAEHIL programme every year. Since its introduction in April 2016 and up to January 2017, the TAHFIZ programme generated 2,235 Protocol TAHFIZ which benefited 705 enterprises. From January 2017 to December 2017, the programme generated 3,211 Protocol TAHFIZ to the benefice of 1,450 Enterprises.

Data on the percentage of women beneficiaries of the active employment programme indicates that the TAEHIL programme is the one that has the largest share of women beneficiaries followed by the IDMAJ programme. A total of 65

TABLE 5.2 Women beneficiaries of the active employment programmes in 2016

Programmes	Beneficiaries	Percentage of women
IDMAJ	75613	48
TAHFIZ	2235	34
TAEHIL	16542	65
MOUKAWALATI	1904	25

Source: Observatoire National du Marché du Travail, Les initiatives récentes pour favoriser l'autonomisation économique des femmes. Le Monde du Travail Bulletin Mensuel du Ministère de l'Emploi et des Affaires Sociales. Numéro 15, Avril 2017.

per cent of the 2016 beneficiaries of the TAEHIL programme are women and almost 50 per cent of the 2016 IDMAJ beneficiaries are women. The MOUK-AWALATI programme or self-employment programme (auto-emploi) shows the lowest share of women at 25 per cent indicating that few women create their own business. The TAHFIZ programme benefits a smaller share of women at 34 per cent.

The Min Ajliki programme is a Belgo-Moroccan programme to support women's entrepreneurship, the first phase of which spans the 2013-16 period. The project aims to promote Moroccan women by affirming their skills and their ability to enrich and develop the economic network. Support is provided to women who wish to enter the entrepreneurship sector, women entrepreneurs already entrepreneurs and women who wish to enter the formal sector. The results achieved by the programme indicate that 18,769 women were sensitised to entrepreneurship, 10,000 were trained and 5,000 were accompanied in the creation of their businesses. A total of 150 projects were incubated in business incubators. Min Ajliki 2 targets both women and men and spans from 2017 to 2021.

Impact of employment programmes on formalization

The evaluation of active employment policies implemented in Morocco remains insufficient and has only a limited influence on public decision-making (Ministère de l'Emploi et des affaires sociales, 2014). However, programme evaluations have been carried out both in terms of realising the quantitative objectives, in terms of integration indicators and in terms of the impact on the career paths of jobseekers. The main results of its evaluations indicate that these programmes do help formalisation for at least a limited number of job seekers (Observatoire National du Marché du Travail, 2017).

The impacts in terms of integration for TAEHIL and IDMAJ were studied on the basis of several methods by the National Observatory of Employment (Observatoire National du Marché du Travail, 2017). These methods include the overlap between the beneficiaries' files (based on ANAPEC data) and the salary declaration files (based on the CNSS), the conduct of follow-up surveys of the beneficiaries of the TAEHIL and IDMAJ programmes and the completion of a survey on the integration pathways of IDMAJ beneficiaries.

The overlap between the beneficiaries' files and the salary declaration files

The inclusion of the beneficiaries of the IDMAJ over the period 2003 to 2008 (updates of this work have been done but are not public) indicate that two-thirds of the beneficiaries of an integration contract are declared to the CNSS. Insertion rates are 65 per cent for higher education graduates, 64 per cent for vocational training graduates and 59 per cent for bachelor graduates (Observatoire National du Marché du Travail, 2017).

Recipient tracking surveys

A survey of IDMAJ beneficiaries conducted in 2009 on a sample of 7,200 job seekers showed that 64 per cent of the beneficiaries of an integration contract have completed their internship at the host company, 83 per cent of those that completed their internship obtain a job in the host company, 80 per cent of job seekers that benefited from the IDMAJ programme have managed to enter the job market and 66 per cent of them have a permanent job contract.

A survey of 2,227 beneficiaries of the TAEHIL programme conducted in 2009 indicates that 35 per cent of beneficiaries of qualifying training or retraining have a paid activity after training, against 70 per cent for the contractual training for employment; 87 per cent of those that were recruited following a contractual training for employment were inserted in less than three months after the training against 56 per cent for the qualifying training or retraining; 83 per cent of those surveyed are generally satisfied with contractual training for employment, compared to 68 per cent of the qualifying training or retraining.

Evaluation of career paths

The IDMAJ programme (Morocco) has also been subject to an impact assessment using monitoring and evaluation methodologies and techniques. The methodology used for the IDMAJ evaluation was based on a statistical survey of 3,000 job seekers; 2,500 jobseekers who participated in IDMAJ, as well as a control group of 500 jobseekers who did not participate in IDMAJ. Firms using the programme (300 companies) were also questioned. Three populations were interviewed: beneficiary job seekers, eligible jobseekers that were not beneficiaries of the programme and companies that used the programme. The main results of this study were cited by Recotillet (2016). The comparison of the employment rate between the reference and the control group indicates a difference of ten points for the benefit of the beneficiaries. The insertion rate of beneficiaries of the IDMAJ programme exceeded 40 per cent at the end of the integration contract and 75 per cent after about 12 months of completion of the integration contract, 63 per cent of them signed a permanent contract. The IDMAJ programme has also reduced the average duration for obtaining sustainable employment: 3.7 months for beneficiaries at the end of the IDMAJ integration contract compared with 12.8 months for job seekers who have not benefited of the IDMAJ programme. Participation in this integration contract has an impact on other integration in-dicators, such as salary, the type of work contract, access to social security cover. The IDMAJ programme has had a positive impact on the quality of the job found.

The impact of the laws aiming at formalisation on specific sectors

Effectiveness of the law on formalising domestic employment

The three implementing regulations of the domestic employees Act, 19-12, which came into force in early October 2018, include the publication in the Bulletin Officiel (BO) of the decree setting out the model employment contract and the one setting out the list of tasks prohibited for the employees under 18 years and a draft decree 2.18.686, setting the conditions of application of the social protection system for the benefit of domestic workers. The Governing Council, meeting 10 January 2019, adopted the draft decree 2.18.686, fixing the conditions of appli-cation of the system of social protection for the profit of the domestic workers. As long as the decree concerning the subjection of domestic employees to the CNSS has not been published in the Official Bulletin, it cannot be applied. The draft decree will first have to be published in the Official Bulletin so that the CNSS can launch the first integration operations.

Today, approximately 300 employment contracts linking a domestic employee to his/her employer have been filed. This number is slightly higher than in mid-December 2018. This particularly low figure comes for a large part from foreign employers residing in Morocco. Domestic workers are reluctant to sign em-ployment contracts. In the case of domestic employees, there is reluctance and wait-and-see attitude by employers and mistrust of employees. Many domestic workers refuse to sign their contract and move from the informal to the formal type of employment. One of the reason is the fear to lose the RAMED discussed above. Employees are also concerned that signing the contract will engage them, and prevent them from quitting their jobs at any time. The role of intermediaries in the hesitation of employees to sign an employment contract was mentioned. In fact, the income of intermediaries (Semsara) is based on the turnover of domestic employees and would be reduced by a greater stability of the situation of domestic employees. The lack of information of the employees was also presented as a possible explanation of the lack of interest for signing a contract which appeared at first very advantageous.

The draft decree 2.18.686 sets the conditions for the application of the social security scheme to domestic workers. This text aims to strengthen the social protection rights of this category, through the determination of the conditions allowing them to benefit from the services of the social security and the basic medical coverage. The draft decree defines the conditions of registration of domestic workers at the CNSS, as well as the conditions of affiliation of their employers to the fund, besides the measures that the CNSS must take in the cases of non-affiliation of an employer or non-registration of domestic workers. The said project also fixes the basis for calculating the contributions due to the CNSS.

Law 19-12, the main purpose of which is to allow full social security coverage for domestic workers, is struggling to gain public support and have a significant impact on domestic workers. Law 19-12 in fact obliges the house employer and his employee to unite under a clearly defined and established contract of employment. However, the scope of this law is greatly diminished by the lack of application of the provisions allowing affiliation to the CNSS of the house employer and registration at the same fund of his employee. Despite the adoption of the draft decree 2.18.686, fixing the conditions of application of the social protection system for the benefit of the domestic workers, by the Government Council, the fact that it has not yet been published, prevents the law 19-12 to have a real impact. This delay in the publication in the Official Bulletin of the draft decree 2.18.686 is explained by the constitution of a working group within the executive body which aims to amend several provisions considered by the Government as too complex for its applicability. Amongst the changes contemplated is first of all the desire to postpone its entry into force and the idea that the employee must pay the contributions to the CNSS, the employer's burden being paid directly by the employer, with the employee's obligation to pay his dues to the CNSS.

After the publication of the draft decree in the Official Bulletin, the CNSS will be able to start integrating domestic employees. It is expected that the affiliation will allow the employee to access social benefits from the CNSS which are both short-term benefits and long-term benefits. The long-term benefits will cost 11.89 per cent of the salary of which two-thirds will be borne by the employer and one-third by the employee. In the event of an accident at work, a disability pension will be paid to the beneficiary. Beneficiaries will also be entitled to retirement and survivor's pension. Family allowances, taxed at 6.4 per cent of the salary and at the expense of the employer will be paid according to the number of children of the employee. The short-term benefits will cost 1.57 per cent of the salary and will also be borne by both parties, two-thirds will be borne by the employer and one-third by the employee. The CNSS also provided for the reimbursement of medical expenses as well as the payment of sick leave benefits. The health insurance will be applied at the rate of 6.37 per cent of salary: 4.52 per cent paid equally between the contractor and the contracted and 1.85 per cent paid by the employee. And in case of delivery, the daily allowance is scheduled for 14 weeks.

Even before it could start, the formalisation of domestic employment was delayed and complicated by the non-publication of the draft decree 2.18.686. Other issues might arise from the fact that the domestic employment law only seem to address one type of domestically employed person. As Mechouat (2017) mentions, there are different categories of domestic workers. Her study distinguishes four categories. The first category includes women who permanently live with their employers and work without remuneration and only receive food, clothing and on occasion limited amount of money. The women in this category are sometimes relatives of their employers. The second category includes women who work for a monthly wage well below the minimum wage. These women, often young, do not always negotiate or receive the wage that can be given directly to their parents. The negotiation can be conducted by a broker (Semsar) who sets wage and work conditions. The third category is comprised of women that hire themselves out for a day from a well-designed place called the Mouqaf. The fourth category receives a weekly or monthly wage for a whole day of cleaning. It will be difficult to ascertain the rights of the women relatives working as domestic employees or to give even 60 per cent of the minimum wage to domestic employees living outside the major cities.

Effectiveness of the law on self-entrepreneurs at formalisation

The objective of the Law on the status of self-employed is to encourage self-entrepreneurs to enter the formal sector through, eventually, provision of social security. This law hopes to reduce the role of the informal economy by making business creation easier and cheaper through legal, fiscal and social benefits and by extension creating formal jobs. This status of the auto-entrepreneur has attracted a large number of candidates. The aim of the self-entrepreneur status was to have 100,000 self-employed entrepreneurs between 2017 and 2020. The self-employed population reached 86,169 persons in 2019 which is below target. According to the tax department, 27,109 people gained self- entrepreneur status in 2018, an increase of 46 per cent over 2017.

The status is attractive especially for young people. Indeed, more than half of self-entrepreneurs are between 15 and 34 years old. Two-thirds are men and one-third are women. In general, 40 per cent of self-employed entrepreneurs are in commerce and 32 per cent in services. Auto-entrepreneurs have the option of not having a dedicated premise. As a result, more than half of the registered self-entrepreneurs practise from their homes and 84 per cent work permanently. While the Law on self-entrepreneurs alone is not sufficient to significantly reduce informality, it has given the opportunity to many to formalise their activity.

V Youth and informal employment

This section is based on the results of a survey of youth carries out by SAHWA, a research project on Arab Mediterranean Youth. Its aim is to study youth prospects and perspectives in a context of multiple social, economic and political transitions in five Arab Mediterranean countries (Morocco, Algeria, Tunisia, Egypt and Lebanon). The Moroccan part of the youth survey was carried out amongst 1,854 young people in Morocco of which 1,207 are men and 647 are women in 2016. The questionnaire covers a wide range of research questions. These include questions concerning education, employment and social inclusion, political mobilisation and participation, culture and values, international migration and mobility and gender.

The set of variables provided in the survey allows us to investigate a series of issues. First, it allows us to explore men and women youth informal employment characteristics. In doing this, we start by looking at the "work values" that men and women have in both formal and informal contexts. The hypothesis to be verified here is that those working in the informal employment tend to have more conservative values and to be less supportive of women work and empowerment when compared with those working in formal employment. We then analyse the extent of informality by gender, by age, by area of residency, by various measures of educational backgrounds, by marital status and by the parental work status. Second, the data permit us to investigate the implications of informality both in terms of job satisfaction and in terms of remuneration. Third, we examine the mobility between work status and the extent to which the respondents were aware of the employment formalisation programmes discussed above. In this study, we are interested in the comparison between those in the formal and informal employments. Formality and informality are measured in two different ways in the survey. First, one can consider those employed and having social security related to their work as formally employed and those employed without benefitting from social security as informally employed. Another possible measure, not used in this chapter, is given by data on contract availability.

Using availability of social security as an indication of formality, there were 473 persons employed, 21 per cent being formally employed and 79 per cent informally employed. Among the 473 employed persons, 379 are men (of which 22 per cent being formally employed and 78 per cent informally employed) and 94 are women (of which 15 per cent being formally employed and 85 per cent informally employed).

The survey identified several characteristics of youth in formal and informal employments, including work values. The results on values were separated in two groups: those that deal directly with employment and those that are indirectly related to work. The results were somewhat surprising, showing that differences in "values" were stronger by work status than by gender. Furthermore, men in the formal and informal sectors showed similar values, whereas the values of women in formal and informal employments were quite different. The differences between men and women were smaller with respect to work but wider on issues indirectly linked to employment.

There was a significant difference between genders regarding whether men and women should be given same job opportunities and salaries; 74 per cent of women and only 65 per cent of men agreed that men and women should be given the same job opportunities and salaries, a difference of 9 percentage points. Similarly, more men (64 per cent) than women (61 per cent) agreed that men should have more right to a job in case of job scarcity, but the difference was smaller. Men were still believed to be the main provider in the family by both men and women: 70 per cent of men and 67 per cent of women agreed with this.

There were some differences between those in formal and informal employments regarding whether men and women should be given same job opportunities and salaries; 73 per cent of formally employed youth and 65 per cent of informally employed agreed that men and women should be given the same job opportunities and salaries. Similarly, 68 per cent of formally employed and 62 per cent of informally employed agreed that men should have more right to a job in case of job scarcity. Men were widely believed to be the main providers in the family by the majority of the workers, whether in formal employment (71 per cent) or informal employment (69 per cent). A total of 86 per cent of formally employed women and 73 per cent of informally employed women agreed that men and women should be given the same job opportunities and salaries, a 13 percentage point difference. There was also a 21 percentage point difference between formally and informally employed women about whether men should have more right to a job in case of job scarcity; 79 per cent of the women with a formal job and 58 per cent of the women with an informal job believed that men should be given priority in employment. Men were still widely believed to be the main provider in the family by the majority of the women formal workers (71 per cent) and women informal workers (69 per cent).

The differences between men and women and between those in formal and informal employments were larger with respect to issues indirectly related to work, that is, those that influence job opportunities and real participation in the job market such as the importance of education, whether similar upbringing should be given for boys and girls, whether women should be authorised to travel alone and whether men should be contributing to housework.

The SAHWA survey suggests that the informally employed represent 87 per cent of young workers in rural areas and 74 per cent of young workers in urban areas. Informality among young female workers in rural areas was as high as 97 per cent, and in urban areas it was lower but still 78 per cent. For young male workers, the ratio was 84 per cent in rural areas and 72 per cent in urban areas.

It is already evident that the youth are more likely to be informally employed than older workers. The survey found that formal employment shares among the youth population increase with age, from 14 per cent in the 15-17 years age group to 20 per cent for 18-22 years, 21 per cent for 23-26 years and 24 per cent for 27-29 years. However, the results do not hold for female taken separately.

It is generally expected also that more education leads to a greater probability of obtaining a formal job. In Morocco, it seems that only higher education protects young workers from informality. Primary, middle and secondary education show similar shares of formal employment at around 18 per cent, whereas 52 per cent of the youth with higher (tertiary) education had formal jobs. It is possible that workers with higher education probably find formal employment in the public sector, which questions the ability of the private sector ability to create jobs for youth. Higher education protects both men and women from being informally employed but is more important for women.

Two other aspects of education were investigated. It was found that being in the private school increased the chance of being formally employed, but this was true mainly for men. Men who attended private schools had more chance of being formally employed (33 per cent) compared to men who attended government schools (25 per cent). This was true for women but to a smaller extent: 25 per cent of women who attended private schools were formally employed compared to 19 per cent for women who attended government schools. The language of schooling used also had some impact, but it was small and worked only for men. 37 per cent of youth educated in French medium were formally employed compared to 23 per cent of youth with Arabic as the medium of instruction. Men who studied using French as the main language had significantly more chances of being formally employed (41 per cent) compared to men schooled in Arabic (23 per cent). The reverse held for women. Only 17 per cent of women who were schooled in French medium were formally employed compared to 20 per cent of women who studied using Arabic as the main language.

Informality was common among both married (89 per cent) and unmarried young workers (83 per cent). Informality was less common among male married workers (72 per cent) compared to single male workers (81 per cent). Informality was also less widespread among female young workers who were married (67 per cent) compared to single female workers (80 per cent).

The idea of intergenerational links in employment formality is based on the intuition that people working in the formal sector benefit from a network of relations that are likely to provide information's on job openings, are also more aware of the requirements for getting a job in the formal sector and accordingly better prepare their children to obtain these jobs. The parent holding a formal job increased the probability that the person's employment would be formal rather than informal. This held true for both men and women, but the mother's job status has more influence on women's job status, indicating that formally employed women could act as role models for their daughters. The share of youth in formal employment increased from 16 per cent when the father was not insured by social security to 41 per cent when he was insured. For male workers, it rose from 17 per cent to 43 per cent and for women, it increased from 10 per cent to 33 per cent. The share of youth in formal employment increased from 18 per cent when the mother was not insured by social security to 56 per cent when she was insured. For male workers, it rose from 20 per cent to 53 per cent and for women grew from 8 per cent to 64 per cent.

The average wage of informally employed youth (2,314 dirhams per month) was lower than that of formally employed youth (3,150 dirhams per month). The difference was even larger for the previous month's average wage.

Overall, formally employed youth were mostly satisfied (54 per cent) or very satisfied (36 per cent) with their jobs. Only 10 per cent were either dissatisfied (5 per cent) or very dissatisfied (5 per cent) with their job; 31 per cent of the informally employed declared being dissatisfied (22 per cent) or very dissatisfied (9 per cent) with their job. Women formally employed youth were particularly satisfied (79 per cent) or very satisfied (14 per cent) with their jobs. Only 7 per cent of the formally employed women were dissatisfied (7 per cent) and none was very dissatisfied with their job. By contrast, 20 per cent of informally employed women and 8 per cent were very dissatisfied with their job. For formally employed male youth, 49 per cent were satisfied and 40 per cent were very satisfied. Only 5 per cent of formally employed young men were dissatisfied and 6 per cent very dissatisfied with their job. Among informally employed young women, 22 per cent were dissatisfied and 8 per cent very dissatisfied with their job.

As expected, the level of awareness of active employment programmes was higher for those in formal employment. The employment programmes discussed above have been at the beginning targeting the job seekers with at least high school degrees, as well as graduates of vocational education schools and university graduates.

We use data from the Sahwa survey to undertake a logistic regression analysis in order to explore the effects of a set of variables on youth informal employment. The dependent variable is a measure of informality defined as the job not being insured by the social security system. We seek to evaluate and quantify the chance of being in the informal sector, based on the explanatory variables. These variables consist of the following[4]: gender, education level, marital status, age, place of residency, father insured by social security, job position and sector of activity. These variables stem from the descriptive statistics discussed above. We expect that a number of characteristics such as being a woman, single, young, rural, having a father working without social security, being a temporary worker, being in some specific sectors such as construction increase the chance of informality.

A simple logistic regression model with eight qualitative variables is tested. The dependent variable informal employment being binary, the required model is a simple logistic regression. The analysis included 471 individuals. All the independent variables are significantly correlated with the dependant variable. However, and because of the potential correlations between them, some explanatory variables were excluded from the final logistic regression model. The Chi-2 test goes in the same direction and approves the existence of a significant association between the dependant and independent variables.

The results of the analysis are given in Tables 5.3 and 5.4. The results are mostly as expected. A woman is 2.8 times more likely to be in the informal sector than a man. All the levels of education reduce the likelihood of being in informal employment compared to no education at all. Those that have a father working in a job with social security insurance are 2.4 times more likely to be in formal employment. The likelihood of being informally employed decreases when one works in the industrial or health services sector. Compared to the employer only the permanent employment increases the likelihood of being formally employed. Those that are single are more likely to be informally employed compared to the married ones. We expected that the likelihood of being

TABLE 5.3 Logistic regression model of informal employment

Youth characteristics	Odds ratio
Urban/Rural	
Rural	1.631
Urban	I
Gender	
Female	(★★) 2.881
Male	I
Education	
Pre-school	0.53
Primary	(★★) 0.274
Middle	0.648
Secondary	(★) 0.480
Higher	(★★) 0.264
No education	I
Parents Social Security Insurance	
Father no insured by Social security	(★★) 2.495
Father insured by Social security	I
Activity sector	
Industry	0.783
Building and public works/construction	(★★) 5.475
Health services	0.544
Education	1.648
Trade	(★★) 2.422
Other commercial services	(★★) 2.686
Administration, non-commercial services	1.182
Agriculture	I
Age	
Agé entre 22 ans et 29 ans	1.245
Agé entre 15 ans et 22 ans	I
Job position	
Permanent employed	(★★) .394
Temporary employed	(★) 1.848
Apprentice	1.807
Others (family support,…)	1.627
Employer/Self-employed	I
Marital Status	
Single	1.648
Divorced/Separated/Widow(er)	0.407
Married	I

(★) Significant at 10 per cent (sig < 0,1), (★★) Significant at 5 per cent (sig < 0,05)

formally employed increase with age, which is not the case here; but distinguishing those that are 15-22 from those that are 22-29 appears not to be significant (Table 5.3).

Table 5.4 gives the results of a model that retains the most important variables. These are gender, father insured by social security, sector activity

TABLE 5.4 Final logistic regression model of informal employment

	Odds ratio
Sex	
Female	(**) 2.296
Male	I
Activity sector	
Industry	(*) 0.503
Building and public works/construction	(*) 4.168
Health services	0.323
Education	1.141
Trade	(**) 1.819
Other commercial services	(**) 2.163
Administration. non-commercial services	0.778
Agriculture	I
Father Work Status	
Father insured by SS	(**) 3.448
Father not insured by SS	I
Job position	
permanent	(**) 0.382
temporary	(**) 2.106
Apprentice	1.984
Others (family support. ..)	1.461
Employer/Self-employed	I

(*) Significant at 10 per cent (sig < 0,1); (**) Significant at 5 per cent (sig < 0,05)

and the job position held. In this final model, the four explanatory variables are all significant and the statistics of adequacy and strength of association are all acceptable in particular the Hosmer and Lemeshow test. A woman is 2.3 times more likely to be in the informal sector compared to men. Being in the construction, trade and other commercial services gives you a larger likelihood of being informally employed compared to agriculture. Working in the industry makes more likely to be formally employed. If your father has social security, you are 3.4 times more likely to work formally. If you are a temporary employee, you are 2 times more likely to be informally employed.

VI Conclusion

A wide range of policies of economic and trade liberalisation were adopted in Morocco during the last two decades. They succeeded in achieving growth but they did not create the type of growth that is capable of generating sufficient employment for a growing population where youth represents a large share. Sectoral policies that lacked both a time framework and overall coherence were introduced, each setting its own ambitious goals of employment creation that for the most part remained unrealised. There are important differences in the structure and evolution through time of the population between men and women and between young and older people. There are also differences in the mobility of labour across type of employment status. Women are more likely to move towards more unfavourable status such as informal and unprotected employments and men are more likely to move to more favourable status. Whether measured by the lack of work-related medical coverage, the absence of pension, the nonexistence of a contract or by the fact that work is unpaid, informal employment is highly prevalent among both men and women and particularly dominant among the youth.

Significant efforts have been devoted to attempt to reduce informality among Moroccan workers. The elaboration of an employment strategy did help to identify the issues at stake and it defined a strategy that seeks to promote decent employment, enhance human capital and insure active employment programme effectiveness. When studying the active employment programmes, it was found that well-designed active employment programme can help secure employment to a number of job seekers. However, it was also found that the more educated have a higher likelihood of benefitting from these programmes and that women can be relegated to the least interesting programmes. The active employment programmes in Morocco provide incentives to firms to provide job seekers with formal employment. The incentives include tax and social charges exemption or both and training of job seekers. These programmes have been evaluated using different methods by the Ministry of Employment. Quantitative measures of beneficiaries highlight the share of women beneficiaries in each programme. The women usually are not in the programmes that have the highest likelihood of employment generation. The career evaluation path based on a comparison of a group of beneficiaries of a programme and a control group of no beneficiaries indicated that the IDMAJ programme, for example, had a positive impact on insertion but also on time delay before finding employment, on salaries, on social security and on the type of contract obtained.

When studying two laws seeking employment formalisation, it was found that promulgating the law is not sufficient to ensure that a given category of workers will move from informal to formal jobs. In the case of the domestic employment law, we show that its formalisation impact was delayed by the non-publication of the decree concerning the conditions of application of social security, the surprising reluctance of domestic workers to sign contracts, the possible resistance of the domestic employee's intermediaries through disinformation and the fact that domestic workers are not a homogeneous group. Furthermore, having to renounce to the RAMED might appear too costly to RAMED recipient who might prefer to keep it and stay informal. In the case of self-entrepreneurs, despite the numerous advantages and procedure simplifications introduced by the law and despite some success, the objective in terms of the self-entrepreneurs interested by this status was not achieved.

The analysis of youth in informal employment gives somewhat surprising results because the differences in "values" are stronger when different work status are considered than when gender is taken into account. Agreements or disagreements with statements dealing with whether men and women should be given the same job opportunities and salaries, whether men should have more right to a job in case of job scarcity, whether men should be the main provider and whether married women should work outside the house are rather similar between men and women but are quite different among women formally and informally employed and slightly different between formally and informally employed men. It was also found that the questions directly related to work do not indicate wide differences between men and women but that questions indirectly related to work do. Questions that deal with the importance of education, whether similar upbringing should be given for boys and girls, whether women should be authorised to travel alone and whether men should be contributing to housework seem more controversial.

At the aggregate level, the share of young female workers who were informally employed was higher than that of young male workers. The informally employed represent a higher percentage of young workers residing in rural areas compared to young workers residing in urban areas. The young rural female workers were almost all informally employed (97 per cent). Formal employment in the youth population increases with age and education. The type of education received also seemed to matter in terms of access to formal jobs: attending private school increased the chance of being formally employed and studying in the French language increased the chance of men being formally employed. Parental job status was a good predictor of formal versus informal employment among youth. The fact that the father or mother held a formal job increased the probability that the person's employment would be formal. This held true for both men and women. However, the mother's job status had more influence on both sons and daughters. The average wage of informally employed youth was significantly lower than that of the formally employed youth. Overall, formally employed youth were for the most part satisfied or very satisfied with their jobs. The level of awareness of active employment programme was higher for those in formal employment.

The regression analysis supports these results and allows us to identify the most pressing issues. The issue of informality is more important for women, for some sectors in the economy such as construction and trade, for some type of employment such as temporary employment and for the most vulnerable such as the families where the household providers works informally.

Notes

1 According to the CGEM survey, "The informal economy: Impacts on the competitiveness of enterprises and proposals for integration measures," carried out in 2014 and published in 2018, the informal sector weighs more than 20 per cent non-agricultural GDP and employs 2.4 million people.
2 "Annual compilation of public funding instruments and programmes for Startup and TPME," Ministry of Economy and Finance, Kingdom of Morocco, 2018.
3 2015-2020 programme contract between the State and Maroc PME. signed on 13 July 2015. Its roadmap aims to promote entrepreneurship, job creation and inclusive growth.
4 Gender (Male and Female); education level (No education, Pre-School, Primary, Middle, Secondary and Higher Education); marital Status (Married, Single, Divorced/

Separated/Widow); age (Aged between 15 and 22 years old, Aged between 22 and 29 years of age; place of residency (Urban, Rural); father Insured by social security, job position (employer/self-employed, permanent contract, temporary contract, apprentice, others such as family support; sector of activity (Agriculture, Industry, Building and public works, Health services, Education; Trade, Other Commercial Services, Administration, non-commercial services).

Bibliography

Aaibid, M., 2018. La protection sociale selon les données de l'enquête nationale sur l'emploi, Les Brefs du Plan, N°. 6, 11 novembre 2018, HCP.

Angel-Urdinola, D. F., Barry, A. G., Guennouni, J., 2016. Are Minimum Wages and Payroll Taxes a Constraint to the Creation of Formal Jobs in Morocco? Policy Research Working Papers No. 7808 World Bank.

Angel-Urdinola, D. F., Kuddo, A., 2010. Key Characteristics of Employment Regulation in the Middle East and North Africa. Social Protection Discussion Paper No. 55674. The World Bank, Washington, DC.

Aujourdhui le Maroc, 2019. Personnel domestique: L'immatriculation à la CNSS obligatoire, février 09, 2019. aujourdhui.ma.

Ben Amar K ., 2019. Voici Où En Est La Nouvelle Loi Sur Le Travail Domestique, le 05 Mars 2019. http://m.le360.ma/societe/exclusif-voici-ou-en-est-la-nouvelle-loi-sur-le-travail-domestique-185315.

Bureau International du Travail, Ministère de l'Emploi et des affaires sociales, Agence Espagnole de Coopération pour le Développement, 2014. Etude de diagnostic sur la situation de l'emploi au Maroc, Préalable A La Formulation De La Stratégie Nationale de L'Emploi, Rapport Global.

Crétois, J., 2019. Maroc: le parquet veut faire appliquer la nouvelle loi sur le travail domestique 02 Janvier 2019, Jeune Afrique. www.jeuneafrique.com

Dassouli, A., 2019. Pourquoi la Loi sur les travailleurs domestiques n'est pas appliquée La Tribune, 22 Mai 2019. https://Int.ma/loi-travailleurs-domestiques-nest-appliquée/.

Freund,C.,Theodore, M., 2017.Multinational Investors as Export Superstars: How Emerging-Markets Governments Can Reshape Comparative Advantage. Working Paper. Peterson Institute for International Economics.

Hassan, E. A., 2019. Auto-entrepreneuriat: Le statut a du mal à séduire Par Hassan EL ARIF | Edition N°: 5424 Le 03/01/2019. https://www.leconomiste.com/article/1038819-auto-entrepreneuriat-le-statut-du-mal-seduire.

Haut-Commissariat au Plan, 2019. Note du Haut-Commissariat au Plan Relative aux Principales Caractéristiques de la Population Active Occupée en 2018. www.hcp.ma

Hosmer, D. W., Lemeshow, S., 1989. Applied Logistic Regression. John Wiley & Sons, Inc., New York.

ILO, 2015. La Stratégie Nationale Pour L'emploi Du Royaume Du Maroc Document De Synthèse. www.ilo.org wcms_420201.pdf.

Infomédiaire, 2019. Travailleurs domestiques: Le Maroc applique un régime de sécurité sociale. https://www.infomediaire.net/travailleurs-domestiques-le-maroc-applique-un-regime-de-securite-sociale/.

Kingdom of Morocco, 2004. Labor Code of the Kingdom of Morocco: Law Number 65-99.

Lagtati, K., La loi n° 114-13 relative au statut de l'autoentrepreneur Un texte situé à l'intersection de problématiques juridiques, sociales et fiscales. Revue Marocaine de la Prospective en Sciences de Gestion, n1 May 2018. http://revue.imist.ma/ndex.php/RMPSG/article/view/12421.

Le Boursier, 2019. Loi sur les travailleurs domestiques: la surprenante résistance des employés de maison, 22 Janvier 2019. http://www.leboursier.ma/Actu/3609/2019/01/22/loi-sur-les-travailleurs-domestiques-la-surpenante-resitance-des-employes-de-maison.html.

Mechouat, K., 2017. Moroccan women in the domestic services sector: recognizing the unrecognized: Fez as a case study. Eur. Sci. J. 13 (17), http://dx.doi.org/10.19044/esj.2017.v13n17p17

Media 24, 2019. Immatriculation du personnel de-maison a la CNSS: Voici le detail du projet de decret. https://www.medias24.com/MAROC/SOCIETE/188944-Immatriculation-du-personnel-de-maison-a-la-CNSS-Voici-le-detail-du-projet-de-decret.htm.

Observatoire National du Développement Humain, 2017. Évaluation du Régime d'Assistance Médicale (RAMED) Rapport. www.ondh.ma rapport_ramed_fr.pdf.

Observatoire National du Marché du Travail, 2017. Les initiatives récentes pour favoriser l'autonomisation économique des femmes. Le Monde du Travail Bulletin Mensuel du Ministère de l'Emploi et des Affaires Sociales. Numéro 15, Avril 2017.

OCEMO, 2014. Enquête OCEMO sur les attentes de la Jeunesse—premiers enseignements. http://www.academia.edu/22192740/ENQUÊTE_OCEMO.

Ouraich, I., Tyner, W., 2018. Moroccan agriculture, climate change, and the Moroccan Green Plan: a CGE analysis. AfJARE 13 (4), 307-330.

Présentation Min Ajliki - Centre Mohammed VI, www.cm6microfinance.ma/wpcontent/uploads/2018/.../Présentation-Min-Ajliki.pdf.

Recotillet, I., 2016. Promouvoir le suivi et l'évaluation de programmemes actifs pour l'emploi comme un objectif stratégique dans la région MENA.

Royaume du Maroc, Ministère de l'Emploi, Bilan Social 2015, 2017 et 2018.

Shehu, E., Nilsson, B., 2014. Informal employment among youth: evidence from 20 school-to-work transition surveys February 2014, Youth Employment Programmeme, Employment Policy Department, Work4Youth Publication Series No. 8 ILO.

6

THE SOCIO-ECONOMIC COMPLEXITIES OF FORMALISATION OF WOMEN'S EMPLOYMENT IN THAILAND

Jessica Vechbanyongratana, Yong Yoon, Warn Nuarpear Lekfuangfu and Peera Tangtammaruk

I Introduction

Thailand's economy has undergone a process of serious structural transformation that began in the 1960s. The government has made concerted efforts to develop the non-agricultural sectors of the economy by encouraging, for example, the development of the domestic automobile and textile industries in the late-1960s and 1970s, enacting market liberalisation policies and further actively attracting foreign direct investment in the 1980s and 1990s. Concerted efforts at developing the tourism industry and other services have also been made in the 1990s and 2000s. As such, Thailand experienced a steep decline in the agricultural share of gross domestic product (GDP) from 45 per cent to 10 per cent and a steady increase in the non-agricultural share of GDP from 55 per cent to 90 per cent between 1950 and 2015 (National Economic and Social Development Council, 2019).

Despite the modernisation of the economy and the government's attempts to formalise businesses and jobs, the pace of employment formalisation in Thailand—where formal employment is defined as having employer-provided social insurance and protections under the labour law—has been slow. As of 2016, about 70 per cent of the overall workforce remains informally employed. While most informal workers are own-account workers, 35 per cent of workers in an employee relationship (private firm workers and government employees) remain informally employed. Unemployment in Thailand has remained perennially low, hovering between 1 and 2 per cent over the last decade, while the labour market remains especially tight in manufacturing and other sectors dominated by lower skilled jobs. Given this, it is puzzling as to why informal employment persists, that is, why do so many workers choose informal employment when plenty of formal jobs are available?

This chapter explores various facets of informal work in Thailand. The chapter starts with a summary of Thailand's economy and labour market trends over the past few decades. The following section summarises various policies implemented by the Thai government aimed at formalising enterprises and employment, as well as social protection policies aimed at covering those workers who remain outside the formal employment system, and potential gendered consequences of such policies. Case studies on three sectors—domestic work and cleaning services, sex work, and manufacturing—all of which have high levels of women's employment and informality, is then discussed. The discussions are meant not only to explore differences between formal and informal work within each sector, but also to explore reasons why workers may prefer informal work even when formal work may be available. We close the chapter with a discussion about the gendered aspects of work formalisation and policy implications in the Thai context.

II Thailand's economic context

Macroeconomic trends

Efforts by the government to attract and promote industry during the 1980s and 1990s were largely successful. As shown in Figure 6.1, the share of GDP attributed to agriculture declined from 29 per cent in 1969 to about 8 per cent by 2018. In contrast, manufacturing grew rapidly, with the manufacturing share of GDP overtaking agriculture by 1981 and peaking at 31 per cent in 2010. The share of services to GDP has grown rapidly since 2010 and stands at 57 per cent in 2018. Annual real GDP growth has averaged 5 per cent over the period of 1990 and 2017, with real GDP (2015 baht) reaching 15,253,661 million baht (US$464,382 million) in 2017, when per capita real GDP (2015 baht) stood at 225,466 baht (US$6,864) per person, making Thailand an upper middle-income country (National Economic and Social Development Board, 2017; World Bank, 2019).

Labour market trends

Labour force participation rates for workers between the ages of 15 and 64 are around 75 per cent, which is slightly higher than the average among all upper middle-income countries at 71 per cent (World Bank, 2019). Men's labour force participation stands at 82 per cent, while women's labour force participation is around 67 per cent. Women have consistently made up around 45 per cent of the workforce over the past three decades. Remarkably, the unemployment rate in Thailand has remained at less than 1 per cent since 2010.[1] Even during the 1997 Asian Financial Crisis and its aftermath, the unemployment rate never rose above 4 per cent. Men's and women's unemployment rates have diverged very little over the last decade, indicating that both men and women can find work relatively easily in Thailand's fast-growing economy.

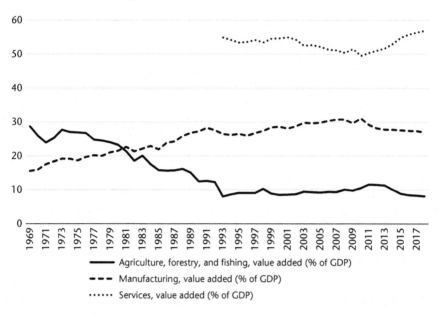

FIGURE 6.1   Sectoral value added (% GDP) in Thailand, 1969–18
Source: (World Bank, 2019).

Figure 6.2 shows the level of employment and average wages for both men and women in the top ten industries in terms of employment. These ten industries employed approximately 78 per cent of Thailand's labour force (National Statistical Office of Thailand, 2019). There are slightly more men employed in manufacturing and wholesale and retail trade, and disproportionately more men working in agriculture, public administration and defence, and transportation and storage. Women dominate employment in education, accommodation and food service, human health and social work and financial and insurance activities. Interestingly, within industries, there is little in terms of gender gaps in wages, with a female advantage in wholesale and retail trade, public administration and transportation and storage. It is important to note that men dominate in industries that generally have lower average wages. Women, on the contrary, are employed in larger numbers in fields with higher average wages, including education, human health and social work and financial and insurance activities. The gender split across industries is one of the reasons why the overall gender wage gap is "reversed" in Thailand. In 2018, women have a 1.8 per cent advantage in the overall raw gender wage gap (National Statistical Office of Thailand, 2019).

Despite rapid industrialisation and economic growth over the past four decades, Thailand's labour force remains highly informal. Although there are many dimensions of informality, for the purposes of this case study, we follow the Thai government definition. According to the Thai government, a worker is considered formally employed if they are covered by social security or another employer provided social welfare programme, such as the civil servants' welfare

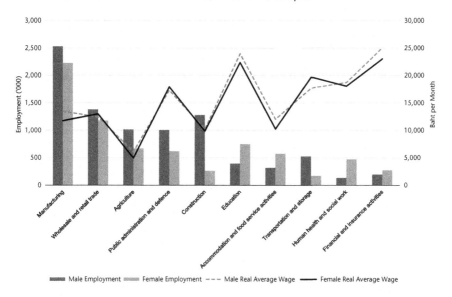

FIGURE 6.2   Employment and wages by industry and gender, 2018
Source: Authors' calculations from the 2018 third quarter Labor Force Survey statistical reports (Table 15; National Statistical Office of Thailand, 2019).

scheme. If one considers all types of workers in the economy, including public and private sector employees, employers, own-account workers and unpaid family workers, the incidence of informality by this definition has remained steady at around 70 per cent between 2011 and 2016. The incidence of informality is very similar among both men and women. In 2016, 71 per cent of men workers and 69 per cent of women workers were informally employed. If one considers only wage and salaried workers (i.e. employees working for the government, public enterprises and private firms), the overall incidence of informality dropped from 38 per cent to 35 per cent between 2011 and 2016. Informality was more common among male employees (39 per cent) then female employees (31 per cent) in 2016.

On average, formal workers earn more than informal workers, which is not surprising. However, there are some interesting patterns worth noting. First, the real wages for both full-time formal and informal workers saw significant increases over the 2011 to 2016 period. Second, the wage gap between full-time formal and informal employees has declined somewhat over the period from 56 per cent to 51 per cent. Third, between 2012 and 2013, the Thai government rolled out a new nationwide minimum wage of 300 baht per 8-hour day that officially applies only to formal workers. Given that the pre-2012 minimum wages set in each province ranged from 159 to 221 baht per day, 300 baht represents a significant increase in the minimum wage across the country. Even though the minimum wage officially only applies to formal workers, full-time informally employed workers also saw a significant bump in monthly labour income after the implementation of the 300 baht minimum wage, suggesting spillovers to other parts of the labour market. Note also that the average monthly labour income for both formal and informal workers is higher than the new 300 baht minimum wage from 2013, suggesting that informal work is not necessarily poorly paid work in the Thai context. Finally, the gender wage gap among formally employed workers closed over the 2011–2016 period. In contrast, although both informally employed men and women saw increases in real wages, the gender wage gap among the informally employed remained constant. Figure 6.3 depicts these patterns.

III Thailand's formalisation policies

Thailand has progressively pursued various formalisation policies, particularly over the last 30 years. This section provides an overview of policies aimed at formalising workers, providing informal workers social protection and bringing informal enterprises more firmly under government regulation.

Formalisation of workers through expanding social security

Although civil servants have long enjoyed a comprehensive welfare scheme, social security for private sector employees emerged much later with the industrialisation of the Thai economy starting in the 1970s. The Workmen's Compensation Fund, which provides protection against work-related injury, death and sickness, was

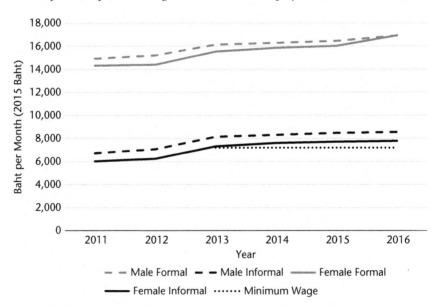

FIGURE 6.3 Monthly labour income for formal and informal workers, 2011–16
Source: Authors' calculations from the 2011–2016 Thai Labor Force Surveys.

established in Bangkok in 1974, and was expanded nationwide in 1988 (Schmitt et al., 2013). The Social Security Act (SSA) B.E. 2534 (1990) was enacted in September 1990. The aim of SSA Section 33 is to provide an additional safety net to formal workers between the ages of 15 and 60 employed in the non-agricultural sector. Social Security Fund (SSF) benefits currently include non-occupational injury or sickness benefits, maternity, invalidity, death, unemployment, old-age and child support. Tripartite contributions fund the scheme, with contributions from the employer and employee equalling 5 per cent of pre-tax labour income and the government making a 2.75 per cent contribution (Schmitt et al., 2013, 6-7).[2] In theory, all employees in firms employing one or more workers should be covered by social security, although in practice many firms do not register or pay contributions for their employees. As of 2017, there are 10,791,655 individuals registered under Section 33 of the SSA (Social Security Office Thailand, 2019).

There are two voluntary social security schemes that were established with the SSA. Section 39 of the SSA provides continuation of social security coverage for workers who have left social security-covered employment. Section 39 allows workers to transition in and out of unemployment, formal employment and in-formal employment without losing social security coverage. As of 2017, there are 2,497,619 individuals registered under Section 39 of the SSA (Social Security Office Thailand, 2019).

Finally, Section 40 of the SSA—which was enacted more recently in 2008—extends voluntary coverage to informally employed workers. Any in-dividual between the ages of 15 and 60 who is not covered by Sections 33 or 39 of the SSA or other government social welfare schemes is eligible for this scheme (Schmitt et al., 2013, 9). Since this scheme targets informal workers, there is no contribution from the employer, and thus would not fit the International Labour Organization's definition of formal employment. Simply put, this scheme attempts to bridge the gap in social protection between formal and informal workers by providing a social safety with similar coverage to informal workers. There are three different social security packages offered under SSA Section 40. The basic package, which costs 100 baht per month (70 baht from the insured and 30 baht from the government), provides sickness, invalidity and death coverage (Schmitt et al., 2013). The second package, which costs 150 baht per month (100 baht from the insured and 50 baht from the government), provides the same coverage as the basic package, but also includes an lump-sum old-age payment (Schmitt et al., 2013). Finally, a third package that was first offered in 2018 has benefits most similar to those enjoyed by formal workers under SSA Section 33 and 39. The monthly contribution for package 3 is 450 baht (insured person contributes 300 baht and the government supports 150 baht) and provides child payments in addition to the other benefits listed above (Social Security Office, 2017). As of 2017, 2,251,842 people are voluntarily covered under Section 40 of the SSA (Social Security Office Thailand, 2019).

Alternatives to social security: universal and targeted social protection schemes

Given high rates of informality in the Thai labour market, the government has had to find alternatives to providing social protection outside of employment arrangements. Some of the protections are targeted at special populations, including a disability allowance, an HIV/AIDS allowance and a recently established cash card (commonly known as the "poor card") for low-income households. Since we are most interested in protections normally provided within formal work arrangements, we briefly summarise the two most important universal social protection programmes in Thailand covering health and old age. These programmes are specifically designed for the informally employed and family members who fall outside of formal schemes.

The National Health Security Act B.E. 2545 (2002) established the Universal Health Care System (UHCS), also commonly known as the "30 baht scheme." This scheme is administered by the National Health Security Office and it aims to provide healthcare services to individuals not covered by the civil servant medical benefits scheme, social security scheme or other schemes provided by the government. Any Thai citizen with a 13-digit national identification number has the right to avail this service through a local service provider. Therefore, this provision significantly alleviates the financial burden related to medical services for informal workers and those with relatively low income. The scheme is financed by tax revenue to provide for various medical benefits, including outpatient and inpatient treatments, maternity care, birth delivery, dental care and emergency care (Schmitt et al., 2013, 10). The implementation of the UHCS in Thailand has made a significant contribution to expanding the state's healthcare provision at a national level. Due to this universal scheme, nearly 100 per cent of the Thai population has health coverage (National Statistical Office of Thailand, 2019).

The Thai government also provides a universal pension to those who do not qualify for pensions under other government schemes. The Universal Non-contributory Allowance for the Elderly was established by the Old Age Act B.E. 2546 (2003), but it came into effect only in 2009. Under this scheme, Thai nationals who (1) are 60 years and above, (2) have registered and applied for the old-age allowance at their local government office, (3) have their domicile registered in the local government district in which they applied for the allowance, and (4) receive no other old-age benefits provided by the government. The allowance ranges from 600 to 1,000 baht and is based on age (Schmitt et al., 2013, 11). In 2018, there are 8,408,498 elderly persons receiving allowance (National Economic and Social Development Council, 2019).

Other recent approaches to formalisation

A recent approach to formalising enterprises targets online businesses and small and medium enterprises (SMEs) that have flourished in response to the rise of

Thailand's digital economy. Social networking sites (e.g. Facebook, Line and Instagram) and e-commerce websites have led to a rapid increase in the number of online shops. Although many online shops operate on a small scale and provide only supplementary income, a large number of online shops and SMEs do earn significant revenues while operating in the shadow economy. According to an announcement of the Ministry of Commerce regarding registration of e-commerce on 10 November 2010, any individual or legal enterprise situated in Thailand that (1) sells products or services via an online platform using an internet connection, (2) provides an internet service and/or webhosting or (3) operates as an e-Market place are required to register themselves with the Department of Business Development (DBD) within the Ministry of Commerce within 30 days of commencing operations. By registering, these online enterprises can enjoy various benefits, such as displaying the logo "DBD registered" to project goodwill and trustworthiness to potential customers (DBD). In turn, this formalisation increases confidence among customers regarding the trustworthiness of the transactions as there are many fake commercial websites plaguing the e-commerce world. However, according to the data from DBD (as of April 2018), there are only 37,491 online shops registered as e-commerce enterprises with the DBD (Department of Business Development, 2018).

Another recent approach to formalising business activities is the Prompt-Pay programme, which is a project under the National e-Payment Plan that provides convenient and secure transfer of money (National Epayment, 2016). The system is optional and open to both individuals and legal entities. To register, interested persons or legal entities need to associate their bank account with their 13-digit identification number and mobile phone number. The system is considered to be more convenient than the traditional money transfers since money can be wired to a recipient (who also uses Prompt-Pay) with their national identification number or mobile phone number. In addition, registration for Prompt-Pay offers reduced cost transactions for both individuals and legal entities. Another benefit of registration for Prompt-Pay is that it is integrated into other government structures and can be used to receive government subsidies, state provisions and tax refunds (National Epayment, 2016). Although the initiative has provided a platform for convenient cash transactions that can complement business activities, since the scheme requires registration via a unique national identification number and a mobile phone number with a bank account, it is possible that the Prompt-Pay platform will be used as a formalisation tool for income tax collection in the future. However, the scheme is relatively new and there has yet to be any initiative to utilise Prompt-Pay for income tax collection.

IV A Gendered perspective on Thailand's formalisation policies

It is generally accepted that formalisation of employment provides various financial and social benefits for workers. But are the benefits enjoyed equally by both men and women? Does formalisation impact men and women differently? We evaluate Thailand's major formalisation programmes and social protection schemes for the informally employed through a gendered lens.

Social security schemes

We evaluate four facets of Thailand's social security schemes from a gendered perspective: (1) social security coverage; (2) social security benefits; (3) gaps in coverage due to interrupted careers; and (4) gaps in coverage due to transitions between the formal and informal employment. In many countries, one of the weaknesses of social security schemes provided through formal employment is that women are much less likely to be formally employed and therefore less likely to be covered by social security. Although approximately 70 per cent of all workers are informally employed in the Thai economy and are thus not eligible for SSA Section 33 coverage or protection under the civil servant scheme, of those who are formally employed, the majority are women. For workers in an employer-employee relationship, 69 per cent of women are formally employed and eligible for SSA Section 33 benefits compared to 61 per cent of men. In this sense, employer provided social security does not favour men over women.

In terms of the benefits, SSA Section 33 provides woman-friendly benefits including a 13,000 baht maternity allowance, partial pay during maternity leave and medical care associated with pregnancy and childbirth. Furthermore, SSA Section 33 provides a small monthly child allowance to help offset the costs of care until the child reaches six years of age. The social security scheme also provides a pension for retirees over 60 years of age, which is important in the context of an aging population where women generally live longer than men (Schmitt et al., 2013).

While these benefits are progressive from a gendered perspective, women may face problems associated with low levels of benefits and access issues. For example, the pension scheme has low contribution rates with a reference salary ceiling of only 15,000 baht per month. Furthermore, benefits are not indexed on inflation, which means that the pension payments are low with the real value eroding steadily over time (Schmitt et al., 2013). Since the retirement age is low at 60 years of age and women generally live longer, women covered by the social security pension will need to make do with limited benefit payments over long periods of time in the future if no adjustments are made to the programme.

A more serious issue is one of access. Women are more likely to move in and out of the workforce throughout the lifecycle because of their caring roles. To access maternity benefits, the worker (or their spouse) has to have contributed at least seven months over the last 15 months to be eligible for the benefit (Schmitt et al., 2013). Thus, workers new to the formal labour force or workers who are returning to the formal labour force after long absences might find themselves without coverage. Old-age benefits are potentially more problematic. To qualify for the old-age pension, workers must contribute at least 15 years. Contributions made for fewer than 15 years but more than 1 year will result in a lump-sum payment in lieu of a pension at the age of 60 (Schmitt et al., 2013). With women more likely to have lapses in social security coverage due to entering and retreating from the formal labour force throughout their life cycle, women are more likely to find themselves without or very limited old-age protection at retirement. SSA Section 39 coverage is voluntary coverage meant to cover gaps between stints in formal employment, but even these premiums may be difficult to cover if women have dropped out of the labour force even temporarily because of care responsibilities.

Although formal schemes, such as SSA Section 33 and the welfare scheme that covers civil servants, go a long way to providing social protection to women in the formal sector, the fact remains that the majority of women workers—69 per cent—are informally employed and not covered by these schemes. As detailed above, the voluntary schemes developed by the Social Security Office under Sections 39 and 40 of the SSA provide protection to informal workers. With the recent addition of child payments under SSA Section 40 package 3, informal workers potentially have access to benefits similar to formal workers through a combination of voluntary social security, the UHCS, and the Universal Non-contributory Allowance for the Elderly. From a gendered perspective, these schemes are consistent with filling gaps and providing support for women whose caring roles may not allow for full and/or consistent participation in the formal labour force.

The SSO has made several attempts to ease access issues. For example, the SSO has made voluntary contribution payments easier by increasing the number of payment outlets (i.e. commercial banks, malls, convenience stores and post offices). For those under SSA Section 40, individuals can pay for future contributions in the current period, helping those whose income may not be consistent (Social Security Office, 2017). Despite these efforts, the failure to comply with periodic contributions seems to pose problems for informal workers and the unemployed, resulting in ineligibility to receive benefits or termination of status. For example, contributors under Section 39 of the SSA are terminated if no contributions are made for a period of three continuous months. Likewise, the membership is terminated if registered individuals fail to contribute for 9 months within a 12-month period (Social Security Office, 2017). Such inflexibility of the law may impose burdens for female workers in the informal economy, especially those who are pregnant or have children. Fortunately, the SSO has taken these issues seriously into consideration. A short-term remedy has been implemented regarding such terminations by allowing for 777,228 individuals registered under Section 39 to have their status restored (Social Security Office, Ministry of Labour, 2018). These individuals, whose membership had been terminated, can file a petition and make contributions during 20 April 2018 and 19 April 2019 to restore their status (Social Security Office, Ministry of Labour, 2018). In the long run, the government should consider relaxing contribution clauses, or perhaps pursuing options for flexible payments. Likewise, it would be helpful if the contribution clauses could be relaxed for women informal workers because they may be financially vulnerable during pregnancy and the post-partum period. Since informally employed women are not eligible for 90-day maternity leave and 45-day wage compensation after birth like formally employed women, extra flexibility in meeting contribution obligations may be warranted.

Despite progress made in social security access and social protection coverage for the informally employed, women who move in and out of the labour force or in and out of formal and informal employment are still likely to have lower levels of coverage than men throughout their life cycles. To date, there is still little continuity between mandatory and voluntary social security schemes. Since women are more likely to transition from the formal to the informal sector during their work life, they are at risk of losing access to higher levels of benefits as a result of the transitions.

Formalising online enterprises and developing online payment platforms

Another area of recent government formalisation efforts is to formalise online enterprises (both wholesalers and retailers) and online payment platforms. As detailed earlier, efforts to register online business and develop Prompt-Pay may pave the way for future regulation and tax collection, which may have disproportionate impacts on women working informally in retail trade. While both formalisation policies target online wholesalers and retailers (both individual and legal firm), this particular informal sector employs a large proportion women workers. From the 2016 Labor Force Survey, the majority of female informal workers engages in agriculture, wholesale/retail trade and accommodation and food services, accounting for 44 per cent, 20 per cent, and 13 per cent of all women informal workers, respectively. In addition, the status of most women working informally are self-employed (38 per cent) and contributing family workers (37 per cent). As a result, formalising online traders may impose relatively heavy costs on women workers in the informal economy since they may be required to report their income to the state for tax purposes. While paying taxes in and of itself is not bad and is in fact needed to continue to finance the government's social protection programmes, the danger is that women will be disproportionately burdened by tax payments if formalisation efforts are concentrated on industries with high proportions of women workers.

V The interaction between formalisation and gender in Thailand: three case studies

The previous section provided a gendered perspective on national-level formalisation policies, including the expansion of social security, Prompt-Pay and mandated registration of online businesses. This section looks in more detail at three industries that employ significant numbers of informally employed women workers, including domestic work and cleaning services, sex work and manufacturing. The line between formal and informal work may be different across industries, and that line is often blurred. Because of the nature of work, some industries have developed their own unique set of formalisation policies, while workers in other industries are formal on paper, but may face barriers to accessing benefits due to work stigma. These case studies provide insights into the complexities at the intersection of formality and gender.

Case study 1: domestic work and cleaning services

Domestic work and cleaning services are common forms of employment in Thailand, representing 7 per cent of all women workers working in an employee relationship in 2016. Domestic work takes place largely within informal contexts. This section covers: recent government efforts to formalise aspects of domestic work, general trends in work conditions between formally and informally employed domestic workers and cleaners and findings from interviews conducted in Bangkok regarding work conditions and reasons for working in formal or informal situations.

Government policies and domestic work

The Labour Protection Act B.E. 2541 (1998) covers many aspects of employment protection, including wages, hours, paid leave, etc. The Act primarily covers employees in formal work situations (such as cleaners employed by hotels and other private firms), but does not specifically cover domestic workers working in households in informal situations. In 2012, the Royal Thai Government enacted Ministerial Regulation No. 14, B.E. 2555 (2012), which decreed that some provisions of the Labour Protection Act B.E. 2541 (1998) would be extended to domestic workers informally employed in households. These provisions include: domestic workers are entitled to at least one weekly holiday (Section 28); at least 13 paid traditional holidays including Labour Day (Section 29); six personal leave days annually after the worker completes a full year of work (Section 30) and up to 30 days of sick leave (Section 32). In terms of pay, domestic workers are entitled to regular pay in Thai currency at least once per month (Sections 70 and 54), and workers who work on a weekly, traditional, or annual holiday are entitled to an extra day's wages (Sections 62 and 64). In terms of termination from employment, domestic workers are entitled to notice of termination (without cause) at least one pay period in advance (Section 17) and is entitled to any outstanding pay within three days of termination (Section 70). If the employer fails to give advance warning of termination, the domestic worker is entitled to wages that should be paid during the notice period (Section 17). Finally, domestic workers must meet the minimum age requirement for employment of 15 years of age (Section 44).[3]

While Ministerial Regulation No. 14, B.E. 2555 (2012) provides informally employed domestic workers several workplace protections, there are some notable exclusions. First, the provisions that cover domestic workers do not mandate a maximum number of work hours or mandatory rest periods per day. Since there is no mandated maximum number of work hours, it follows that there is no provision for hourly overtime pay. Second, domestic workers employed in homes are also not entitled to severance pay. Third, informally employed domestic workers are not covered by minimum wage laws.

As discussed earlier, the Thai government implemented the Social Security Act, B.E. 2533 (1990), which initially provided social security protections to formally employed employees (under Section 33) and on a voluntary basis to people formerly insured under Section 33 and have subsequently left employment (Section 39). Cleaners and helpers working in business settings (provided the businesses are following labour regulations) are eligible for coverage under Section 33 of the SSA, leaving most informally employed domestic workers and cleaners working in private homes without social security coverage. Informally employed domestic workers and cleaners working in homes and unregistered businesses generally rely on the UHCS and the Universal Non-contributory Allowance for the Elderly for healthcare and pensions, respectively. These workers are also eligible for voluntary subscription to Section 40 of the SSA for further protections, but as discussed above, the available packages provide lower levels of protection compared to Section 33 and the take-up rate is low (Schmitt et al., 2013).

Statistical overview of domestic work in Thailand

We provide a statistical overview of the domestic worker and cleaner market in Thailand based on the Thai Labor Force Survey, in particular the third quarter data, from 2011 to 2016. For the purposes of this case study, domestic work includes individuals performing work consistent with the International Standard Classification of Occupations 2008 (ISCO-08) codes 5152 (domestic housekeepers), 9111 (domestic cleaners and helpers) and 9112 (cleaners and helpers in offices, hotels and other establishments).[4] In 2016, just over 550,000 workers worked as domestic workers or cleaners, of which 96 per cent were women. A total of 63 per cent worked in firms, such as offices and hotels, while the remaining 37 per cent worked in private homes. Domestic workers in Thailand tend to be older with low levels of formal education. A total of 64 per cent of domestic workers and cleaners were older than 40 years of age, and only 14 per cent were under 30. Approximately 68 per cent of domestic workers in Thailand completed primary education or less, and only 14 per cent of workers completed secondary school or higher. Domestic workers and cleaners regularly work about six days per week and have seen real wages grow by about one-third over 2011 to 2016. Compared to all other private firm workers in the economy, domestic workers and cleaners on average worked approximately the same number of hours per week and earned almost 70 per cent of the average private firm employee in all other sectors. The growth in monthly income and real hourly wages also mirrors the growth among private firm workers in all other industries.

Formal versus informal domestic and cleaning work in Thailand

This section covers differences in work conditions between formal and informal domestic workers and cleaners. Due to data constraints, we follow the Thai government's definition of informality, which is based on whether or not an individual has access to social security coverage (Sections 33, 39, or 40) or coverage though other social insurance programmes, such as the welfare programme that covers civil servants.[5] Figure 6.4 shows the incidence of informality among workers engaged in domestic work and cleaning services.

Domestic housekeepers, as well as domestic cleaners and helpers, largely work inside private homes and are overwhelmingly informally employed. In fact, 71 per cent of domestic housekeepers and 91 per cent of domestic cleaners and helpers are informal employees without any type of social security coverage. In contrast, 80 per cent of cleaners and helpers in hotels and other businesses are employed formally. Private firms who have one or more employees by law are required to register their employee(s) for SSA Section 33 coverage and make contributions to the SSF. Thus, it is not surprising that this occupational category is largely formal. However, the fact that 20 per cent of cleaners and helpers in hotels and other businesses are informally employed may point to the fact that many businesses evade labour laws in order to avoid paying social security and other business taxes.

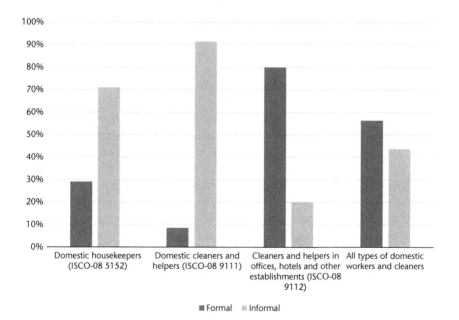

FIGURE 6.4   Incidence of informality by worker type, 2016

For the following analysis of work conditions, we group all types of domestic workers and cleaners together (regardless of workplace) and compare work conditions across the formal and informal designations. Table 6.1 provides the distribution of hours, monthly labour income and hourly wages for full-time (35 or more work hours per week) formally and informally employed domestic workers and cleaners.

In terms of weekly work hours, there is little difference between full-time formal and informal workers. On average, informal workers work 47.6 hours per week compared to 46.4 hours per week for formal workers, which works out to a 1 hour 12 minutes longer average workweek for informal workers. Both types of workers work 48 hours per week—the equivalent of a six-day workweek—at the median. The distribution of hours between formal and informal workers is also similar with slightly more variation at both ends of the distribution for informal workers.

Turning to earnings, formally employed domestic workers and cleaners on average earned more than the informally employed by 1,510 baht per month in 2016, representing a wage gap of about 17 per cent. Across the entire monthly labour income distribution, formal domestic workers and cleaners earned more than informal workers, with the gap ranging from 5 per cent at the 75th percentile to 24 per cent at the 10th percentile, suggesting that labour income gaps are generally higher at the lower end of the income distribution. Note that the labour income gaps within domestic work and cleaning services is much lower than the overall formal-informal wage gap of 51 per cent in 2016, suggesting that within occupation differences for formal and informal labour income are much lower than the gap across workers in general. We see a similar pattern across hourly wages. At the mean, formal workers earn 48.3 baht per hour compared to 39.2 baht per hour for informal domestic workers and cleaners, representing a gap of 19 per cent.

A new nationwide 300 baht daily minimum wage was implemented over 2012 and 2013, which represents an increase in the previous provincial minimum wages by 36 per cent to 89 per cent. The 300 baht daily minimum wage is equivalent to 7,200 baht per month (based on a 6-day workweek) or 37.5 baht per hour. At the mean, both formal and informal workers earned more than the minimum wage in terms of monthly labour income and hourly wages in 2016. Among formal workers—who should be covered by minimum wage laws—83 per cent earned at least the minimum labour income, and 85 per cent earned at least the minimum hourly wage. Even though informally employed domestic workers and cleaners are not covered by minimum wage laws, we find that 51 per cent have monthly labour income greater than 7,200 baht per month, and 55 per cent have hourly wages greater than 37.5 baht per hour.

The third quarter Labor Force Survey has a series of supplemental questions about additional work conditions that may vary across formal/informal status. We analyse the following questions: (1) Do you have any problems at work? (2) Are there problems with the work environment? (3) Are there any problems with

TABLE 6.1 Distribution of hours, monthly labour income, and hourly wages for formally and informally employed full-time domestic workers and cleaners, 2016

	Weekly work hours			Real monthly labour income (2015 baht)			Real hourly wage (2015 baht)		
	Formal	Informal	Gap	Formal	Informal	Gap	Formal	Informal	Gap
Mean	46.4	47.6	-2.6%	8,842	7,332	17.1%	48.3	39.2	18.9%
10th Percentile	38.0	35.0	7.9%	6,587	4,991	24.2%	36.4	24.4	32.9%
25th Percentile	42.0	40.0	4.8%	7,785	5,989	23.1%	40.5	31.2	23.1%
Median	48.0	48.0	0.0%	8,983	7,486	16.7%	46.8	39.2	16.2%
75th Percentile	48.0	49.0	-2.1%	9,482	8,983	5.3%	52.8	46.8	11.4%
90th Percentile	54.0	56.0	-3.7%	11,029	9,482	14.0%	62.4	53.5	14.3%

Source: Authors' calculations from the third quarter 2016 Labor Force Survey.

workplace safety? Problems at work include problems with pay, arduous work, working outside normal hours, lack of continuity, too many hours of work, no holidays, cannot take leave or vacation, and no benefits. Problems with the work environment include crowded conditions, uncleanliness, bad air circulation, atmosphere (i.e. not friendly), dusty/smoky, loud or too bright. Finally, problems with workplace safety include presence of chemicals, presence of dangerous machinery, potential for ear and eye damage, work that is high/underwater/underground and unrest at the workplace.

In most cases, the responses to these questions on work environment were similar between formal and informal workers. Informal workers were more likely to report problems at work over the 2011 to 2016 period, with 22 per cent reporting problems compared to 16 per cent of formal workers. Issues with pay was the most common complaint (69 per cent of overall complaints) among both formal and informal domestic workers and cleaners. Although informal workers are slightly more likely to report problems at work, they are just as likely to report poor work conditions (6 per cent for formal and 5 per cent for informal) and safety issues (3 per cent for formal and 2 per cent for informal). The overall picture that emerges is that formal and informal domestic workers and cleaners face similar work conditions in several dimensions, including work hours, work environment and workplace safety. Formal and informal workers diverge in terms of labour income/wages and the incidence of workplace problems, but it is important to note that the gaps across these work conditions are relatively modest.

Interviews with "Mae Baan" working in Bangkok

This final section is devoted to the analysis of interviews with 20 *"mae baan"*—women working as domestic workers or cleaners—working in Bangkok, including ten women working as domestic workers in private households and ten women working as cleaners in firms or government offices. The purpose of these interviews was to gain deeper insights into the choices these women have made about working in formal or informal settings. We also wanted to ask additional questions about work conditions and workers' knowledge about their labour rights.

The 20 respondents were chosen by snowball sampling. After interviewing each domestic worker or cleaner, we asked if she could refer us to another acquaintance working in a similar position. All respondents are Thai nationals who work in Bangkok, but are spread across different parts of the city. We collected information on worker characteristics to see if the group was similar in composition to what we found in the Labor Force Survey. In our sample, 80 per cent of the respondents were over the age of 40 and 60 per cent had completed education at the primary level or lower. The profile of older female workers with low levels of education is in fact similar to what we found in the nationally representative sample. Among these workers, 75 per cent had more than ten years of experience working as a domestic worker or cleaner.

We asked the workers about the number of workdays they normally work and whether they receive government holidays, personal vacation days and paid sick leave. Employees, regardless of their work status, are entitled to at least one weekly holiday, at least 13 government holidays, six days of vacation leave (after the first year of employment) and up to 30 paid days of sick leave. Half of the 20 respondents indicated that they normally work seven days per week, many of whom do not receive compensation for working on weekly holidays. Interestingly, workers in private homes more often received government holidays, personal days and sick leave afforded to them by law than workers in firms. Four respondents working in firms indicated that they received no or only some government holidays compared to only one in a private home. Out of the 20 respondents, 6 indicated that they receive no or only unpaid vacation leave each year. Finally, four workers in firms were afforded unpaid or no sick leave, compared to only one worker in a private home. Overall, it seems that employers both in private homes and in firms are not strictly adhering to the labour laws, and that informally employed workers in private homes are not necessarily worse off in terms of leave. It also became clear that many did not know their rights to paid leave afforded to them by law.

The ten workers in private homes were asked, "if given the option, would you choose to work in a firm rather than a private home?" Three respondents said they would prefer work in a firm, while seven answered that they prefer to remain working in a private household. For the three respondents who would consider working in firms, the main reason why they would like to move is that *mae baan* in offices have fewer or different duties. When they elaborated on why they do not try to find work in a firm, two of the three answered that they were too old to start a new job. One responded that a firm would have to offer her higher pay to entice her to leave her current position. Finally, one of the respondents felt that her level of education was too low to be considered for work in a company.

Even though the statistics in the Labor Force Survey indicate that workers in private firms command higher pay, the majority of workers we talked to in private homes prefer not to find work in firms. This begs the question of why workers choose to remain working in private homes with lower pay, longer hours, less access to social security and fewer legal protections. When the workers in private households were asked why they prefer to stay where they are, they supplied the following reasons:

- *Work atmosphere*—Several of the respondents said the work atmosphere in private homes is much better than in an office. One respondent referred to the office environment as too intense and too crowded. A couple of workers described working in a private home as "comfortable" or in their "comfort zone." Flexible hours were another reason why working in a private home is preferred to work in a firm.
- *Relationship with the boss*—The relationship with one's boss was an important factor as well. One woman sums up the sentiments of several workers when

she said, "welfare depends on the boss; a good boss comes with good welfare." One respondent who used to work in a firm said that she did not get along with her boss at the firm, so she prefers working in a private home. Another woman mentioned that her boss was very nice and gave advances on her pay if she needed it. This informal source of credit is important because, as the respondent elaborates, it means she does not have to seek loans from loan sharks. She could not approach her boss for informal loans in the same way if she were working for a firm.

- *Tasks*—One respondent mentioned that her former boss in a firm regularly assigned work outside her job description. Another said that the work in firms is too difficult, which is why she prefers to work in a private home. Another mentioned that working in a private home is much easier.
- *Costs*—One issue that came up a few times was transportation and living costs. One respondent said that she is more comfortable working in a private home because she lives there and does not have to travel. Another worker pointed out that workers in firms have high expenses associated with traveling to work and other things. The Labor Force Survey does not collect information on travel costs faced by workers, thus reported compensation does not take into consideration the expenses associated with formal sector work.

The main conclusion is that the decision to work in private homes has little to do with the pay and more to do with preferences over the work environment. Work in private homes seems to provide a calmer and more comfortable atmosphere, long but more flexible hours, and lower costs associated with travel. A good working relationship with one's boss and the ability to approach the boss on private matters also seems to be a reason why some of the workers continue to choose to work in private homes rather than find formal work in firms.

For the ten workers interviewed from private firms and other organisations, they were asked the question, "if given the option, would you choose to work in a private home rather than a firm or organisation?" All ten respondents answered that they prefer working in a private firm. The reasons for preferring work in private firms or other organisations are summarized below.

- *Work hours*—By far the most common answer was that the women preferred to have fixed hours. Five of the respondents noted that there are no fixed hours when working in private homes. Also, one worker mentioned that when working in a firm they have the option of refusing overtime hours, which they cannot easily do when working in a private home. Two respondents felt that *mae baan* in private homes have no freedom.
- *Family obligations*—In a related issue, three of the respondents mentioned that they value time with their children. Working in a private home comes with long work hours with little flexibility. A guaranteed 8-hour workday at a firm allows the workers to meet family obligations. One of the respondents noted

that they felt only older workers and those with no family burdens could work in private homes with long work hours.

- *Risk of bad boss*—Two of the respondents mentioned that there is a high risk of getting a bad boss in a private home compared to a firm or organisation. One was concerned about being accused of stealing if she misplaced anything in a private home. Another had a bad experience with a bad boss in a private home in the past and thus prefers working in a firm.
- *Tasks*—Two of the respondents mentioned that they perceive *mae baan* work in private homes to be more detailed and difficult than work in firms.
- *Compensation and benefits*—Interestingly, none of the workers said that the reason why they prefer to work in firms is higher pay. Only one respondent said that they prefer working in a firm because they receive benefits.

To summarise, all the workers interviewed who work in private firms or other organisations prefer to stay in their current employment situation. The main reasons are firms have shorter and more regular hours and work in private homes is perceived to lack flexibility, making meeting family obligations difficult. There is also a perception that the probability of getting a bad boss in a private home is high. Finally, wages and benefits are generally not important reasons for preferring work in firms over private homes.

Concluding remarks on domestic workers

This case study shows that despite relatively higher wages and benefits for formal workers and the availability of formal work given Thailand's low unemployment rate, preferences for formal or informal work go beyond wages and benefits. For example, if formalisation strategies push maid services out of private homes and into firms specialising in cleaning services for hire, women who prefer working in a "comfortable" home environment and receiving in-kind payments that lower living costs, such as room and board that often accompanies live-in contracts, would be worse off. Thus, when considering various formalisation strategies, one must think beyond the impact of these strategies on wages and benefits only. The results of this case study point to the importance of considering preferences over other workplace amenities that are more easily provided in an informal setting than in a formal setting.

Case study 2: sex work

Sex work, or the exchange of sexual services for money, although hardly unique to Thailand, is today rampant in Thai society. Documented history of prostitution in Thailand goes back at least six centuries, mentioned in the Sukhothai Kingdom law in 1361, and later by the Chinese voyager Ma Huan (1433), and subsequently by European visitors (Van Neck, 1604; Gisbert Heeck, 1655, and others). Current estimates put the number of sex workers in Thailand at anywhere between

200,000 to more than 1 million, with many non-venue-based sex workers, part-time and occasional sex workers, migrants and minors (those aged less than 18).[6]

Thailand's approach to sex work has been to criminalise it under the Prevention and Suppression of Prostitution Act 2539 (1996) and Article 286 of the Criminal Code. The law basically forbids selling sex, pimping and running a "prostitution establishment" and punishes the sex worker for selling sex (with a maximum fine of 1,000 baht, but not the customer for purchasing sex—except in cases when minors are involved).[7]

Although the manner in which issues of prostitution in Thailand is brought up in much of the discussions is usually characterized by "exploitation," "coercion" and "human trafficking," the reality is that many women voluntarily work in the sex industry lured by the opportunity to earn a high incomes. An average woman can earn a significant amount, 20-40 times more than what they would earn as factory workers, through sex work (Yoon and Tangtammaruk, 2016). Interviews with sex workers reveal that many engage in sex work to fulfil their duties to their family. In Thai society, grown children are responsible for taking care of their parents and this duty usually falls onto the shoulders of the youngest unmarried daughter. Many uneducated, rural women and migrants from neighbouring countries find that working in the sex industry is the best way to make ends meet, and hence move to more metropolitan areas.[8] Sex work, despite it being illegal, remains rampant catering to both local demand and foreigners, affecting all strands of the country's economic and social fabric. According to Havocscope, a black-market research company, the sex industry in Thailand in 2015 was estimated to be worth US$6.4 billion per year in revenue, accounting for a significant portion of the national GDP (approximately 3 per cent).[9]

Legalisation and formality

It is difficult to separate discussions of formalisation when it comes to Thailand's sex industry without referring to its illegality. Admittedly, being informal does not necessarily mean illegal, but being illegal usually makes formalisation somewhat tricky. There are several negative consequences, especially for women, that arise because sex work is illegal in Thailand. For example: (1) often legitimate "service providers" working in so-called entertainment venues struggle to determine their legal status; (2) illegality allows for the violations of many other sex workers' rights, particularly the rights to equal protection under the law, to work, to have access to social services and the right to the highest attainable standard of health; (3) illegality also becomes as a barrier for sex workers, who want to seek help from local authorities when targeted with violence and harassment but who wish to keep these abuses, along with their work, hidden for fear of being arrested;[10] and (4) there is little done to diminish the physical and mental abuse of sex workers and their human rights, by brothel owners, clients, etc.[11] In 2003, the Thai Ministry of Justice had considered legalising prostitution as an official occupation with health benefits and taxable income, and in fact held a public discussion on the topic.

Legalisation and regulation were proposed to increase tax revenue, reduce corruption and improve the situation of the (sex) workers.[12] However, nothing further was done.

Organisation and type of contract

The literature on the Thai sex industry distinguishes between venue-based and non-venue-based sex work. It is estimated that a majority (85 per cent) of sex workers are venue-based, that is, employed in entertainment establishments (Empower, 2017). Those working directly in entertainment establishments, such as body massage parlours and karaoke bars, are usually registered as "service providers," and are therefore *de facto* under the protection of the Thai Labour Law. Moreover, the entertainment establishments are recognized as legitimate businesses under the Civil and Commercial Code B.E. 2551 and are legally registered under the Entertainment Place Act 1966 (2003). Basically, entertainment establishments such as massage parlours and A-go-go bars provide only their front service as treatment service and entertainment service to customers, respectively, while the sexual services (which are by law prohibited and illegal) are provided discretely.

Full-time workers receive a salary plus extra, or a portion of the fee per client. The Entertainment Places Act places the onus upon the owner of certain types of entertainment establishments if prostitution occurs on the premises, thereby making them criminally liable. That is, if found guilty, sex workers and their business owner are liable to be punished according to the Prostitution Suppression Act. Furthermore, sex workers must also undergo rehabilitation for one year at a reform house upon the completion of punishment for practicing prostitution if caught. Hence, according to a recent report, although the Thai Labour Act and Social Security Act does not specifically exclude people working in entertainment places, many owners of such venues choose not to register their businesses for fear of being prosecuted by authorities.[13] Such a situation then only allows exploitation of workers with impunity, and places sex workers in risky situations as well as preventing them from accessing social benefits, such as the social security scheme and unemployment benefits.

Technically, persons employed full-time by a legally registered entertainment establishment are not excluded from the usual social security facilities, including pensions, maternity/paternity leave and benefits, unemployment benefits and registration with and self-contributions to provident funds. According to Empower, however, in reality, most employers in entertainment establishments avoid registering all their workers, thus barring them from make contributions under Section 33 of the SSA.[14] Moreover, because of the nature of sex work and its illegality, if caught by law enforcement officials, or if found to be infected by sexually transmitted diseases (especially HIV/AIDS), it is common that the sex worker will be asked/forced to leave. The lives of sex workers are tightly controlled by entertainment owners and managers, which is not surprising since a venue's incomes are derived from deducting a portion of the earnings of the sex workers.[15] Additionally, given that sex workers do not usually stay long at a certain establishment, contributions to and subsequent benefits from social security facilities are rather minimal.

Regarding medical coverage, the Thai government provides healthcare services under the UHCS to all Thai citizens without access to other social security schemes. However, patients generally can only receive healthcare services in the district in which they are registered as inhabitants. This practice has hindered sex workers' access to health services since most work in cities outside their hometown and frequently relocate to their working areas. Furthermore, there are issues regarding confidentiality. For example, in prior free Voluntary and Confidential Counselling and Testing (VCCT) at government hospitals, sex workers were asked to fill out a form with personal information and to answer questions, such as the numbers of clients they have had and whether they use condoms or not. Moreover, some government hospitals often do not have strict confidentiality and privacy systems and, consequently, information is easily accessed by anyone in the hospital. Naturally, some sex workers became uncomfortable receiving VCCT or sexual and reproductive health services for fear of disclosures of their work status or health status which could lead to being prosecuted by police and/or stigmatisation from service providers and people in communities.[16]

On the contrary, there are non-venue-based sex workers who keep their working status secret and act as "freelancers" and do not work full-time in brothels or massage parlours under high supervision of owners. Non-venue-based sex workers are often ordinary college students, waitresses, models, dancers, etc., who negotiate directly with their clients. This group of sex workers also includes those working independently in public areas such as the street and parks, and are considered the most vulnerable to violence or harassment, often undergoing greater struggles in redressing difficulties they might have experienced. In addition, many often lack access to proper information and knowledge on STD/HIV prevention and access to healthcare and services.[17]

Legalisation and/or formalisation

Legalising prostitution in Thailand, according to some advocates, will allow sex workers to register with the government authorities, allowing them to undergo regular medical checks for sexual transmitted diseases. They would also then be subject to taxation and labour laws and contribute to social security schemes. Regulation also would make it easier to control the minimum age of those entering the trade. Some argue that prostitution may even reduce marital rape.[18] There are others who oppose, however. For example, Rahab Ministries feels that legalisation will not help women in prostitution and will rather put more money and power in the hands of the procurers, pimps and brothel owners. Legalisation, they argue, will also put women at risk of increased sexual harassment, contribute to further family breakdown and lead to younger and younger girls becoming involved. Legalisation of prostitution also gives men the "Go ahead; it's OK to sexually abuse women" signal (Raymond, 2004).

The debates about the merits of sex work as a legitimate form of labour will of course continue. But what about formalisation and/or regulation? Those favouring regulation of prostitution and its ancillary activities believe this could enhance the social and physical protection of sex workers, clarify the legal framework in which enforcers operate, increase income for the government and facilitate the detection and eradication of excesses. But reality poses some serious challenges.

Thailand is a predominately Buddhist country with a culture that values non-confrontation and emphasizes the need for the individual to strive for smooth relationships in the family, community and society. There are distinct hierarchies and roles based on age, gender and wealth that individuals generally comply with.[19] Those who break or defy social mores in Thailand are not directly challenged but rather they are ignored and rejected from society. Social alienation in Thailand is often a very subtle, but an extremely painful and debilitating force for those who experience it. Women working in the sex industry are commonly marginalised, stigmatised and criminalised by the society in which they live. The idea of promiscuous acts in the sex trade is against the beliefs and morals of the general public in Thailand and this has resulted in labelling sex workers as "dirty" and "vectors of disease." Hence, most sex workers conceal their work status for fear of being arrested by police and being stigmatised and discriminated against in society since the perception towards sex workers is generally negative. As such, many sex workers feel that formalising and regulating (or indeed legalising) sex work will not change the situation much because many would insist on keeping their anonymity, both for financial reasons (i.e. untaxed earnings) and societal reasons (i.e. taboo and stigmatisation). Some argue that formalisation could drive prostitution further underground rather than reducing it, thereby making it even more dangerous.

Moreover, it may be argued that The Prostitution Act, in a way, has fuelled an environment where police and local authorities feel emboldened to take abusive actions against sex workers based on outdated or unrelated laws and policies, such as laws directed at social order policy and public nuisance policy. Frequently, police run entrapment or sting operations in direct contradiction to police policy which only authorises such actions for the investigation of serious drug or weapons crimes.[20] In some cases, even the possession of condoms has been used as evidence to prosecute sex workers for committing a crime.[21] According to Jomdet Trimek, a leading criminology professor at Rangsit University, bribes to law enforcers range from 200,000 to 400,000 baht a month. The National Economic and Social Advisory Council found in a 2003 study that A-go-go bar and massage parlour owners in Thailand pay a 3.2 billion baht (US$80 million) a year in police bribes regardless of whether they are breaking any laws or not. Although such fraudulent practices are an open secret, they are maintained by the slack enforcement of social law, which partly results from a lack of political will to intervene in the sector.

Taken together, any attempts at formalising Thailand's sex industry head on will be extremely difficult. Having said this, however, this does not mean that nothing can or has been done to influence/regulate the sex industry effectively. It is worth mentioning that in the midst of the HIV/AIDS epidemic in the 1990s, top-level political commitment and multi-sectoral strategies mobilised funds and human resources to implement various policies and programmes to combat the epidemic (e.g. the Thai government's HIV/AIDS Prevention and Control Program has promoted 100 per cent condom use in commercial sex encounters). The country's sex industry became the major focus of campaigns aimed at HIV prevention and treatment due to the perception that sex workers were seen to be responsible for the spread of AIDS. As a result, there was significant behavioural change with increased condom use in sex establishments rising from about 10 per cent of sex acts in the late-1980's to 95 per cent by 1994. This resulted in a 90 per cent reduction of the sexually transmitted disease rate and the rate of new HIV infections dropped by 80 per cent in 1995.[22]

Concluding remarks on sex work

Many commentators argue that the Thai law as it applies to the sex industry is old and outdated. There seems to be an urgent need to revise legislation to actively protect the rights of individuals that enter into the sex industry without being criminalised, stigmatised and marginalised. Legalisation and indeed formalisation and regulation, however, remain elusive on a practical level not least because of social stigma, discretion and crime, but also because there seems to a general lack of political will to drastically change the industry. Perhaps, providing more job alternatives for sex workers would help? However, many come from the vast rural areas of Thailand without proper education or employment opportunities locally. There is therefore a need to support alternative professional training for sex workers to transition out of the industry. Perhaps this is where some kind of formalisation can begin? Be as it may, finding alternatives does not directly help resolve the many perennial issues for those who remain active in the industry as sex workers.

Case study 3: manufacturing

We provide a brief summary of Thai's manufacturing sector with special attention to women's work participation, informal employment and wage gaps. Overall, informal workers earned less than formal workers in manufacturing, with the wage gap higher for women workers compared to their male counterparts. Informal workers in the manufacturing sector also reported that they were less happy about the general work conditions, especially safety. We also look more closely at three manufacturing subsectors, namely, manufacture of textiles and wearing apparel (ISIC 13 and 14, respectively), processing and preserving of fish and fish products, fresh, chilled or frozen (ISIC 1021) and manufacture of bakery products (ISIC 1071), where informality and women's participation are important. The discussion shows that the manufacturing sector is by no means homogenous with respect to wages and working conditions of informal employment for both women and men workers.

Using data from 62,564 observations between 2011 and 2016 (six years) from the Thai Labor Force Survey (including the informal sector supplement), we find that the average real monthly wage for formal and informal manufacturing workers were 11,642 and 7,204 baht per month, respectively. Over this period, formal employees in the manufacturing sector earned about 62 per cent more than their informal counterparts. We also find that the wage gap between formal and informal workers is larger for female workers than male workers, with formal workers earning 65 per cent and 59 per cent more than informal workers for women and men, respectively.

Overall the manufacturing sector employs as many men as women in formal and informal employment; however, important variations are observed across different subsectors in manufacturing. For example, 80.1 per cent women are in the manufacturing of wearing apparel, compared to only 12.3 per cent of women in the repair and installation of machinery and equipment. Furthermore, when considering the manufacturing sector, 72 per cent of workers are engaged in formal employment, while only 28 per cent are informal workers. However, these ratios vary depending on subsectors, such as the manufacture of wearing apparel, the manufacture of wood and wood and cork products (except furniture) and the manufacture of articles of straw and plaiting materials, in which about 50 per cent were informal workers, compared to the manufacture of machinery and equipment (including electrical equipment), the manufacture of motor vehicles, trailers and semi-trailers, as well as the manufacture of chemicals and chemical products, which registered less than 10 per cent informal workers.

Across the Thai manufacturing sector, the mean age of workers over our sample period was 35.5 years old. The average age for men in formal and informal employment were similar (35.3 and 34. 2 years, respectively), while informal women workers' average age was 37.3 years compared to their formal counterparts at 35.4 years. Interestingly, education of both men and women manufacturing workers were similar (4.9 and 4.8 years). However, informal workers had lower education on average than formal workers (a difference of about 2.5 years of schooling) and this difference was similar for both men and women. About 66 per cent of all workers were married, with slightly more formal workers married than informal workers (67 per cent compared to 64 per cent). While marriage rates were similar for men and women formal workers, interestingly, 68 per cent of female informal workers were married compared to 60 per cent married in the case of male informal workers.

Moving on to describing the real wage gap, Table 6.2 shows the real wage gap of formal and informal workers for each manufacturing subsector (according to ISIC codes) for men and women, as well as the gender wage gap for formal and informal workers. Overall, the wage gap between formal and informal employment is higher for women than for men (65 per cent compared to 59 per cent), but

TABLE 6.2 Real monthly wages for Thai manufacturing subsectors by gender, 2011–16

N (m/f)	ISIC	Male			Female			Gender wage gap	
		Formal	Informal	Gap	Formal	Informal	Gap	Formal	Informal
6756/7922	10	11,044	7,556	1.46	9,444	6,405	1.47	1.17	1.18
832/566	11	12,936	7,558	1.71	11,986	6,359	1.88	1.08	1.19
28/51*	12	3,946	2,078	1.90	3,607	3,106	1.16	1.09	0.67
1044/1571	13	10,775	7,375	1.46	9,537	5,219	1.83	1.13	1.41
906/3657	14	10,241	7,957	1.29	9,071	5,883	1.54	1.13	1.35
405/816	15	10,897	7,156	1.52	8,793	6,559	1.34	1.24	1.09
954/576	16	10,310	7,163	1.44	9,617	5,506	1.75	1.07	1.30
758/523	17	13,429	9,121	1.47	10,946	7,230	1.51	1.23	1.26
406/302	18	13,558	9,036	1.50	12,250	8,025	1.53	1.11	1.13
186/78*	19	25,610	10,453	2.45	19,564	10,178	1.92	1.31	1.03
1125/748	20	16,681	8,562	1.95	14,614	8,408	1.74	1.14	1.02
133/248*	21	16,192	9,698	1.67	16,854	9,607	1.75	0.96	1.01
2131/1979	22	11,896	8,164	1.46	10,185	7,621	1.34	1.17	1.07
2561/1497	23	13,458	7,411	1.82	10,881	6,165	1.76	1.24	1.20
976/337	24	13,831	8,843	1.56	12,171	7,574	1.61	1.14	1.17
2671/763	25	11,712	7,981	1.47	10,639	8,195	1.30	1.10	0.97
1663/3580	26	13,580	12,153	1.12	10,838	10,587	1.02	1.25	1.15
743/832	27	13,847	10,289	1.35	11,030	8,861	1.24	1.26	1.16
941/809	28	14,303	11,218	1.28	11,896	10,127	1.17	1.20	1.11
818/78*	29	14,822	11,318	1.31	12,394	10,511	1.18	1.20	1.08
319/231	30	13,452	7,741	1.74	10,420	7,710	1.35	1.29	1.00

N (m/f)	ISIC	Formal	Informal	Gap	Formal	Informal	Gap	Formal	Informal
1154/6588*	31	10,716	8,246	1.30	10,541	6,586	1.60	1.02	1.25
1186/1657	32	12,716	8,675	1.47	10,517	5,744	1.83	1.21	1.51
636/89	33	13,420	8,853	1.52	13,158	5,986	2.20	1.02	1.48
Manu. Avg.		**12,735**	**8,024**	**1.59**	**10,550**	**6,379**	**1.65**	**1.21**	**1.26**

Note: N(m/f)—sample size (male/female); * 2012–16; ISIC—International Standard Industrial Classification of All Economic Activities.

there is variation when considering subsectors. For example, the formal–informal wage gap for men and women range from over 2 per cent to 200 per cent, with some subsectors exhibiting larger differences for men and others for women. Interestingly, the gender wage gap in the formal and informal sectors are similar, with men earning 21–26 per cent more than women on average. Looking at the subcategories, men do not consistently earn more than women. What is interesting to note is that those subsectors in which the real wage gap is higher for men than for women workers also exhibit a higher gender wage gap in the formal sector. Furthermore, we found a small negative correlation (-0.07) between the proportion of women workers in each subsector and the informal gender wage gap, but a positive correlation (0.12) with the formal gender wage gap.

The Labor Force Survey also asks various questions related to work conditions, including work environment, safety and whether they experienced any injuries, among other things. Overall, in the manufacturing sector, 41 per cent of informal workers compared to 25 per cent of formal workers had some concern about their work conditions. More specifically, 32 per cent of informal workers compared to 28 per cent of formal workers complained about safety, with 37 per cent of informal and 26 per cent of formal workers stating that they were injured (or fell ill or were wounded) at work in the past 12 months. Also, 26 per cent of informal and 13 per cent formal workers stated there were work problems with allowance, difficulty of work, long hours, no vacations, etc., while 19 per cent of informal and 13 per cent of formal workers, respectively, disliked work conditions (small, restricted work space, unhygienic, smoke, dust, poor lighting, etc.). In sum, formal workers' work conditions seem more favourable than working conditions for informal workers with regards to safety, job conditions and working environment.

Manufacture of textiles and wearing apparel

The two subsectors, manufacture of textiles and manufacture of wearing apparel (ISIC 13 and 14, respectively), were once traditionally important sectors in the Thai economy. For the past few years, the competitiveness of Thailand's clothes and textile industry has eroded, and it is now considered a "twilight" industry. However, this sector continues to have a proportionately larger number of women workers (about 60 per cent and 80 per cent, respectively) compared to other subsectors. Textile manufacturing consists of 32 per cent informal workers, while wearing apparel manufacturing has 47 per cent informal workers. Textile manufacturing firms have become increasingly formalised over the years, with many growing (more than half of workers in our sample work in firms of 200 or more) and integrating into the global supply chain. Among the wearing apparel manufacturing firms, as much as 32 per cent of firms employ fewer than 10 workers, compared to only 15 per cent for textile manufacturing.

The category of manufacture of wearing apparel, except tailoring and dressmaking (1,411), consists of: manufacture of work wear including school uniforms (14,111); manufacture of outerwear (14,112); manufacture of underwear and nightwear (14,113); manufacture of babies' garments (14,114); manufacture of sportswear (14,115); and manufacture of wearing apparel made of leather or composition leather (14,116). According to our calculations using the LFS 2011–2016, 27 per cent employees work in firms that employ fewer than ten workers. The majority of these workers (90 per cent) are informal workers, and 80 per cent are women earning about 6,345 baht per month.

With the smaller manufacturing firms employing proportionally more informal workers, many are based at home and are independently managed, with funds usually originating from personal or family sources and have their operations within domestic markets. There is often close communication with staff and customers. The organisational structure is typically simple and, to a large extent, the owner determines whether their business fails or prospers. For details, Charoenloet (1992) provides a lucid account of informal shophouse ready garment manufacturing in Bangkok. Overall, informal workers in the small garment shophouses often came from the poorer rural areas in the northeast of Thailand. The owners and workers often built close personal relations (hence most working together would come from the same rural town), but work remained usually flexible and productivity low. After a few years, a worker could gain some substantial skills to join the formal sector. Although this occasionally happened, most sooner rather than later returned to informal work unhappy about fixed working hours, strict rules and regulations, and generally were not able to adjust to the formal work environment.

We also spoke to the CEO of a popular Thai brand based in Buriram province that manufactures and sells high-quality handmade designer bags, among other items. With a long history of over 30 years, about 60 per cent of the products are made by network home producers, some located in the remote mountain communities. The company provides materials to the home-based manufacturers, consisting largely of informal workers, who would stitch and/or provide new designs, after which they are collected and taken to one of three factories for further processing or packaging before being distributed to retail outlets. According to the CEO, many individuals and families have been positively impacted by this informal network manufacturing system. The challenge, however, remains for future generations, as many of the younger generation do not wish to continue their family's line of business and would rather move to the cities.

Manufacture of food products

Another interesting subsector is the manufacture of food products (ISIC 10), which consists of about 54 per cent women workers. Overall, 38 per cent of workers in this subsector are informal workers earning about 6,918 baht per month compared to their formal colleagues earning 10,195 baht per month. If we scope down to the processing and preserving of fish and fish products, fresh, chilled or frozen (ISIC 1021), the subsector consists 51 per cent informal workers (of which 65 per cent are women) and 49 per cent formal workers (of which 74 per cent are women). There are proportionately more female workers in formal employment than informal employment in this subsector.

We visited a factory in the province of Samut Sakhon (which exports baby octopus, employing some 200 persons) and made some observations: (1) plants were very clean and work flows were well organized; (2) there was little to distinguish between the formal and informal (part-time and seasonal) workers, and (3) workers were generally punctual, and worked at a relaxed, consistent pace (although productivity seemed to increase when the owner was around). Here, accompanying a specialist, we appreciated the legacy of Japanese production systems in the Thai fish processing sector. Quality of plants/work were of high standard, but somewhat outdated. Processes needed to be upgraded to meet international standards.

The manufacture of bakery products (ISIC 1071) subsector provides yet another contrasting picture of Thai informal manufacturing. With about 50 per cent formally employed, there are proportionately more female workers in the informal sector (76 per cent) than in formal employment (60 per cent female). As with other firms in other sectors, smaller firms engage more informal workers (i.e. 70–85 per cent informal in firms employing fewer than ten workers) than larger ones (34.5 per cent of firms employ fewer than ten workers, while 30 per cent employ more than 200 workers). Real monthly wages are also higher averaging about 10,463 baht per month in formal employment compared to 6,558 baht per month for informal workers.

Concluding remarks on manufacturing workers

The Thai informal manufacturing sector is by no means homogenous. We find that different subsectors attract different gender workers, and the proportion of formal and informal employment varies depending on the type of manufacturing. Overall, however, wages are generally lower for informal work, and this gap is larger for women workers compared to their male counterparts. Although the proportion of men's and women's employment is about equal overall, women's employment remains high in the manufacture of wearing apparel sector, which continues to face many challenges related to poor work conditions, poor skill upgrading and lack of competitiveness. What is also interesting to note is that informal workers continue to face huge barriers if and when they do find formal employment, and as such often find informal work more attractive. As such, the importance of informal employment in Thailand cannot be underestimated nor should it be ignored.

VI Conclusions

In this chapter, we have presented a complex picture of Thailand's informal work landscape. Despite rapid industrialisation and the availability of formal employment amidst persistently low unemployment, we see varied and often high rates of informality across different industries. Not surprisingly, we find on average that formal workers earn more than informal workers in the economy as a whole. However, the case studies on domestic work and cleaning services and on manufacturing show there is significant variation in formal-informal wage gaps within industry. Also, the incidence of workplace issues and safety were remarkably similar between formal and informal workers in domestic work and cleaning, but diverged significantly between formal and informal workers in manufacturing.

Given the macroeconomic context of Thailand, workers often have a choice of whether to work formally or informally. Currently, there are shortages in lower skill formal and informal jobs, including domestic work/cleaning services and manufacturing. Given this fact and what we know about formal-informal wage and benefits gaps, it is puzzling to find so many people informally employed. The case studies on domestic work and manufacturing suggest that wages and benefits may not be the most important factors that influence work decisions. The work environment, demands of the job, social capital and flexibility especially for women who need to meet other domestic responsibilities may be important factors in their decision. Furthermore, formalisation can sometimes have negative consequences. The case of sex work provides a case where fully regulating and formalising may have the unintended consequence of pushing the industry even more underground. Informality by choice and access to government-provided social protection protects women from further stigma while allowing them to access basic services and benefits.

Given the heterogeneity of informality, it is difficult to characterise "problems" of informal work that are consistent across Thailand's informal labour force. Given this complexity, one may ask again whether formalisation (i.e. registration of enterprises and employer provision of social security) be pushed as a policy issue, especially when considering a gendered perspective? Evasion is rife in Thailand, as in many emerging economies. Given Thailand's current levels of enforcement, many workers who rely on employers for social protection are excluded, as exemplified by all three of the case studies where large proportions of workers, especially in small firms, are excluded from social security. This is especially true in the case of sex workers where registration is rare in an industry that operates in a legal grey area. Also, current rigidities in the SSA Section 33 (contribution periods; limited portability between schemes; low levels of benefits) are not particularly woman-friendly given life-cycle patterns of work, both from the perspective of moving in and out of the labour force, as well as moving in and out of formal employment.

As this book goes to press, Thailand, like the rest of the world, struggles with the coronavirus pandemic, registering 3,031 cases and 56 fatalities (as of 18 May 2020). The country has been under a state of emergency since 26 March 2020, which is ongoing at least until 31 May 2020, with several measures implemented nationwide including the temporary closure of schools and many businesses.[23] A curfew implemented since April 3 has restricted movement between 10 p.m. and 4 a.m.

Although businesses generally have been negatively impacted by the COVID-19 crisis and government emergency measures, the impact on the informal sector has been somewhat mixed. Gig economy food delivery services have skyrocketed, while Airbnb may not survive. Many domestic workers saw little change to their terms of employment, while others lost jobs or faced pay cuts due to employers' own job loss, salary reductions or business failures. The sex industry has been hit particularly hard due to the collapse of the tourism industry amidst international travel restrictions, as well as the mandatory closure of entertainment venues following government orders.

While informal workers have access to several types of social protection, including universal healthcare and pensions, one of the issues that has been brought to the fore by the COVID-19 crisis is that informal workers lack systematic protection from job loss. The Thai government moved quickly to make adjustments to the social security system to ensure that temporarily or permanently unemployed formal workers would quickly receive enhanced unemployment benefits. However, an attempt to provide cash assistance to informal workers affected by the crisis was largely unsuccessful. The Thai government rolled out an emergency cash assistance scheme called "No One Left Behind," which was initially designed to provide 5,000 baht (US$150) per month for three months to informal workers whose jobs were negatively affected by the COVID-19 crisis. The government originally budgeted for 3 million affected people, but nearly ten times that number applied for the cash assistance, many of whom have been deemed ineligible—including sex workers—and will likely never receive a payment.

In normal times, Thailand seems to have found a happy medium of sorts. The government has made social protection a right rather than a privilege of the (stably) formally employed. Given the fallout of the COVID-19 pandemic, the government may need to consider revising its current voluntary social security package for informal workers to include protection against severe economic crisis. Funding issues and low levels of benefits also need to be addressed, but as a whole, the suite of social protection packages offered by the Thai government ensures that women are not excluded from protection because of their work status. The takeaway from the Thai case is that blanket formalisation is not necessarily good for everyone. An approach that incorporates social norms and the balance of women's labour force participation and care work across the life cycle will likely lead to more favourable gendered outcomes.

Notes

1 Thailand uses the International Labour Organization's definition of unemployment. Specifically, a worker who is without work or is employed less than one hour in a week and is seeking employment is considered unemployed (Bangkok of Thailand, 2019). The United States uses a more stringent definition, namely individuals who work at least 15 hours a week as an unpaid worker in a family business are also considered

employed. Even with this adjustment to the definition, unemployment in Thailand remains very low at under 2 per cent as of 2018 (Bangkok of Thailand, 2019).

2 The maximum salary for calculating contributions is 15,000 baht per month, which means that the employee and employer contributions are capped at 750 baht per month, while the government contribution is capped at 412.5 baht per month.

3 https://www.ilo.org/wcmsp5/groups/public/@ed_protect/@protrav/@travail/documents/publication/wcms_208703.pdf.

4 According to the International Labour Office (2012), workers in both the 5152 and 9111 classifications do much of the same work. "The key difference is that domestic housekeepers take responsibility for the organisation and supervision of housekeeping functions in private households, as well as carrying out some or all of these functions themselves. Domestic cleaners and helpers, on the other hand, carry out these functions under the supervision ether of a person employed as a domestic housekeeper of a member of the household who takes responsibility for the organisation of housekeeping functions" (International Labour Office, 2012). Workers classified as 9112 perform similar work to those in 9111, but perform the work inside buildings, such as offices or hotels.

5 Although the Thai government includes workers covered by Social Security Sections 39 and 40 as "formally employed," this coverage is in fact voluntary and does not provide the same level of protection as Section 33 (e.g. there is no unemployment coverage). The researchers consider employees with voluntary coverage paid for entirely by employees as informal employment. Unfortunately, for the years 2011-15 the Labor Force Survey does not identify which type of social security coverage an employee has. The 2016 survey, however, identifies the social security plan. Only 1 per cent of the sample of domestic workers and cleaners has Section 39 or 40 coverage; thus, inclusion of this group in "formal workers" likely has little impact on the reported results.

6 See Phongpaichit et al. (1998) for an overview of Thai's underground economy.

7 Prostitution incidentally was legal in the Ayutthaya period (1350-1767) when sex work establishments had to pay tax to the government (called the road maintenance tax). In the modern era, when Thailand became a democracy and a member of the United Nations, the government declared the Prostitution Suppression Act in 1960 which ruled all sex work establishments as well as all commercial sex activities as illegal.

8 https://www.endslaverynow.org/blog/articles/history-of-prostitution-and-sex-trafficking-in-thailand.

9 In December of 2003, the sex trade was reported to be a US$4.3 billion per-year industry. "Sex debate: Prostitution is a $4.3 billion industry in Thailand," Agents/CNN, http://www.thaivisa.com.

10 A perennial issue is harassment at the workplace. According to one report, physical and sexual violence against female sex workers by clients and brothel supervisors remains still a major problem. Another 2007 study of 815 female sex workers highlighted that 15 per cent had experienced violence in the week before the survey.

11 Issues such as discrimination (against, for example, pregnant workers and those who are overweight, have HIV/AIDS and migrants), work environment and safety, and child prostitution (and trafficking) are prevalent but remain extremely difficult issues since the sex worker has hardly any access to the law as she is de facto a criminal by engaging in sex work.

12 "Thailand mulls legal prostitution". Theage.com.au. 2003-11-26. Retrieved 2018-10-28 https://www.theage.com.au/national/thailand-mulls-legal-prostitution-20031127-gdhv3l.html. A 2012 UN survey of sex workers in 48 Asian countries drew the conclusion that decriminalizing prostitution would be beneficial in terms of the workers' rights, safety and health.

13 See "A Joint UPR Submission on the Human Rights of Sex Workers in Thailand" submitted jointly by the Planned Parenthood Association of Thailand and the Sexual Rights Initiative.
14 (Empower, Moving Towards Decent Work, 2016).
15 The "easier" work conditions such as hours of work and breaks during work are often met and minimum wages is usually not an issue for high-end sex workers. Empower reports however that most entertainment places pay workers less than the minimum wage and that there is also an embedded culture in the Thai Entertainment Industry of imposing salary cuts as a way to punish and control workers.
16 See "A Joint UPR Submission on the Human Rights of Sex Workers in Thailand" submitted jointly by the Planned Parenthood Association of Thailand and the Sexual Rights Initiative.
17 It is estimated that the prevalence of HIV infection among freelance or street-based female sex workers is between 20 per cent and 45 per cent (Manopaiboon et al., 2013).
18 Mataluk, a Thammasat University law professor and expert on laws governing women and children. http://www.nationmultimedia.com/detail/national/30353452.
19 Kevin Bales in "Disposable People: New Slavery in the Global Economy" addresses the role of religion and gender stratification in sustaining the practice of prostitution in Thailand. https://www.endslaverynow.org/blog/articles/history-of-prostitution-and-sex-trafficking-in-thailand.
20 Empower (2017) reports that "police also have sex with women to create evidence to arrest them on charges of prostitution." In 2003, the Thai National Human Rights Commission recognized that police entrapment often leads to serious human rights violations, especially against women in the sex industry and recommended it should only be used under a clear and precise system that prevents such human rights abuses.
21 Empower (2017).
22 Thailand's "Mr. Condom," Mechai Viravaidya, is often credited for having saved millions of lives by raising awareness of HIV/AIDS. In 1990, Thailand had 100,000 new cases of HIV infection and just three years later, the number of cases had jumped to around a million, with 97 per cent of all cases of HIV infection linked to sexual transmission from sex workers. Mechai Viravaidya assumed the job of launching a public information campaign that included the airing of anti-AIDS messages every hour on the country's 488 radio stations and six television networks. All this was accompanied by a significant jump in funding (The HIV/AIDS budget for preventive activities increased almost 20-fold to US$ 44 million in 1993.)
23 The Thai government declared a state of emergency under the "Emergency Decree on Public Administration in Emergency Situation B.E. 2548 (2005)" ("EPAES"), which provides more enforcement power to the Prime Minister with the approval from the Council of Ministers to perform actions and impose policies in unusual circumstances.

References

Bangkok of Thailand, 2019. Implications of Low Unemployment rate in Thailand. Bank of Thailand, Bangkok. Retrieved from https://www.bot.or.th/English/MonetaryPolicy/MonetPolicyComittee/MPR/BOX_MRP/BOXMPR_EN_March2019_01.pdf.

Charoenloet, V., 1992. "The shop-house ready-made garment manufacturing: a case study of the informal sector in Bangkok," in Phongpaichit, P. and Itoga, S.(eds.), *The Informal Sector in Thai Economic Development*. Institute of Developing Economies-Japan External Trade Organization, Chiba.

Department of Business Development, 2018. Registration of Online Businesses and Services [Karn Jot Tabian Turakij lae Karn Hai Borikarn Tang Elektronik]. Retrieved from Department of Business Development: https://dbd.go.th/ewt_news.php?nid=469409729&filename=index.

Department of Business Development, 2019. (n.d.). *Trustmark Thai.* Retrieved from Trustmark Thai: https://www.trustmarkthai.com/index.php/component/dbd/main/10?layout=knowledge.

Empower Foundation. 2016. *Moving Toward Decent Sex Work: Sex Worker Community Research Decent Work and Exploitation in Thailand.* Empower University Press, Nonthaburi.

Empower Foundation. 2017. *Sex Workers and the Thai Entertainment Industry: Submitted by Empower Foundation to the Committee on the Elimination of Discrimination against Women Sixty-Seventh Session 3–21 July 2017.* Empower Foundation, Chiangmai. Retrieved from United Nations Human Rights Office of the High Commissioner: https://tbinternet.ohchr.org/Treaties/CEDAW/Shared%20Documents/THA/INT_CEDAW_NGO_THA_27511_E.pdf.

International Labour Office, 2012. *International Standard Classification of Occupations: Structure, Group Definitions and Corresponence Tables.* ILO, Geneva.

Manopaiboon, C., Prybylski, D., Subhachaturas, W., 2013. Unexpectedly high HIV prevalence among female sex workers in Bangkok, Thailand in a respondent-driven sampling survey. Int. J. STD & AIDS 24 (1), 31–38.

National Economic and Social Development Board, 2017. National Income of Thailand 2017 Chain Volume Measures. Retrieved October 5, 2019, from National Economic and Social Development Board: https://www.nesdb.go.th/nesdb_en/ewt_dl_link.php?nid=4374&filename=national_account.

National Economic and Social Development Council, 2019, October 21. Income Secuity (Table 4). Retrieved from National Economic and Social Development Council: http://social.nesdb.go.th/SocialStat/StatReport_Final.aspx?reportid=175&template=1R2C&yeartype=M&subcatid=47.

National Epayment, 2016. Prompt Pay - The Series. Retrieved October 2019, from National Epayment: http://www.epayment.go.th/home/app/media/uploads/files/PromptPay_the_Series_05082016.pdf.

National Statistical Office of Thailand, 2019. Access to the Health Services System [Karn Khao Theung Rabop Borikarn Sukapap]. Retrieved October 9, 2019, from National Statistical Office of Thailand: http://statbbi.nso.go.th/staticreport/page/sector/th/05.aspx.

National Statistical Office of Thailand, 2019, October 6. Statistics from Major Surveys. Retrieved from National Statistical Office of Thailand: http://www.nso.go.th/sites/2014en/statistics-from-majo-survey.

Phongpaichit, P., Piriyarangsan, S., Treerat, N., 1998. Guns, Girls, Gambling, Ganja: Thailand's Illegal Economy and Public Policy. Silkworm Books, Chiang Mai.

Raymond, J. G., 2004. Ten reasons for not legalizing prostitution and a legal response to the demand for prostitution. J. Trauma Pract. 2(3–4), 315–332.

Schmitt, V., Sakunphanit, T., Prasitsiriphol, O., 2013. Social Protection Assessment Based National Dialogue: Towards a Nationally Defined Social Protection Floor in Thailand. International Labour Organization, Bangkok.

Social Security Office. 2017. SSO's Secretary Announces Coverage Expansion for Members under Section 40 of the SSA (In Thai). *SSO J.* 23 (12), 2–3.

Social Security Office Thailand, 2019, October 7. Statistics on the Social Security Fund [Khormul Sathidti Kong Tun Prakarn Sangkhom]. Retrieved from Social Security Office Thailand: https://www.sso.go.th/wpr/main/knowledge/ข้อมูล สถิติ กองทุน ประกันสังคม_category_list-label_1_168_0.

Social Security Office, Ministry of Labour, 2018. SSO Restores Membership for Individuals under Section 39 of the SSA to Receive 6 types of Benefits (In Thai). Social Security Office, Bangkok.

World Bank, 2019. The World Bank in Thailand. Retrieved from The World Bank: https://www.worldbank.org/en/country/thailand/overview.

World Bank, 2019. World Development Indicators. Retrieved from The World Bank: https://databank.worldbank.org/source/world-development-indicators.

Yoon, Y., Tangtammaruk, P., 2016. "Taking risk in the era of HIV: a closer look at selling sex in Thailand. Pertanika J. Social Sci. Human. 24, 175–188.

INDEX

Note: Page numbers in **bold** indicate a table.

Aaibid, M. 146
Abeberese, A. B. 92
Accra Metropolitan Assembly 120
Accredited Social Health Activists 14
Ackah, C. G. 92
active employment programmes, Morocco
151–3, 158–60, **159**
Adaawen, S. A. 121
Adom-Asamoah, G. 119, 122
Afrane, S. 114
Africa, incidence of informal employment
in 1, *3 see also* Ghana; South Africa
African Reclaimers Association (ARO) 74
agriculture: in Ghana 18, 30–1, 88, 93, **93**, 97,
98–100; modernisation of 99; and Morocco
economy 21; rural women recognized
workers in 40; smallholder production 109
Agyei-Mensah, S. 113
Ahiable, G. 114
Ahsan, R. N. 35
Akurang-Parry, K. O. 113
Akyeampong, E. 113; Allman, J. 113
Amanor, K. S. 121
Amin, S. 111
Anyidoho, N. A. 111, 114, 118, 119
artisanal mining, in South Africa 77–9
Asuming, P. O. 92

Baah-Ennumh, T. 119, 122
Bairagya, I. 35
banking 36, 59–60; reforms in domestic
trading 114–8, *115–8*
Baviskar, A. 35

Below Poverty Line (BPL) workers 44, 45
Benso Oil Palm Plantation (BOPP) 104
black market 78
Blue Skies Ghana Limited 102, 106
Bob-Milliar, G. M. 120, 121
Bogoev, J. 93
Building Businesses on Values, Integrity and
Dignity (B-BOVID) Company Limited
104–5, 106

Caltech Ventures Limited 103, 106
Carre, F. 13, 29
Central Guarantee Fund (CGF) 149
Chakraborty, S. 39
Charoenloet, V. 203
Chen, M. A. 5, 6, 13, 29, 71, 113
Chi-2 test 167
civil society organisations 2
Clark, G. 113, 118, 119
cleaning work, in Thailand 187–90
CNOPS (National Fund of Social Welfare
Organizations) 156–7
CNSS (National Social Security Fund/
Caisse Nationale de Sécurité Sociale)
152, 156–7, 162
Code 92 38
Code 93 38
Collective Retirement Allowance Plan 158
commercial banks 36
Compulsory Health Insurance Plan 156
The Consolidated Bank Ghana Limited 115
contract farming, in Ghana 18–20, 100–2;
Blue Skies Ghana Limited and 102;

Building Businesses on Values, Integrity and Dignity Company Limited and 104–5; Caltech Ventures Limited and 103, 106; farmers involved in 106; labour relations of 108–9; regulation of. *see* regulation, of contract farming; Serendipalm Company Limited and 103–4, 106
contractual employment, in Morocco 147
Convention on Domestic Workers (ILO) 23
Coronavirus Alleviation Programme (CAP) 126
costs, of compliance 9, 10–1
COVID-19 pandemic 31, 40, 43, 62–3; gendered impact of 80–3; in Ghana 126–31; impact on domestic workers 82

Damodaran, S. 35
Darkwah, A. 118
Decardi-Nelson, I. 120, 122
demonetisation 13, 37, 49–50, 59–60
Department of Durban Solid Waste (DSW) 74
Deshpande, A. 63
Deshpande, S. 35
de Silva, S. J. 95, 97
digitisation, of payments 13, 49–50, 59–60
discrimination, social 35
Dladla, N. 74
domestic trading, in Ghana 20–1, 110–24; activities 110–1; feature of 111; gender segmentation of 113; regulation of. *see* regulation, of domestic trading in Ghana; segmentation of 119; women's predominance in 112, 113
domestic workers: employment law in Morocco 153–5; impact of COVID-19 pandemic on 82; law on formalising in Morocco 23–4, 161–3; in South Africa 17, 75–6; in Thailand 26, 185–93
domestic workers, in Thailand 26, 185–95; analysis of interviews 190–3; formal *vs.* informal *187*, 187–90, **189**; government policies 185–6; statistical overview 186–7

e-commerce 181
economic boom, India 36–7
economic responses, to formalisation 10
Egyir, I. 114
Employees Provident Fund Organisation (EPFO) 48–9, 57

Employees' Provident Funds and Miscellaneous Provisions Act, 1952 48
Employees State Insurance Corporation (ESIC) 57
employment: formalisation of. *see* formalisation, of employment; informal. *see* informal employment; low productivity 12; in Morocco 142–4; patterns, in Indian labour market 36–40
enterprises: formalisation of. *see* formalisation of enterprises; informality, and employment 7, *7*
Entertainment Place Act 1966 (2003) 195
EPF (Employees Provident Fund) 48
Extended Public Works Programme 73

false formalisation 8, 20
FDI (Foreign Direct Investment) 100
female unionisation 15–6
Fertiliser Subsidy Programme 98
financial abuse 78
financial institution: account, access to 114–5, *115*; and reforms in domestic trading 114–8, *125*–18; savings at 115, *116*
formal employment 57–9
formal enterprises, in India 41–3, **42**
formalisation, of employment 2–4; approaches 7–11; benefit of 2, 9–10; formalisation of enterprises *vs.* 29–30; in Ghana 17–21; impact on women workers 4–5; in India 11–4; insights and policy recommendations 27–32; laws/regulations 30–1; macroeconomic context 28; in Morocco 21–5, 23; policies, gendered impact of 4; regulation of contract farming and 109–10; role of government in 8; in South Africa 15–7; in Thailand 25–7; trajectories of 8
formalisation, of enterprises 2–3; economic responses to 10; formalisation of employment *vs.* 29–30; government's policies towards 13; policies, in Morocco 148–9
formalisation policies, in India: demonetisation 49–50; Goods and Services Tax 51; Maternity Benefits Act 44–6; Pradhan Mantri MUDRA Yojana 46–7; Stand Up India 47; Street Vendors (Protection of Livelihood and Regulations of Street Vending) Act, 2014 47–9; Unorganized Workers' Social Security Act 43–4
formalisation policies, in Thailand 178–84;

gendered perspective on 181–4; recent approaches 180–1; social security expansion 178–9
formal workers *vs.* informal workers 2
Freund, C. 140

gender: and formalisation policies in Thailand 181–4; impact of formalisation policies 4; informal employment by 1, *2*, 10, 22; participation in non-agricultural activities 1, *3*; segregation, in nature of work 54; wage gaps 39–40, **40**
gender differences 5, 10; in Indian labour markets 35–6
gender segmentation 88; domestic trading in Ghana 113
Ghana: agriculture in 18, 30–1, 88, 93, **93**, 97; anti-COVID-19 measures 129–31; beneficiaries of Government of responses 128–9; contract farming in. *see* contract farming, in Ghana; Coronavirus Alleviation Programme (CAP) 126; COVID-19 in 126–31; debt owed by 92–3; domestic trading in. *see* domestic trading, in Ghana; economic growth, trends in 91–3; economy, changes in structure 93; formalisation of employment in 17–21; government response to COVID-19 127–8; Highly Indebted Poor Country (HIPC) initiative 91; informal economy in 18, 88–91; informal employment in **96**, 95–8; labour market in 93–5; Multilateral Debt Relief Initiative (MDRI) 91; pro-poor programmes 91–2; Single Spine Salary Policy 92
Ghana Commercial Agriculture Project (GCAP) 98
Ghana Living Standards Survey (GLSS) 94, 111
Ghana Oil Palm Development Company (GOPDC) 100
Ghana School Feeding Programme 91–2
Ghana Statistical Service (GSS) 92
Ghana Sugar Estates Limited (GHASEL) 100, 101
Gini Coefficient 68
Goods and Services Tax (GST) 13, 37, 51
governments: intervention in informal activities 16; local, and regulation of domestic trading 118–21; policies towards formalisation, in India 13, 36; role in domestic trading 21; role in formalisation 8

government schemes, awareness among workers 60–2
Graham, Y. 91

Handloom Weavers' Comprehensive Welfare Scheme 44
Haque, T. 93
harassment 4; by police 83
Hart, K. 88, 95
Hassan, E. 71
health insurance scheme, Morocco 156–7
Highly Indebted Poor Country (HIPC) initiative 91
Hill, P. 111
Honorati, M. 95, 97
Horn, P. 69, 85
Hosmer, D. W. 169
Hosmer and Lemeshow test 169

IDMAJ programme 23, 151–2, 158, 159, 160–1
illegal miners, in South Africa 17, 77–9
India: commercial banks in 36; conditions of employment in 43, **43**; demonetisation in 13, 37, 49–50, 59–60; economic boom 36–7; formalisation of employment in 11–4; formal sector activity in 41–3; Goods and Services Tax in 13, 37, 51; government's policies towards formalisation 13, 36; growth and employment in 11–2; incidence of informal employment in 1, *3*; informal economy in 12–3, 35; informal sector activity in 41–3; labour markets. *see* labour market, in India; official strategies for formalisation. *see* formalisation policies, in India; survey of workers in Delhi NCR 51–62; unemployment rates 12; worker–population ratios 37, *38*
informal economy: and agricultural-related activities 98; defined 5; in Ghana 18, 88–91; in India 12–3, 35; in South Africa 68–9
Informal Economy Monitoring Study (IEMS) 73
informal employment 57–9, 137; defined 6, 95; formalisation of. *see* formalisation, of employment; gender differences in 1, *2*, 10; in Ghana 17–21, **96**, 95–8; global incidence of 1–5, *3*; jobs types as 7; in Morocco 21–5, 144–8; in non-agricultural activities 1, *3*, 15–6; share in total employment *2*; in South Africa

15–7; by type of production unit 7, 7; types of 6; youth and 163–9, **168**, **169**
informal enterprise 9; economic responses to formalisation 10; formalisation of. *see* formalisation, of enterprises; in India 41–3, **42**
informal production units (IPUs), NSIS survey 144–5
informal workers: benefits of formalisation to 9–10; formal workers *vs.* 2; women 4, 15–7, 80–3
Integrated Business Establishment Survey (IBES) 112
Integrated Child Development Scheme (ICDS) 14
internally generated funds (IGF) 119
International Labour Organization (ILO) 1; Convention on Domestic Workers 23; Recommendation 204; relevance for South Africa 79–80
International Monetary Fund (IMF) 91

Jan Dhan Yojana 61–2
Jerven, M. 92
jobs, by status in employment 7, 7
Jorgensen, S. H. 120

Kanbur, R. 10
Kasapreko Company Limited 103
Kesar, S. 35
King, R. S. 120, 122
Kingsuwankul, S. 95
Kohn, L. 72
Kolavalli, S. 92
Kolavalli, S. L. 122
Kuznets-Lewis trajectory 8

Labor Force Survey (2016) 184
Labour Act 2003 103, 106
Labour Code (2004) 141, 154
labour force participation rate (LFPR) 93
Labour Force Survey 94
labour market: in Ghana 93–5; in South Africa 68–9; in Thailand 175–8
labour market, in India: employment patterns 36–40; formal and informal sector activity 41–3; gender-based differences in 35–6; overview 34–6
labour market, Morocco 137–8; legislation 141–2
Labour Protection Act B.E. 2541 (1998) 185
labour relations, of contract farming 108–9

Law 19-12 162
Lekfuangfu, W. N. 95, 136
Lemeshow, S. 169
Linking Environment and Farming (LEAF) 102
Livelihood Empowerment against Poverty 92
logistic regression model, of informal employment 167–9, **168**, **169**
loss of employment benefit, Morocco 158
Lourenzani, A. E. B. S 110
low productivity employment 12
Lund, R. 119, 122
Lyon, F. 122

Mahamallik, M. 35
Mander, H. 35
Manopaiboon, C. 208
manufacturing sector, Thailand 198–206; food products 203–4; textiles and wearing apparel 202–3; wages gaps formal and informal workers 198–202, **200–1**
Maternity Benefits Act 14
Maternity Benefits Act (1961) Amendment 2017 44–6
Mechouat, K. 163
Medical Assistance Plan (RAMED) 157
men: employment rates, in Morocco 22, 142; in informal employment 1, 2; in non-agricultural employment 15; participation in economic activities, in Ghana 18; unemployment rate, in South Africa 70; worker-population ratios 37, 38; working in registered enterprises 55–6, **56**
Metro Mass Transit 91
MGNREGA programme 40
Micro and Small Loans Centre 116
microenterprises: benefits of formalisation to 9; and costs of compliance 10–1
microfinance institutions (MFIs) 122, 123
Minimum Wage Act 61
mining, in South Africa: informal workers in 17, 77–9
Ministerial Regulation No. 14, B.E. 2555 (2012) 185–6
Mitra, D. 35
Mitra, S. 40
mobile money account, access to 115, *116*
Moroccan Inter-Professional Retirement Fund 158
Morocco: active employment programmes

151–3, 158–60, **159**; contractual employment 147; domestic workers in 23–4; employment in 142–4; formal employment in youth 22–3; formalisation of employment in 21–5; health insurance scheme 156–7; labour market 137–8; laws aiming formalisation 153–6, 161–3; loss of employment benefit 158; macroeconomic trends 138–41; National Employment Strategy 149–51; NLFS, informal employment in 145–7; NSIS, informal employment in 144–5; pension system 158; population of 142; retirement benefits 146–7; unemployment/youth unemployment in **139**; wage employment 143–4, 147; work-related medical coverage 146; youth and informal employment 163–9, **168**, **169**
MOUKAWALATI programme 151, 153, 159
MUDRA Yojana 46–7
Mukherjee, A. 35
Multilateral Debt Relief Initiative (MDRI) 91

National Agency for Employment and Skills 152
National Agency for the Promotion of Small and Medium Enterprises (NAPSME) 149
National Employment Strategy (NES) 138, 149–51
National Health Insurance Scheme (NHIS) 91
National Health Mission 14
National Labour Force Surveys (NLFS) 138; informal employment in 145–7
National Sample Survey Organisation (NSSO) 41; 73rd Round survey of Unincorporated Non-Agricultural Enterprises 41
National Social Security Fund 152
National Survey of the Informal Sector (NSIS) 138; informal employment in 144–5
Ndebele, N. 77
Negi, P. 35
neither in employment nor in education (NENE) 143
non-agricultural activities: share of informal employment by gender 1, *3*, 15–6; women workers in 40
non-venue-based sex work 195, 196

Norpalm Ghana Limited 104
Norwood, C. 123
Not in Employment, Education or Training (NEET) 70
NULM 45–6

Obeng-Odoom, F. 120, 121
Oduro, A. 128
online enterprises: formalising 188; registeration of 181
open unemployment rates: in Ghana 18; in India 12, 40; in Morocco **139**; in South Africa 15, 69, 70, 81; in Thailand 175
organised/formal sector activity, in India 41–3, **42**
Overa, R. 113
Owusu, G. 119, 122

Paiva, N. S. 110
Pakampai, W. 95
Pape, J. 113
pension system, in Morocco 158
person protective equipment (PPE) 81–2
Plange, N. K. 121
Planting for Food and Jobs programme 99
police, harassment by 83
Pradhan Mantri Jan Dhan Yojana 61–2
Pradhan Mantri MUDRA Yojana 46–7
Prasitsiriphol, O. 179, 180, 182, 183, 186
Prevention and Suppression of Prostitution Act 2539 (1996) 194
Prompt-Pay 181
prostitution, in Thailand. *see* sex workers, in Thailand
Prybylski, D. 209

RAMED (Medical Assistance Plan) 157
Raymond, J. G. 197
recession, in South Africa 69–70
reclaimers, in South Afriica 16, 73–5
Recommendation 204 (ILO) 79–80
Rees, R. 75
regulation, of contract farming 100–1; company regulation 106–7; and formalisation of employment 109–10; global certification bodies with key influence on **110**; labour 106, 107–8; nature of 105; state 106
regulation, of domestic trading in Ghana: banking and financial sector reforms 114–8, *116*–8; local government and 118–21; state regulatory actions 114–8, *115*–8; traders' associations 121–4

retirement benefits, work-related, in Morocco 146–7
reverse trajectory 8
Robinson, E. J. Z. 122
Rogan, M. 71
rotating savings and credit associations (ROSCA) 123
Rubber Out-growers Plantation Project (ROPP) 101

Sahu, P. P. 35
SAHWA survey 163–9, **168**, **169**
Sakunphanit, T. 179, 180, 182, 183, 186
Samson, M. 74
savings, at formal financial institutions 115, *116*
Scheduled Castes/Scheduled Tribes (SC/STs), Stand Up India for 47
Schindler, K. 121, 123
Schmitt, V. 179, 180, 182, 183, 186
Sekhwala, M. 74
Self-Employed Women's Association (SEWA) 60–1
Self-Employed Workers Association 69
Self-Employed Workers Union (SEWU) 69
self-employment 4, 5, 9, 25–6; in Morocco 22; in non-agricultural activities 12
self-entrepreneurs, formalisation law in Morocco 155–6, 163
Self Help Groups (SHGs) 45–6
Senapati, C. 35
Serendipalm Company Limited 103–4, 108
73rd Round survey of Unincorporated Non-Agricultural Enterprises (NSSO) 41
Sexual Harassment Act 61
sex workers, in Thailand 26–7, 193–8; formalisation legalisation 194–5; legalising prostitution 196–8; non-venue-based 199; type of contract 195–6; venue-based 195
Shah, G. 35
Shepherd, A. W. 122
Singh, S. 106
Single Spine Salary Policy 92
skilled workers 40
Skills Training and Employment Programme 117
Smallholder agriculture production 109
Smith, G. 93
Smith, J. 99
social discrimination 35
social networking sites 181
social security 11, 12, 23, 26, 43, 44, 56–7,

57; formalisation of workers through expansion 178–9; schemes 182–4
Social Security Act (SSA) 179, 182–3, 186
Social Security Fund (SSF) 25, 179
Social Security Office (SSO) 183
Solomon-Ayeh, B. E. 120, 122
Sort at the Source (S@S) 73, 74
South Africa: domestic workers in 17, 75–6; economic recession in 69–70; formalisation of employment in 15–7; formal sector in 71; ILO Recommendation 204 79–80; impact of COVID-19 pandemic on informal workers 80–3; informal/illegal miners in 17; labour market 68–9; open unemployment rate in 15; sectoral shares in GDP and employment 70; social protection indicators in *71*; street vendors in 16, 72–3; trajectory from formalisation 69; waste pickers and reclaimers in 16, 73–5
South African Diamond Exchange and Export Centre 78
Special Agricultural Schemes (SAS) programme 100
Stand Up India 47
Steel, W. F. 111, 128, 119
Streetnet 79
street vending 111
street vendors: in Ghana 21, 119; in South Africa 16, 72–3
Street Vendors (Protection of Livelihood and Regulations of Street Vending) Act, 2014 47–9
Structural Adjustment Programme (SAP) 91
Subhachaturas, W. 208
Sundaram, A. 35
survey of workers, in Delhi NCR 51–62; demonetisation/digital payments/banking 59–60; respondents, profile of **52**, 52–3; social security levels 56–7, **57**; union participation/awareness of laws and government schemes 60–2; wages and conditions of work 53–6, **54**, **56**

TAEHIL programme 23, 151, 152, 158–9; beneficiaries of 160
TAHFIZ programme 152
Tangtammaruk, P. 95, 136, 194
taxation 121
Terkper, S. 116
Thailand: domestic workers in. *see* domestic workers, in Thailand; economy 174;

formalisation of employment in 25–7; formalisation policies. *see* formalisation policies, in Thailand; labour market 175–8; macroeconomic trends 175, **176**; manufacturing sector. *see* manufacturing sector, Thailand; sex workers in 26–7, 193–8
Theodore, M. 140
30 Baht for All Scheme 25, 180
Thorat, A. 35
Thorat, S. 35
TNC (Transnational Corporations) 99
Town Vending Committee (TVC) 47
traders' associations, and domestic trading 121–4
trade unions 2
trading activities 110–1
trajectories, of formalisation 8, 69
Tsikata, D. 113, 120, 121, 128
Twifo Oil Palm Plantation (TOPP) 100, 101

Ujoranyi, T. D. 119
unemployment rates. *see* open unemployment rates
union participation, of workers 60–2
United States Agency for International Development (USAID) 98
Universal Health Care system 25
Universal Health Care System (UHCS) 180
universal social protection, requirement of 31–2
unorganised/informal sector activity, in India 41–3, **42**
Unorganized Workers' Social Security Act (UWSSA), 2008 14, 43–4, 62
unpaid labour/employment 4, 22
unskilled workers 40
urban planning 121

Valiana, S. 77
Vechbanyongratana, J. 95, 136
venue-based sex work 195
Vigneri, M. 92
Vyas, M. 40

wage gaps: formal and informal workers 198–202, **200**–1; by gender 39–40, **40**
wages, workers 53–6, **54**; in Thailand 177–8, **178**
wage work/employment: in Morocco 21–5, 143–4, 147; types of 6
Waitrose Care Trace 108
Waste Management Strategy, Johannesburg 73
waste pickers, in South Afriica 16, 73–5
Watanabe, K. 110
Whitfield, L. 91
WIEGO 16, 74, 79, 82
Women's Development Fund 116
worker-population ratios 37, *38*
workers: domestic. *see* domestic workers; formal 2; formalisation of. *see* formalisation, of employment; impact of formalisation policies on 4–5; informal 2, 6; and knowledge of legal provisions 14; self-employed 4; *see* self-employment; survey in Delhi NCR 51–62
Workmen's Compensation Fund 178–9
work-related medical coverage, Moroccan population 146
World Bank 91, 98, 105
Wrigley-Asante, C. 123

Yoon, Y. 95, 136, 194
youth: formal employment 22–3; and informal employment 163–9, **168**, **169**

Printed in the United States
by Baker & Taylor Publisher Services